CRADLED

Gently in the Arms of God

May you find rest in His arms

Lois Williams
Deuteronomy 33:27

LOIS WILLIAMS

"Come to Me, all you who labor and are heavy laden, and I will give you rest. Take my yoke upon you and learn from Me, for I am gentle and lowly in heart, and you will find rest or your souls." Matthew 11:28-29

A 365-Day Devotional

CRADLED: Gently In the Arms of God

www.LoveLettersFromLois.com

This title is also available as an eBook.
Published with help from Creative Force Press, Olympia, WA

ISBN: 978-1-939989-32-1

Cover Photo: ID 128944540 © Momoleif | Dreamstime.com
Author Photo: Fredrick L. Williams
Printed in the United States

"I'm delighted and appreciative of the quality and content in *Cradled: Gently in the Arms of God.* I'm transported to a quiet peaceful place - sensing the nearness and love God has for me. Lois has an ability to communicate with clarity the emotions that reflect my heart and soul. She softly weaves God's truth and grace in practical words that lift me up to His perfect ways and brings me closer to "the God who faithfully comforts those who seek Him."

If you find it difficult sometimes to "feel God is there," this is a book you will value and deeply appreciate as you read the short and concise daily reflections for each day."

– Richard A. Gordon,
Pastor of Living Springs Church, Brandon South Dakota

"*Cradled* is a treasure of encouragement and inspiration. Lois Williams has words of wisdom and insightful analogies. Prepare to be uplifted with these verses and devotional thoughts."

– Pastor Tim Olson

"Lois writes with such a lovely voice. Her work is spiritually rich and thought-provoking, a delight to sink into and savor each page."

– Laura Frantz, Author, Christy Award Winner

ACKNOWLEDGEMENTS

For a long time I have wanted to share the joy and fulfillment that a daily devotional time can bring. My own life has been touched by using a devotional guide in my mornings with God. Putting these thoughts together has been an exciting, yet massive, undertaking and I have many people to thank! To my family, especially my husband, Fred, my life's companion, the one who stands beside me, loving me with his encouraging support. There aren't words enough to say a proper thank you, but Honey, I know you are breathing a sigh of relief that the book is done!

I wish to mention the members of my Small Group Bible Study by name—Randi Bley, Janice Erikson, Frank and Delta Culhane, Joe and Donna Gilfillan, Patrick and Janis Sokoloski. As well as my beloved prayer partner, Joyce Walker. These precious friends have faithfully prayed, pushed, encouraged and lifted me when I wanted to quit. Thank you, too, to Ray and Janet Smith for your help and support. It's difficult to adequately express my gratitude. And to Nancy Anderson, who spent so many hours poring over the manuscript, correcting my mistakes and who, in hundreds of ways, has made it better. I treasure you and value your insight. Special thanks to Krista Dunk for all you do.

To my beloved pastors, Tim Olson, Thomas Yarrington, Thomas Magnuson and Richard Gordon, I extend my thanks. You all have taught the truth consistently from the pulpit and walked the walk of true disciples of Jesus. I have learned from you, been encouraged by you and appreciate you more than I can say.

Saving the best for last, humble praise-filled gratefulness to My Heavenly Father, whose loving arms cradle me consistently and gently. Creator of words, the Word Himself, breathes His words of truth and care over my life in uncountable ways. May He be honored with what I have done with them.

Soli Deo Gloria!

From the Author

The following paraphrase of Psalm 139 is God's message to you, and it is the purpose of this book to help you learn to know His heart toward you. May you truly come to know what it means to be cradled gently in His arms.

Beloved,

I know you. I have always known you. I am intimately acquainted with all your ways. I know your thoughts, your comings and goings. Even before you speak I know what you will say. I have laid My hand upon you…because I love you.

There is no place you have gone, no place where you might go, that I am not there. Every memory of pain, each moment of sadness; I understand. I was there. Even your darkness is not hidden from Me. I see you only in My light…because I love you.

I was there at your conception. I formed you, your inward parts; wove them together to create you, special and unique, fearfully and wonderfully made. My thoughts toward you are precious and you could never count them all. I long for you to know Me…because I love you.

January 1

TRANSITION

See, I am doing a new thing! Now it springs up; do you not perceive it? I am making a way in the desert and streams in the wasteland.
Isaiah 43:19 (NIV)

There is a moment of transition, a pause between exiting the past year and entering the new; a moment filled with emotion, mixing nostalgia with expectancy. A conscious moment, when I go from being sad that the year is over, having passed so quickly, to the anticipation of the new year beginning. It beckons with possibilities and as yet unwritten events and adventures; a time of reflection, and resolutions.

I am poised on the threshold once again. It is midnight, and the familiar moment approaches with its conflicting tug at my heart. Overriding it, though, is a sense of praise that fills my thoughts, enlarges my heart, inhabits my prayers and paints my reflections with colors that delight the senses. In looking back I see how God has moved in me, protected and carried me, blessed me in thousands of ways, and shown me His cherishing, loving grace. Grace that covers all the things I didn't do, and magnified what I did do so that He could bring glory to His name.

So now I go from joy-filled reflections to hope-filled resolutions, because He promises the same, and more, for this new year. With only a glance back, I close the door to the old year; and gratefully turn to open the portal of the new, watching for the new thing He is doing. Quenching my thirst in the streams He provides, I will make this poignant transition.

Heavenly Father, help me hold Your hand as this year unfolds and I learn to revel in the streams of refreshment You have promised. Amen.

January 2

HOVERING

In the beginning God created the heavens and the earth. The earth was without form, and void; and darkness was on the face of the deep, and the Spirit of God was hovering over the face of the waters.
Genesis 1:1-2

It is the beginning of a new year. A time of anticipation as well as retrospection. I began my "read-thru-the-Bible" discipline this morning, looking once more into the marvelous story of creation. I know I've read it at least a hundred times, but this morning I noticed the word *hovering*.

It made me stop for a moment and think about the Spirit of God, as a living cloud, resting above the darkness; hovering, covering, watchful, intent on what He was going to do. What a beautiful picture!

And I thought of this new year. Darkness seems to cover the earth, and we are often burdened by despair. The precious Word from God to me today, this burgeoning new year, is that He still hovers over the earth. His presence still watches, lingering and poised, intent on His plans.

He said in the beginning, *Let there be light.*[1] Now He says to us, the Light has come, and I am still here, My Spirit hovering. Let Me lift your darkness, and shine My love upon you.

Oh, my Heavenly Father, My heart responds with welcoming joy! Please make me more aware of that precious hovering presence. Amen.

---

[1] Genesis 1:3

January 3

THOUGHTS ON LOOKING AHEAD

Your ears shall hear a word behind you, saying, "This is the way, walk in it". Whenever you turn to the right hand or whenever you turn to the left. Isaiah 30:21

There are always deep thoughts in my mind as strains of Auld Lang Syne fade away; sighs replacing the merriment of a New Year's Eve celebration. A hush of fresh expectancy fills me as a new year spreads before my eyes.

Though I can't see beyond the bend, I am aware that unmarked pages and unwalked paths await. It is serious, a time of wonder and consideration. Each mark I make, each step I take will form the pattern God has intended. Though I will weave the times and places into a fabric all my own, I like to ponder what I will leave upon the hearts of all of those I've loved and known.

Upon my annual introspection of when this year is done, and I look back at the plans and deeds that made up the year that is *now* ahead of me, will I find satisfaction stemming from these encounters and see the rhythm that holds true for my life? Because there are so many ways to walk along the road I see on the days stretched ahead of me.

Father God, You have given another year! As always I look forward to great things. But what I pray when I look back at what has occurred, it may be a joyful remembrance of growth in my relationship with You, but also with those whom you place in my path. Amen.

January 4

HELD

For the Lord your God, He is the One who goes with you; He will not leave you nor forsake you. Deuteronomy 31:6b

He has put a new song in my mouth – praise to our God; many will see it and fear, and will trust in the LORD. Psalm 40:3

There is such a sense of expectancy and anticipation at the beginning of any change; and a new year or a new journey always brings change. As I struggle with remembering to write a new date for this year, I am reminded that it is a new year. Even though last year passed like lightning, I knew there was growth and healing; yet I long for more.

I begin this year with yearning: yearning for more and more of God; to know Him better, love Him more, accept His love for me and pass it on. The most important thing to remember is the truth of the above scripture. He holds me; and has a never-ending grip on me.

There is such joy in this realization. It makes me want to burst into the new song He gives. He wants me to sing this song for others to hear, but if I am to sing it, I must be sure to hold tightly to the hand that holds me! A famous author writes.' "If there are any regrets in Heaven, perhaps they will be that, given such beautiful music to play, i.e., the gospel, most of us have practiced so casually."[2]

Please, God, I want to grip Your hand, You who will never forsake me. May I go forth in this new year to share Your song of praise with all I meet. Amen.

---

[2] Ruth Bell Graham (1920-2007)

January 5

GOING OUT

By faith Abraham obeyed when he was called to go out to the place which he would receive as an inheritance. And he went out, not knowing where he was going. Hebrews 11:8

I often use this verse at the beginning of a new year. Sensing that there is a journey ahead as the months unfold, I put my own name in place of Abraham, and consider all that that implies. And as I ponder, I ask myself, "Have I come any closer to the kind of faith Abraham showed, leaving all he had known, unsure of where he was headed?'

Going forward without a stated goal takes enormous courage, I think. But within the context of going forward, there is the fact of going out *from*. I have many times in my life packed up and moved on, having been married to a military man. We always knew however, where we were going.

What a difference there is in going out *from* and going *to*. In a spiritual sense, out *from* takes more trust, more faith; it's abandoning the self and whatever I have always depended on, and resting in God's energy and purpose. It's simple, yet difficult.

Some years ago I wrote the following as we prepared for yet another big move: "It's raw – the bleeding wound of parting, stinging with the salt of tears. Hugs offered with murmured appreciation attempt to comfort, but serve only to intensify the loss of what I am leaving behind. I want to go. I don't want to leave."

I wonder…does God feel that reluctance in me each time He calls me out from the familiar into the unknown, trusting Him?

Dear Father, grant me the courage to heed Your invitation to follow, whatever the cost, to the unknown wonder of all You promise. Amen.

January 6

BEGINNINGS

In all their affliction He was afflicted, and the Angel of His Presence saved them; in His love and in His pity He redeemed them; and He bore them and carried them all the days of old. Isaiah 63:9

As this is a brand new year, I've been thinking about the subject of beginnings. There's a wealth of possibilities inherent in the word. A freshness seems to permeate my thoughts even though, looking down the road, a murky mist veils the path ahead. I know from years past that sunshine and excitement await to counteract the dimness as the year progresses.

But I pause to ponder on so many beginnings in my life…my own beginning as the first-born, and the birth of my siblings, as each one changed the dynamics of the family. My first day of school, graduation, first date, first kiss. Leaving home, my marriage, my first child, first grandchild…my first job, my last job that began the altered way I saw my world without feeling significant in the workplace.

Life is about beginnings; each step, each turn, each change, is a passage into a new beginning. Marked by growth and struggle, pain and triumph, I have felt the hand of God as He has ached with my pain and rejoiced in my victories, and gently carried me through each beginning and each ending.

Father, at the cusp of this new year, I can ask no more than what I already have, the joy and peace of Your Presence, as You bless for me this new beginning. Amen.

January 7

GOLD

But He knows the way that I take; when He has tested me,
I shall come forth as gold. Job 23:10

Often the road is bumpy. It seems that what lies ahead is full of danger, darkness and difficulty. There are pitfalls awaiting; I know this from experience, and discouragement dogs my steps.

My Heavenly Father is quite aware, however; aware of what's ahead, aware of my fear and trepidation; most definitely aware of His goal, His will; set out for me before I took my first breath.

How very comforting to read here Job's testimony. Faced with unutterable loss, He holds with incredible stubbornness to His faith. I wish to emulate him, clinging to the knowledge of purpose in my dark road, a purpose of refinement, of growth; a Hand holding mine until a gleam of pure gold bursts through the night, a reflection of His glory I am privileged to share.

Please, Father, refine me, use the testing in my life, but may the testing not obscure the goal…GOLD. Amen.

January 8

WONDER

Eye has not seen, nor ear heard, nor have entered into the heart of man the things God has prepared for those who love Him.
1 Corinthians 2:9

The New Year is truly upon us, and is filled with adventures yet to come. At least that's what I am choosing to believe. God wants His children to live in anticipation of what He has in store for us. Doesn't that fuel your mind with excitement?

Last year, God met me at every turn, for every need. He showed me Himself over and over. As a result I love Him more and am many times more grateful. And even while I move forward into a new year, I pray that I continue to long for Him, even as He fills my heart with the wonder of His love. I like the word *wonder.* Not a questioning wonder, but an awe-filled wonder as I learn to view Him as He really is. Someone dear to me once posed this thought, "If we ever could truly glimpse God in all His brilliance, majesty and glory, our lives would never be the same."

And so I want my life to be changed. I want that glimpse of Him to fill me, so that I will not take Him for granted, or esteem Him too lightly. Then my life will reflect lovely, awe-struck wonder. May we all open our eyes to the wonder of all He is! I am excited! Excited to experience all He has prepared for His people.

Majestic Father God, Help me to hear Your voice more clearly and respond to Your nudges immediately. I know in doing so I will see wonder upon wonder unfold from Your almighty loving hand.
Amen.

January 9

RENEWAL

Then He who sits on the throne said, "Behold, I make all things new" Revelation 21:5

The sun is rising on a brand new day. Millions of cells are reproducing at God's command and life on earth continues. Plants grow. New life is conceived. Rivers flow, and the ocean tide fluctuates with the waxing and waning of the moon as He spins this tiny planet on the tip of His mighty finger.

It is incomprehensible to me...the power of His sustaining Word. I open my eyes to the wonder of my clean new heart fresh from time with Him. Confession and forgiveness are mine, and restoration has taken place. New attitudes are growing, cells of compassion are reproducing, all because of His cleansing work in me. It is unimaginable, the power of His redemption.

And moment by moment, the edges of time are growing nearer to the dawn of the day when all will become new. New bodies, no more tears, only the brilliant light of His presence. All that He is patiently sustaining now will be done away by the power of His judgment...except for the hearts and souls who've trusted Him.

Father, it brings me such joy to contemplate the day when You, the one who will renew it all, will have Your way. Amen.

January 10

REMEMBER

I remember the days of old; I meditate on all Your works; I muse on the work of Your hands. I spread out my hands to You; my soul longs for You like a thirsty land. Selah. Psalm 143:5-6

It is a new year. Assaulted by hopeful anticipation, having come through a year of hardship in many ways, I have chosen my word for the year...*remember*. Most folks will advocate **not** remembering! But God has impressed upon my heart to consider my life, even last year, and find Him in my memories.

I always choose a *word* for the new year, a word that will infuse me with a goal to discover something new and precious in my life. For instance, the year I experienced heart surgery, I had chosen the word *alive*, not knowing how it would impact that entire year!

Psalm 143 is a real favorite. And as I re-read it, the word *remember* leaps out at me. Because when I get discouraged, I read these verses, and they cheer me on. This time when I read it, I noticed the word "Selah", following. Selah means to look back and ponder on what has just been said. How much clearer could it be? So, *remember* is my new word. I encourage you to find your own word from God.

Abba, this is the position in which I want to be this new year...hands outstretched, on my knees, thirsty, waiting to hear Your voice as I remember, meditate, and muse. Through my journal pages, help me find new scriptures to bolster and recreate the memories. Amen.

January 11

LIVING FORWARD

We should live soberly, righteously, and godly in the present age, looking for the blessed hope and glorious appearing of our great God and Savior Jesus Christ… Titus 2:12b-13

The New Year is well under way. How are we all doing, I wonder, with the hopes and dreams we cherished as it began? I can only speak for myself, but I trust that we are finding God present and active in our lives! The reason I asked the above question so early in the year is that I fully believe that if we don't start right away working to try and keep our resolutions, time has a way of eroding the hopes and plans we made.

We all have hopes and dreams, whether or not we voice them; whether or not we are living in the expectancy of what God is going to do.

I truly desire that this year I will live in anticipation, that I will be open to the wonder of His working in my life. The enemy likes to use his hissing voice to discourage me. Truly that identifies the battle in which many of us are involved. If he can take our joy and our hope, he has won, and we become disheartened and disbelieving. We must cling to the hope God promises, because it brings a different perspective. We belong to Him, therefore we can confidently anticipate what is ahead.

What ***is*** ahead is the blessed hope of Jesus's appearing! Keeping that in the forefront of our minds is how we live forward; shrugging off the disappointment and disillusionment that colors our past. Hope is a wonderful thing!

Heavenly Father, gratitude fills me to consider the sacrifice Jesus made in order for us to be able to confidently anticipate His appearing, and to live forward, celebrating our blessed hope. Amen.

January 12

LONGING

Now to Him who is able to do exceedingly abundantly above all that we ask or think, according to the power that works in us…
Ephesians 3:20

At this time of beginnings, we can benefit by looking at all the possibilities that await during the upcoming months. A new year fosters a kind of journey, and so I'd like to spend a few days examining the bones of just what a journey entails. I invite you along!

A journey, I think, begins with the desire to travel, to leave the place you are and embark upon an adventure. For me, having been stuck in the mire of rebellion for many years, I had not recognized God's voice, His tender drawing of my spirit. But He kept calling and I finally caught His whisper. Feeling empty and unfulfilled, I bowed my head and asked, "God, please make me desire You." Then and only then could my odyssey begin.

As the journey continues—now at the turn of a calendar page, the longing is still deep within. God has shown Himself true and faithful, but the more I know of Him the more I desire.

Where are you on your journey? May I encourage you to ask for more of Him; to embark on a path that is fueled by longing. Longing for more of Him. One of my favorite phrases in Scripture is *exceedingly abundantly*[3] Abundance is wonderful, but *exceedingly* goes way beyond it. And that is what He is able to provide.

So, Heavenly Father, may I once again request that You make me desire You. Build the longing in my soul, and I will continue on this journey as You lead. Amen.

---

[3] Ephesians 3:20

January 13

TRAVEL PLANS

But seek first the kingdom of God and His righteousness and all these things shall be added unto you. Matthew 6:33

I'm headed out upon a journey. It's a new commitment to God to walk with Him; a journey which I am concerned about my ability to complete. So I load my suitcase with carefully set-out goals, well-laid plans, celebrated achievements, and march purposely, fervently into the presence of God. With a satisfied thud I lay the suitcase down and invite Him to come along on my proposed journey, never suspecting that He might have something else in mind!

I am bathed in chagrin as He dumps my suitcase; the contents look pitifully inadequate when stacked against the bounteous provision He offers. When will I learn to bring an *empty* suitcase into the throne room of His majesty...an eager soul in need of filling? When will I cease to load my thoughts with plans that I will never need?

God, please open my eyes to the vista of the next step You have planned. I'd rather simply hold Your hand than lug my heavy suitcase down the road. May my travel plans be Yours. Amen.

January 14

SURRENDER

Search me, O God, and know my heart; try me, and know my anxieties; and see if there is any wicked way in me, and lead me in the way everlasting. Psalm 139:23-24

This journey is one on which many of us hopefully are embarked. There are many parts of this odyssey that we can explore together. Let's take a good look at this step: *Surrender.*

Surrender. Without the commitment to pursue an intimate journey, embarkation never can take place. There are struggles, I know; fear of what may be ahead and what it may cost. But we must determine that we will not turn back. Surrender accepts the yoke which rests easily across our shoulders; Jesus and me. Surrender invites God to examine and root out anything that would hinder my forward steps.

I am learning in more detail just how His Word operates in my life. How His precepts, His law, commands and statutes, if followed and heeded, hold a lot of benefits! Refreshment, wisdom, joy and light, are promised. It's important also to learn how these words of God have the ability to warn and convict. Allowing that truth to permeate our thoughts will keep us surrendered. There are words in an old hymn that convict me, "Take all my will, my passion, self and pride. I now surrender, Lord, in me abide."[4] Yes, surrender. So vital.

Heavenly Father, I pray that I will allow Your word to fill and surround me; that I will accept the discipline of conviction. And that I will ever be surrendered to You. That only occurs as I bury my heart and mind into the Scripture. Amen.

---

[4] Search Me, O God, by J. Edwin Orr

January 15

THE PATHWAY

O God, You are my God; early will I seek You; my soul thirsts for You; my flesh longs for You in a dry and thirsty land where there is no water…because your lovingkindness is better than life, my lips shall praise You. Psalm 63:1 & 3

Still plodding along on the journey! "Faith isn't the ability to believe long and far into the misty future. It's simply taking God at His Word and taking the next step."[5]

This fits right in with my thoughts on keeping moving! The heart of God is an unfathomable mystery. How can one so majestic, so holy, so awesome, be concerned with me? His Word refutes my earthbound thoughts—and reverberates with the truth: the heart of God IS infinitely concerned with me. He beckons, tenderly. I have been talking the talk, yet struggling for so long to be acceptable, not comprehending that He was leaning toward me. He doesn't push or pull. He beckons. To walk the pathway of an intimate journey I have to learn about His grace and acceptance, trusting my hand to His grip.

Beckoning is such a welcoming gesture, indicating the desire for us to be closer. Considering this, my heart's yearning increases …to come, to cling, remain close to His side. My eyes fill with tears of joy to realize I am wanted, loved, and invited with a Divine beckoning to find refuge in His mighty arms. That is why this journey is so important. It is an answer to our every longing.

Heavenly Father, I sense You calling me, and everything in me desires to draw nearer to You. Please help me to focus on the steps I need to take to keep moving forward to the sanctuary of Your arms. Amen.

---

[5] Joni Eareckson Tada (1949 -)

January 16

ROADBLOCKS

But he gives more grace. Therefore he says, "God resists the proud, but gives grace unto the humble." Submit yourselves therefore to God. James 4:6-7

As we travel we have to realize that it is not always a smooth road. No destination is ever reached without encountering roadblocks, barriers thrown up by the enemy of my soul who does not want me to travel this road. Often I think I am going backward faster than I am moving forward. However in the struggle of His determined love against my determined will, there are victories.

Patience, for instance, to endure a detour, strength to leap hurdles, and courage to go back to the path. We all struggle against the obstructions along the way. Often I find myself fighting the same issues now as in the past, wondering if they will ever be resolved.

But as I ponder my journey, I realize that roadblocks, in most cases, are for our protection. Perhaps they are guiding us around something dangerous to us. We often fail to understand the "Why". But God asks us to lean on Him anyway.

Father, I want You to be pre-eminent in my life, but I find myself fighting too hard to bring about my goals. The victory lies in surrender; and from there comes the strength to overcome roadblocks. I sense a tender victory awaiting. May I claim the promised God-infused strength and power You offer, and love that will not let go, wrapping me in everlasting arms. Amen.

January 17

THE HIGHWAY

And the ransomed of the Lord shall return, and come to Zion with singing, with everlasting joy on their heads. They shall obtain joy, and gladness, and sorrow and sighing shall flee away. Isaiah 35:10

I read somewhere that a *highway* is a path defined as being raised up above the surrounding land, in order that travelers may walk without soiling their feet.

It is this concept that I am endeavoring to realize in my journey…walking in holiness with God's help. In our walk to the heart of God there will be roadblocks along the way; obstructions that can cause distress and disappointment and storms that cause us to slip, muddying our feet. But the contrast to that is the thrill of walking the high way.

It is in the climb toward His heart that we most experience His blessing. There is peace in walking obediently. Indescribable peace, what the Scripture calls peace that passes understanding. I know, because I have been disobedient for most of my life, fighting against the call of my Savior to follow Him. Anxiety, stress and pain increased in the heartache of the struggle that formed the rocky path I walked. This new road I walk, though often bumpy, is filled with contentment and joy. And yes, peace.

The highway is the link-up of God's grace and human responsibility. Our responsibility is to walk it; His is to pour the blessing of His grace upon us to give the strength, courage and willingness to do so. And He will; He promised.

Father God, I claim Your promised blessing as I set my feet upon the high way. And I look forward to the hope of eternity and Your everlasting joy. Amen.

January 18

SNOWFALL

Through the LORD's mercies we are not consumed, because His compassions fail not. They are new every morning; great is Your faithfulness. Lamentations 3:22-23

Summer and winter, and springtime and harvest, sun, moon, and stars in their courses above, join with all nature in manifold witness to Thy great faithfulness, mercy and love.[6]

As I stare out of the window, I see the snow falling. A part of me feels afraid, threatened, somehow, and unsettled because plans need to be changed, situations reorganized. Schedules must be altered because life beats a different cadence to match the slowing rhythm that a big snowfall brings. Yet how lovely it is…the white blanket that softens jagged edges and harsh angles.

I am thinking of Your faithfulness to me, God, through all the seasons of my life, now that my winter approaches. And I feel a bit unsettled because I realize changes are coming. Some of my life's plans will be altered…my dreams must adjust to the new rhythm of my days, for I can no longer accomplish all the tasks I used to do.

But with my winter, I hope, will come a richer covering of Your grace to blanket me and soften the rough edges, smooth the harsh angles of impetuosity with Your wisdom and deepen the beauty of Your life in me.

Dear Father, there is much to anticipate because I know that as surely as spring will follow, (it always does, for You are faithful) the end of my winter will open the door to Spring eternal. Great is Your faithfulness. Amen.

---

[6] Great Is Thy Faithfulness – T. O. Chisholm (1866-1960)

January 19

COTTON CANDY

For all have sinned, and fall short of the glory of God.
Romans 3:23

Do I see my sin? Do I see myself as a sinner? The question challenges me. Sometimes I have seen the thoughts that lurk beneath the levels of consciousness where I live my life, and I have acknowledged those thoughts. But for the most part I think I consider myself as pretty nice. Any mention of sin usually elicits a recitation of my good deeds.

And so I am aware this morning that I have an incredible amount of sugarcoating spinning around in the whirling center of my mind, ready to build a big cone of cotton candy to sweeten the taste and appearance of my sinfulness and offer it to God for a bite.

It may look pretty to me, and appetizing, but it is a bad taste in His mouth. He wants only my repentant heart, confessing, throwing my sin on His altar. Will I allow that brokenness to be humbly laid at His feet? Begging for, and receiving His forgiveness?

Dear God, for the sake of my healing, please forgive my apathy, my blind complacency. I am a sinner. Help me to begin anew with this realization. Amen.

January 20

BABY STEPS

The LORD preserves the simple; I was brought low, and He saved me. Return unto your rest, O my soul, for the LORD has dealt bountifully with you. For You have delivered my soul from death, my eyes from tears, and my feet from falling. I will walk before the LORD in the land of the living. Psalm 116:6-9

I was thinking, when I read this verse, of our early days of grand-parenting and how much fun it was to watch those beginning steps of independence. I remember writing in my journal, "Our granddaughter is walking!"

So small, it seemed she had deserted our laps too early. So determined, for weeks she had pulled herself up on every available piece of furniture, testing her leg strength, taking a tentative step, then two. So focused, her attention unwavering on her destination, she fearlessly toddled forth. What joy I feel when she launches herself into my arms after a wobbly run across the space between us!

As I watched her, God showed me the application He wanted me to observe. He draws us to Himself. We wobble and hesitate, needing to be held, carried and picked up when we fall. But experiencing Him infuses divine strength into our baby steps, our legs of faith are empowered.

God has carried me for so long. Even now I still test my legs, often falling. He wants my focus to be on Him, my limbs to strengthen. Not so I can stand alone, but run straight into His arms.

Dear Father, I thank You for the assurance of Your presence when I wobble and waver. I thank You for drawing me to Yourself by adding strength to my weakness, waiting with arms open wide to receive me. Amen.

January 21

TERRIBLE TWOS

For though by this time you ought to be teachers, you need someone to teach you again the first principles of the oracles of God, and you have come to need milk and not solid food. For everyone who partakes only of milk is unskilled in the word of righteousness, for he is a babe.
Hebrews 5:12-13

Remember the *Terrible Twos* when our little ones begin to assert their independence and test their boundaries? I do, even though it was a long time ago. The dictionary defines it as a normal developmental phase experienced by young children that's often marked by tantrums, defiant behavior and lots of frustration. How true is that?

I am a grandmother now, but I remember an incident when I was brought up short, while observing this phenomenon in the lives of our grown children and their offspring. When my 2-year-old granddaughter was told "no", screamed at her daddy, "Go away! I don't want you!" Hurt glazed my son's eyes as he tried in vain to soothe her, hold her and guide her to safe rules for her behavior.

I wanted to weep as I watched the bumps in their relationship. But then, God nudged me gently and I looked into my own heart, saw how often I pushed at Him and, with my behavior said, "Leave me alone. I want my own way." And for a moment I saw the pain in the heart of a loving God who only desired me to bend to His will.

I truly believe neither she nor I want to be as independent as we claim. However, discovering the delight and peace of dependence on God is a lifelong process.

Heavenly Father, as I watched my beloved granddaughter grow and mature, please help me, too, to grow past the Terrible Twos!
Amen!

January 22

EMBERS

Therefore I remind you to stir up the gift of God which is in you through the laying on of my hands. 2 Timothy 1:6

I believe there comes a time in our lives when we really need to experience a rekindling of the flame that we had when we began following our God. Complacency tends to set in, and our routine rules our behavior. Somehow we lose the vivid excitement of what Jesus has done for us and the desire to share with others. Oh, we have embers; the fire is not completely out! But I contend, if you are anything like me, there is a necessity of a fresh blowing from the bellows of God's heart to fan those embers into flame.

Let's look at fire's embers for a moment. Embers are the mature heart of the fire that keeps it going. We often consider them to be the *sad* remains of a dying fire; however, if we look at them from a different perspective, they are the lingering *life* of the fire, not its death. The heat is there, waiting for a fresh infusion of fuel, of oxygen, to once again burst into flame.

If we have allowed things like heartache, disappointment, complacency and struggle to begin extinguishing our fire; if we feel that we are diminished to embers, take heart! There is hope! In the name of God and by the power of Jesus we can shine *like stars in a darkened generation.*[7]

Dear Father, help us to acknowledge our God-given power to change and grow, to be radically alive for You, overflowing with goodness and alight with purpose to draw others to Your flame. Amen.

---

[7] Daniel 12:3

January 23

DIRECTIONS

He left Judea, and departed again to Galilee. But He needed go through Samaria. John 4:3, 4

I often wonder at the situations in my life—pondering on the ways God moves to bring me to any given place I happen to be. It amazes me—God's directing of events.

It appears that Jesus was constantly on the move, obediently following His Father's urging. In the above event the scripture records that He *needed* to go through Samaria—though it was not the normal route—because a divine appointment awaited. I am struck by how often His miracles, His touches, occurred while He was on His way.

I contemplate the steps and stops on my own journey that have brought me to this place in life. The many situations that seem random are really God's positioning. It amazes me to contemplate; making trust in His sovereignty easier when I notice the many ways He urged me on and brought me here.

I want to illustrate this with a few lyrics:

How could I boast of anything I've ever seen or done?
How could I dare to claim as mine the victories God has won?
Where would I be had God not brought me gently to this place
I'm here to say I'm nothing but a sinner saved by grace.[8]

The same Force that propelled Jesus through Samaria, with a mind-rocking stop at a village well, is the One that directs and propels me on my own path.

Oh, God, I am filled with praise. It is so important that I get up and get moving so that I can follow Your needed directions. Amen.

---

[8] Sinner Saved By Grace, Bill and Gloria Gaither

January 24

ENOUGH

And if you say, "What shall we eat in the seventh year, since we shall not sow nor gather in our produce?" Then I will command My blessing on you in the sixth year, and it will bring forth produce enough for three years. Leviticus 25:20-21

How do we live in hope in the midst of this world today when fear seems to be all around us? Do you hear this complaint of the children of Israel? It sounds rather similar to what we hear a lot these days…a lot like what goes through *my* mind.

I realize that there are three conditions that tend to motivate my behavior. The first one has dogged my pathway most of my life: I am not enough. I'm afraid that I never will be! This often leads to paralysis…at least in my life. What's the use? I'll only fail.

The second one is the fear that I will not HAVE enough. It leads to possessiveness; a clutching at what I have, just in case. God promised His children *enough*; and the promise remains true today.

The third thing that motivates me is the fear that God is not enough. This fear must break the heart of God, because it surely brings with it doubt, distrust, unbelief and powerlessness. It keeps me from trusting in His power and provision.

God told the Israelites that He would bless them and bring forth enough in the sixth year to feed them in the seventh. They needed not fear, but confidently trust in His provision. And so must I.

Father, sometimes hope is fleeting and fear overtakes my thoughts. But I must cast aside the anxiousness and lean on Your promises, always, always trusting that You are enough. Help me, please. Amen.

January 25

DISAPPOINTMENT

Your ears shall hear a word behind you, saying, "This the way, walk in it," whenever you turn to the right hand or whenever you turn to the left. Isaiah 30:21

I have heard it said that disappointment is the enemy's spearhead. It is so often how he begins his attack. And it is very effective; for me, at least. He knows well how to derail my thoughts and emotions; how to distract me from trusting God, which is my first line of defense. His goal is to turn my attention from God's love to disgust at my own efforts.

He targets my trust, my line of defense. The weapon is to fill me with disappointment. I begin the journey, hope high, feeling strong from an encounter with God, and before long I stumble over the bumps in the road I didn't expect. It isn't working out the way I thought it would. So, I am disappointed. It is debilitating; it makes me feel like a failure.

What is the cure? What defense would God have me employ to get back on the road? It is walking in obedience, seeking His guidance. Perhaps to accept the reality that it may be His appointment to teach me something. To turn disappointment into His appointment!

Heavenly Father, I too easily become discouraged when I come up against a roadblock. But it is true that You are guiding my steps and my trust needs to be in You, totally. Refusing to be derailed and distracted. I so need to comprehend this, and I know You will help me. Thank You. Amen.

January 26

HOSPITALITY

Then He also said to him who invited Him, "When you give a dinner or a supper, do not ask your friends, your brothers, your relatives, nor rich neighbors, lest they also invite you back, and you be repaid. But when you give a feast, invite the poor the maimed, the lame, the blind, and you will be blessed because they cannot repay you..."
Luke 14:12-14

These verses speak to our motivation in welcoming friends and family into our homes. I am challenged to look at my own issues regarding hospitality! I love to have company, but too often I don't extend an invitation until I feel everything is just right. That the house is clean and organized and delicious food all prepared, so I can greet them with a calm face and a frilly apron!

God appears to have a different idea. So I ask, "Is my home truly His dwelling place, warmed by His presence? Does it offer a space where hearts can be held in a holy embrace?"

I know it is God Who dwells with my family. But is my home, when guests are arriving, filled with God's sweetness that frees from the striving for perfection? And the big question...do I entertain with the thought of repayment? He asks me to bring in the poor and maimed, from whom I cannot expect anything in return, but only to give from a heart that loves and worships Him.

Heavenly Father would You extend a welcome alongside me? And make my home a haven from the cold of an uncaring world? Help me to redefine hospitality with Your terms; that family, friends AND strangers will find here a reflection of You. Amen.

January 27

IMMEDIATELY

And immediately Jesus reached out his hand and caught him, and said to him, "O you of little faith, why did you doubt?"
Matthew 14:31.

We live in a culture of immediacy. Our expectation is that the response to what we are seeking will be ours as soon as we request it. Of course that doesn't always happen, but we expect it. Fast food, instant gratification, the click of a button. We no longer comprehend the need for learning how to wait.

I love to study Jesus as He walked through His life here on earth. Never in a hurry, always patient, even in a culture that was tortoise-like, compared to ours! Yet so many times in the gospels the writers use the word *immediately.* Implying that Jesus is ready to move and willing to move at once. Seeing a need, sensing a longing He stretches out His hand, and healing grace flows, immediately.

Yet, there is another side to this equation. In spite of our expectation of an immediate solution, when it comes to our need of God's intervention, we don't go to Him immediately. We tend to try to fix things ourselves. Going, as my friend once said, "to the phone rather than to the Throne." If He is ready to move in a split second, why aren't we?

Heavenly Father, oh, how grateful I am for Your promise of immediate help. As for my part, I must learn that when I am in need it will behoove me to turn to You, immediately. Amen.

January 28

PERMANENCE

But He, because He continues forever, has an unchangeable priesthood. Therefore He is also able to save to the uttermost those who come to God through Him, since He always *lives to make intercession for them. Hebrews 7:24-25.*

Beneath the shifting sands of our society, in the confusing chaos and erratic ethics of our culture there is a longing for stability. We seek it, dream of it, and check boundaries for something solid in which to place our hopes, our efforts, and our faith. We are ever searching, under the guise of pursuing success.

"Permanence" is not a word that I find used very often. I seem to be much more accustomed to temporary, makeshift, a quick fix, answering the need of the moment, in order to quell the urgent cry of my heart for truth and reliability.

And then, like a freshening shower from heaven I happen upon a verse with words like "forever", "unchangeable", "always", and "to the uttermost", which strike a resonant chord within my soul.

Jesus. Our Savior. Our High Priest. The Truth, the Reliable One, the Stable One, the Eternal Rock of our Salvation; the thirst-quenching response to the dry and changeable winds of our world. He IS permanence.

Dear Father, there is such a settled peace in my heart, contemplating the truth of this. No need to tremble in a spirit of anxiousness. You are my Rock and my soul wells up with Hallelujahs! Amen.

January 29

INFUSION

For it is God who works in you, both to will and to do for His good pleasure. Philippians 2:13

Life. *All* is encompassed in that word…the essence of my soul. Life: the source that holds my past, inhabits my present, and shapes my everlasting tomorrows. God is at work IN me. Have I ever truly stopped to consider what this means?

It is no small thing: eternal life, in the person of the Holy Spirit, is working within me. My imagination has somehow considered Him as simply a tightly coiled Presence waiting to spring into action at my nod. But it is now fired by a new realization of a living, breathing force that infuses every cell of my spiritual being; a pushing, throbbing mist of LIFE!

Life within me. Surrounding me. Inhabiting me. My mind can scarcely absorb what my spirit already comprehends…the presence of vitality, the essence of life…God Almighty infused into me!

God, I believe it. May I live like I believe it. Bring Your life alight in my heart. I rest in You. Amen.

January 30

A LIGHT ON THE PORCH

Then Jesus spoke to them again, saying, "I am the light of the world. He who follows me shall not walk in darkness, but have the light of life." John 8:12

A friend sent us a photo of his front porch light, and it touched my heart in several ways. Shining through frosted crystal, the light is intense against blackness it seeks to dispel. Anchored firmly to its base, (the shelter it promises) it brings warmth, and hope, and beauty into the night. What is more welcoming than a bright light on the porch?

I can't help but look with joy at this contrast between light and darkness. We have just spent hours and days contemplating the Light of the World, Jesus. So this photograph is very meaningful to me, as I look into the unknowns of a new year. I can see Jesus beckoning. Shining through a crystal veil of hope, anchored to the shelter of the rock of faith, warming our hearts with His grace, He brings the warmth of His love into our night.

Jesus, just like this beautiful porchlight shines a welcome, and beckons us, so do You into our hearts. We are grateful for the invitation to enter into the light of Your presence and to bask in it with everlasting joy, Amen.

January 31

THE MORNING WATCH

Watch, stand fast in the faith, be brave; be strong. Let all that you do be done with love. 1 Corinthians 16:13-14

My voice You shall hear in the morning, O LORD; in the morning I will direct it to You, and I will look up. Psalm 5:3

Having spent many years as a Navy wife, I have often been privileged to witness the ceremony honoring a retiring sailor. I am impressed by the focus on his years of keeping the watch. Choosing to stand his duty, knowing full well that if he did not, freedom would suffer. Now he stands relieved, because those he has trained and leaves behind take up the watch.

My own morning watch...a time of quiet communication with God, filled with praise and worship, gratitude and supplication...nurtures my soul; heeding His voice to lift cares and concerns to Him. We are told to keep watch, to be alert; stand and be strong, with love as motivation; love for God and love for others.

Until Jesus returns to claim us to rule and to reign, as His followers we have the watch in the broad scope of our prayer's influence. Let us prayerfully keep it, dear brothers and sisters, morning by morning.

Father, each morning Your voice brings me all Your promises, and I celebrate the truth, and pray You will sustain my heart as I keep watch for You. Amen.

February 1

TEARS

I am weary with my groaning; all night I make my bed swim; I drench my couch with my tears. My eye wastes away because of grief…the LORD has heard the voice of my weeping. The LORD has heard my supplication; the LORD will receive my prayer. Psalm 6:6, 7a, 8b-9

I was chatting with a friend some time ago, and she responded to my "how are you?" question with, "I just can't stop crying." Tears pooled in her eyes even as she spoke. I began to think about our tears, and how much a part of our experiences they are. I found the verse above and it brought many thoughts to mind.

Deep in my being there is an ocean of tears. It comes unbidden, unexpected, not welcome. Like the tide it flows in, piling up the driftwood of remembrance and leaving the debris of pain behind as it rolls back and forth in my heart.

Here on the shore I'm lost in the logjam; tears freshening with each thought, recollection, old memory; reliving hurt, searching for peace. But I am learning that those tears are meant to wash away the refuse that clogs my soul. It is my heavenly Father's cleansing; He washes my heart, as tears wash my eyes, so that I can see Him more clearly. Will I ever cease to weep, I wonder?

And I think that perhaps I never want to reach the place where tears are stopped from flowing; for then I will be hardened, unresponsive, unfeeling.

Heavenly Father, let me keep my tears, so that I will be cleansed by Your presence within me, learning to trust, learning to flow with the tide that frees me to love and accept You; until the day you dry them all forever. Amen.

February 2

ALWAYS, IN ALL WAYS

The LORD has appeared of old unto me, saying, "Yes, I have loved you with an everlasting love; therefore with lovingkindness I have drawn you." Jeremiah 31:3

Some time ago I was preparing a talk for a luncheon. The theme the committee had announced was *Keepsakes*, and I was excited to go back and look at some of my own keepsakes saved over the years.

There were several letters, mostly from my husband when he was at sea; very precious to me. But at the back of the file I noticed a few faded envelopes, their contents torn and worn from many readings. They are all I have left of my father—besides memories—these few letters penned after I had left home rebellious and running, my face turned toward my imagined freedom and my back to the rules.

I had so resented those rules! And I rebelled against all of them. I am sure he never dreamed of all the things I was doing. But at that moment I took the precious scraps of paper, letting my eyes alight on his final words to me, "I love you always, in all ways, Daddy."

As I looked at those letters, I was wrapped in the love from which I had tried to run. I wept to remember he died not knowing that I have returned, repentant, to find my Heavenly Father's arms opened wide. Returned to experience God's beloved words, "*I* love you always, in all ways" signed in the blood drops of His Son on His letter of reconciliation to me.

Dear Father, I tried to outrun Your love, just like I ran away from my earthly father and his rules. I know now those rules were for my good and my protection. How sweet to know Your love never failed through those miserable years. How I love You now. Amen.

February 3

MY TOUCH, HIS TOUCH

Wherever He entered, into villages, cities, or the country, they laid the sick in the marketplaces, and begged Him that they might just touch the hem of His garment. And as many as touched Him were made well. Mark 6:56

I'm discovering we don't have to reach very high to touch the hem of Jesus' garment. In the dregs of pain and misery, desperate for healing, and flat on the floor, we can still reach it. Perhaps that is why this story is included in scripture, letting us know that to reach out and touch…to feel the place where faith meets power…brings healing. The healing is not in the hem of the garment, but comes because of the faith that stretched out the hand.

Even in a crowd He is tuned to the seeking soul. So close, less than a breath away, He senses the slightest reaching movement and power goes out from Him. He is so aware of our pain. My touch is one of faith, His touch is one of power, mercy, grace and unfathomable love.

Why, oh why, do I wait so long, exhausting all other possibilities, to seek His compassion and healing? It just takes my simple touch of faith, to be met by an outpouring of all that He is, in His unimaginably incredible touch!

Heavenly Father, please increase my faith! Stir up the courage You provide and let me experience the healing touch of Your power. Thank You for Your mercy and kindness, Your willingness to offer what only You can give. Amen.

February 4

THE TOUCH

Now when Jesus had come into Peter's house, He saw his wife's mother lying sick with a fever. So He touched her hand, and the fever left her. And she arose and served them. Matthew 8:14, 15

I have been thinking about my mother-in-law lately, reminded of her in an email from a young Navy wife whom we had known in an earlier church. One particular evening many years ago, while her husband was out to sea, my husband and I visited this young woman who was struggling with loneliness and emotional distress. We wanted to offer her our love and support. We took Mother with us and all evening she sat, holding the young woman's hand, just rubbing it gently. "For a girl so far from home, that was encouraging and sustaining to me," she shared in her email.

I long to encourage us all to use what God has given us. We often think that means some big talent or gift, some earth-shaking ministry. Remembering Mother, an amazing woman who truly knew how to love, challenges me. She was an ordinary woman whose life affected many people. She often blessed me with her loving touch and many others have shared a similar experience. This is something every one of us can do. Maybe we think it is too small to matter, but we may never know its long-range result.

We can't all hold each other's hands physically but in simple compassion, by word or deed, we can create a memory that lasts.

Heavenly Father, help me remember how You have touched me, how You hold my hand every day, and seek ways to touch in, even a simple way, another hurting soul. Amen.

February 5

IN THE MIDST OF ME

The Lord your God in your midst, the Mighty One, will save; He will rejoice over you with gladness; He will quiet you with His love; He will rejoice over you with singing. Zephaniah 3:17

Hurting with disappointment, frazzled with stress, *shoulds* and *oughts* hammering at the door of my mind; tasks, duties, urgencies, assault me as I fall headlong into mistakes caused by too many distractions. I am afraid. Afraid I can't do it all, that I will fail…that I already have.

I land with a thud at the Father's feet. I am His whimpering, frightened child, awash in longing for the touch from Him that I've been too busy to feel. I hear, now that I've stopped wailing, these words He breathed through the prophet Zephaniah. They have touched me so many times, yet as I turn the pages to read them once again, I find He is the midst of me… and delighted to be there, it says. He is rejoicing at the center of my being. I so need to be reminded of this. My heartbeat slows, and quiet calm begins to spread, covering all I am with His love.

Father, I now have a different perspective now of my dilemma. Although I am regretting those earlier mistakes, I am comforted by Your presence. You are here. And the joy begins to radiate afresh from the midst of me. Amen.

February 6

THE THREEFOLD CORD

Though one may be overpowered by another, two can withstand him, and a threefold cord is not quickly broken. Ecclesiastes 4:12

There is a longing inside me, a demand for intimacy that, unmet, cuts my heart in pieces. I am learning that God created that yearning. Did He do it when He knit me together in my mother's womb?

Through the years, I have tried to fill that craving with friendships and relationships, struggling to find completion. But now I see in the mirror of my mind that no earthly relationship was ever enough, because my need is God Himself.

God desires to be my friend, in every beautiful sense of the word; to fill the empty longing that I might be whole. And in being whole in Him I can love and be loved.

It takes surrender. It takes giving up the idea that I can fix myself by my own efforts. It takes faith and trust that by inviting and allowing Him into my relationships I will find what's missing.

Father, from the completeness that surrounds my surrender to Your friendship, may I reach outward, cradling no more self-indulgence, to find the third strand that makes the threefold cord. Amen.

February 7

THE COMPASSION OF BOUNDARIES

As a father has compassion on his children, so the Lord has compassion on those who fear Him; for He knows how we are formed, He remembers that we are dust. Psalm 103:13-14 (NIV)

Compassion is not easy for me. So I have to ask God for understanding and tenderness for those who are in my circle of care; to remember the frailty of childhood, the fears and frustrations of adolescence that define the growing process. Because that is how He cares for me. Compassion, knowing me and understanding my frailty.

God asks, *Who shut up the sea behind doors when it burst from the womb; when I fixed limits for it and set its doors and bars in place, when I said, "This far you may come and no farther here is where your proud waves halt.*[9] There is an amazing truth here. God set boundaries for the ocean, and I need to see the necessity of establishing limits; for myself, and for my children, no matter how far in life they've traveled; for friends and others in my sphere. For, as the sea is free to move within its boundaries, so there is freedom within the shelter of God's laws. Without borders, what seems to be freedom can be a frightening unknown pursued in desperation.

Dear Father, I see that limits are a gift, for me as Your child. Thank You for Your law. I pray that my life will consistently show compassion and that I will give, with loving awareness, the gift of boundaries. Amen.

---

[9] Job in 38:8, 10-11

February 8

ASK, BELIEVING

And whatever things you ask in prayer, believing, you will receive. Matthew 21:22

Do you believe this? May I share a miracle with you? Some time ago my husband and I were helping our son stage his fund-raising golf tournament. Unhappily, after months of planning and preparation, there was a monster storm predicted for the weekend reserved at the golf course. Our son refused to cancel, saying, "No, I'm going through with it, and hope that everyone has a good time and sees Jesus in us." So we began praying in earnest for a break in the storm.

I told everyone I believed there would be sunshine during the event. People laughed. "It can't be," they said, "there's a horrible storm that day. It's the storm of the century." But **there was sunshine all day over the golf course!** People showed up to play and donate, even though thunderclouds ringed the area. No drops fell however, until the final putts were sunk! Now what we heard was, "I can't believe it!" Even the golf course personnel were amazed, and we were able to witness a God who is faithful and cares about what perhaps may seem small, but because of His intervention, looms huge in our lives.

Had I *really* believed what I told people I did? Probably not, or I wouldn't have been so blown away by such a vibrantly beautiful answer. I had dreamed of a blue sky and sunshine, but was surprised when that is what greeted us!

Dear God, thank You for the times You let us see You. That day men and women who don't know You were made vividly aware of Your power…and Your love. And therein is the miracle! Help us be aware, watching, so we can share in Your miracles. Amen.

February 9

FOOTBATH

...so he got up from the meal, took off his outer clothing, and wrapped a towel around his waist. After that, he poured water into a basin and began to wash his disciples' feet, drying them with the towel that was wrapped around him. John 13:4-5, NIV

It was a shared meal with curious undertones. Fellowship, yes, but misunderstanding the motives of Jesus, the disciples were no doubt shocked at His very servile activity, washing their feet.

I would have been, too. I think I would have protested, like Peter; that I should be the one washing *His* feet, not the other way around. But I have the blessing of hindsight, and the truth of scripture; knowing what happened afterward. Calvary.

And while my heart rejoices in the fact that His shed blood guarantees my forgiveness, I'm pretty stubborn about receiving the mercy He offers in the basin and the towel. Just as I probably would have protested, had I been there that night, I often resist His ministering grace to me now. I am unworthy, you see. Of course I am. My heart is soiled with daily transgressions and my feet are dirty from walking my earthly path. Jesus brings to me the pure water of forgiveness to wash away the stain; and the mercy of a soft towel to prepare me to go on. Such tenderness, this washing of the feet, the cleansing of the soul. I desperately need it, my own daily footbath.

Father, I think that I should grab a towel and fill a basin with the water of Your Word and begin looking for others who need to sense Your mercy. Jesus did it as an example for me and I must accept it, and pass on the miracle of the footbath. Amen.

February 10

NEVERTHELESS

And he (Jehoshaphat) walked in the way of his father Asa, and did not turn aside from it, doing what was right in the sight of the LORD. Nevertheless the high places were not taken away, for as yet the people had not directed their hearts to the God of their fathers.
2 Chronicles 20:32-33.

Jehoshaphat, one of Israel's good kings, is a great example to us in many ways. I am always struck by the many times God uses the word *nevertheless* in Scripture. I looked it up in the dictionary and it means "in spite of, despite, or however." How could the people, following a wise, Godly king, still maintain the high places? Places where idol worship took place; places that God had ordered them to destroy?

What a contrast there is here. A leader commended for his faithful following of his God, *nevertheless* allowing idolatry by not abolishing the altars of pagan worship.

So I wonder what this says to me? Is there such a contrast in my life? I need to be more and more aware that following God means abolishing the high places in my heart, the altars of self-worship, those high places that take my focus off my God.

My Father, I have so admired Jehoshaphat for his Godly leadership, yet I see now that even he didn't go all the way to obedience. I do want to be obedient, do not want to have a part in nevertheless, but trust you for a purer life of worship. Amen.

February 11

ON TIPTOE

Walk in wisdom toward those who are outside, redeeming the time. Let your speech always be with grace, seasoned with salt, that you may know how you ought to answer each one. Colossians 4:5-6

Somehow I have had the picture of successful Christians as seasoned warriors striding forth waving the Sword as a banner. But here I read that we are to walk in wisdom, and I am thinking that stomping out to the battleground may not be the best plan.

What if in my stomping I crush something or somebody fragile? Or isn't it more than possible to step into something messy or dirty? Or to march so loudly I am unable to hear the voice of my Commander?

No, I think perhaps walking on tiptoe is more what God has in mind. Carefully, circumspectly, cautiously, watchful with wisdom from above—yet confidently moving forward.

It reminds me of a child coming downstairs on Christmas morning: Quietly determined, expectant, prepared for something extraordinary. Yet the child is hesitant, careful in order not to disturb the ecstasy of the moment. Gifts await.

Almighty Father, if we walk on tiptoe, cautious where we step, gracefully obedient, the gifts from above will never disappoint And, I'm sure, we will draw others to You. May we always remember this. Amen.

February 12

BRUSHSTROKES

For we are His workmanship, created in Christ Jesus for good works, which God prepared beforehand that we should walk in them.
Ephesians 2:10

Observing an artist the other day, I was comparing my life to a painting. God saw the finished product in His mind's eye before He ever set the canvas of my days on His easel.

I watch the artist paint—first sketching the design, the vision, applying the first layer, then another and another. Sometimes, at first, it doesn't look like much; the colors muddied, the design unclear, but the process goes on and, little by little, the picture emerges. I begin to see how the dark colors underneath bring the depth and foundation for the highlighting that only the artist can apply to create the completion of his vision.

It's not finished yet, the painting of my life, but one day God will say "Ah, yes, it is done." And He will put His signature in the corner, satisfied and well-pleased with His work.

Consider how sunset wraps the warmth of day in vibrant shades of fire which in turn explode into a night that gives birth to a silver-frosted dawn. Masterpieces, originated by the Creator, proclaiming His glory in vivid blaze and icy alabaster. He is the Painter of contrasts at work in my life, desiring that the sunny colors of joy and the chilly whiteness of pain together will display His glory.

Heavenly Father, though I cannot always discern the brushstrokes, I know that in both hardship and delight, You are painting a masterpiece of love on the canvas of my heart. Amen.

February 13

INTO CAPTIVITY

For the weapons of our warfare are not carnal, but mighty in God for pulling down strongholds; casting down arguments and every high thing that exalts itself against the knowledge of God, bringing into captivity every thought to the obedience of Christ.
2 Corinthians 10:4-5

I have noticed, nearly every time that I reach a new relationship plane with God, that the enemy redoubles his efforts to derail me. He brings sinful thoughts, so much a part of my old sinful nature, into my consciousness. Those familiar emotions and reactions thrust sharp sword points into the tender armor of my new intimacy with God.

An altercation begins, my thoughts against His; the old against the new on the battlefield of my mind. Coexistence is impossible, the defeat of one or the other is inevitable. I must choose the weapons as the fiery darts of the evil one bring envy and bitterness to the front lines. I have available the Sword of the Spirit, mighty through God, able to pierce my darkness.

Here on my knees the battle rages. I have heard of, read of, and even experienced the victory over the foe that is available to me, but obedience is hard and my enemy is clever. I must *capture* the thoughts that threaten to undo me, and obediently draw them to the feet of Jesus where victory is obtainable.

God, please soften my heart with willingness to break the bondage and bring every thought into captivity, obediently responding to Your instructions for victory. And I will thank You and praise You. Amen.

February 14

LIMITS

"I am the Alpha and the Omega, the Beginning and the End," says the Lord, "who is and who was and who is to come, the Almighty." Revelation 1:8

The Almighty God is Everything! He is Omnipotent, Omniscient, Omnipresent. But I've learned that I can limit Him. How can that be? He's all-powerful, all-knowing, all-present, isn't He? Yet one thing remains that He cannot change: my mind. The free will He gave me allows a choice, and the limits come from me.

I discovered this quote that brings me so much comfort. "An infinite God can give all of Himself to each of His children, He does not distribute Himself that each may have a part, but to each one He gives all of Himself as fully as if there were no others."[10] Amazing!

But...does my face turn to Him in joy? Does my spirit yearn for His companionship? Does all else pale in the light of His presence? If not, our relationship is incomplete, and the limits come from me.

Oh, I cannot limit His power, His love or His grace. They're infinite and offered freely; but if He's not *my* everything, our communion is less than He wants it to be. And the limits come from me.

Father, I praise You for Who You are, and I recognize that You desire intimacy with me. Forgive me when I push You away, I really do not want to limit You. Amen.

---

[10] A. W. Tozer (1897-1963)

February 15

AMONG SO MANY

One of His disciples, Andrew, Simon Peter's brother, said to Him, "There is a lad here who has five barley loaves and two small fish, but what are they among so many?" John 6:8-9

I am not sure why this phrase "among so many" rings in my heart. Perhaps it brings to mind the truth that we tend to only look at surface issues, not at our wondrous God who is able to do a miracle. We plod along, merely surviving, instead of walking in anticipation of the seemingly impossible, which God can do.

Jesus's disciples are no different, as we see here! Looking around at the crowd, all they see is the need for food. The offering of loaves and fish seems painfully inadequate in their eyes.

How often I have looked at them in derision...should they not have known the power that Jesus wielded? They were with Him every day, after all! Whoa! As I examine my own life do I not do the same thing when I consider my perceived inadequacy and ask, "Who am I among so many? So many others may have more than I have—more talent, more courage, more skill." It doesn't matter. I only see the obvious human failings, *God* wants me to look to Him for what *He* can do with my small offering.

Heavenly Father, I am convicted of a lack of faith in what You can do. Among so many, Lord, can you use me *and magnify the offering of my life with Your power, that as just Jesus blessed the loaves and fish, it will be enough. I surrender all I am. Amen.*

February 16

THE FRAGRANCE OF VIOLETS

If we confess our sins, He is faithful and just to forgive us our sins and cleanse us from all unrighteousness. 1 John 1:9

A long time ago, I hurt my friend. But learned a lesson. Senior Sneak Day was a tradition we had looked forward to all year. We chartered a bus and headed to the big city leaving at midnight following the class play. In high spirits we were heady with the thrill of being "on our own."

I am not proud of my behavior that night, as I look back upon it. Playing a silly kissing game in the darkened bus seemed harmless enough, but my friend thought I was trying to steal her boyfriend. In school the following Monday she called me aside and told me how I much I had hurt her by monopolizing the boy she really liked. I knew she liked him but I was free with my kisses anyway. She said, "I was so angry with you!"

I was stunned. I felt small and cheap. Unable to defend myself. I stammered, "I'm so sorry." She said something I will never, ever forget. "I forgive you. We were all acting crazy. But you are my friend and I was so disappointed in you. I care about you though, and I forgive you. We can still be friends.

"Forgiveness is the fragrance a violet sheds upon the heel that crushes it."[11] What a lesson I learned that day! Jesus says, "seventy times seven,"[12] which basically means uncountable. Because that is how generously God forgives us.

Father, these words ring in my heart whenever I find myself in a position to forgive, or to be forgiven. Thank you for giving me the opportunity to live surrounded by the fragrance of violets. Amen.

---

[11] Mark Twain (1835-1910)

[12] Matthew 18:22

February 17

THE SCAFFOLD

"And I, if I be lifted up from the earth, will draw all peoples to Myself." This He said, signifying by what death He would die.
John 12:32-33.

Latticework intricately surrounds uncompleted buildings. How often do we look around a construction site, especially where a very high building is being erected, and notice a scaffold? It is a sign of work in progress; a temporary frame to be removed when the labor is done. Its purpose is to support workmen safely, to provide a platform for the necessary tools and supplies. Scaffolding is vital to the successful completion of the planned structure.

High on Calvary's hill a kind of scaffold stood, its rough timbers supporting the incarnate Tabernacle. It is vital to the successful achievement of God's plan. His Son, Jesus, hung there. His efforts completed His appointed task. Calvary's cross, the ultimate scaffold, is no longer visible to our physical eyes. The work is finished, yet to hope-filled eyes it stands forever as a framework for the final sacrifice on which my faith rests.

Dear Father, Jesus was lifted up, for me, upon a painful scaffold, until He could cry "It is finished!" What mercy, what love and what grace! How can I ever say thank you enough? Let my life b one of praise-filled gratitude. Amen.

February 18

THE ENGAGEMENT

And you shall love the Lord your God with all your heart, with all your soul, with all your mind, and with all your strength.
Mark 12:30

I read this verse and sense the challenge deep inside me. Heart, soul, mind, and strength! Focusing on two things here, my strength and my passion; the Scripture says "*all*." Not *some* weak stabs at connecting, but all of me! That cannot happen without passion. Passion that infuses strength, because passivity engenders weakness. God desires my passion because He is passionate about me.

These thoughts bring to mind my engagement ring and how I would wave my hand dramatically at every opportunity so that people would see it and ask about my fiancé. Eloquently, passionately describing the wonder of my love; I was unable to be passive.

Where is that passion now that I am part of the bride of Christ? I'm falling in love with Him. Am I passionate about Him? Living in such expectancy that I want to tell everyone about the wonder of His love for me?

Just like the gleam of my engagement diamond, may His love sparkle from my eyes, shine through my life; so that people will ask about Him and My lips will proclaim Him, Jesus, my Savior passionately, with all my strength.

Heavenly Father, I am coming to know You more and love You better. I want my life to show that, and for it to be so real that the passion is visible, throughout my heart and soul and mind...and definitely, my strength! Amen.

February 19

FOCUS

By this we know love, because He laid down his life for us. And we ought to lay down our lives for the brethren. 1 John 3:16

We love Him because He first loved us. 1 John 4:19

Let's consider some insights on love. We all know the word is cheapened by its overuse these days. We say "I love" about everything from popcorn to our spouses, children, friends. But the true love that motivates our behavior is so much more. This is not news to us!

I've been thinking more deeply and realizing that I, too, use the word loosely more often than not. I heard someone say the other day "love dictates our focus." What we really love grows in magnitude when we examine it under the microscope through which we peer at life.

I'm wondering what is etched on my specimen slide? Is it Jesus? Is it my desire to love like He does? Or do I only observe the selfish needs that demand my attention. I am challenged to examine the specimen called "love" that determines my motivations, fuels my behavior. Perhaps there is a fresh need clamoring for my attention; a need to serve, not myself, but others. It is a *need* to do so from love like Jesus does—seeing lacks, hurts and pain, and reaching out with the right motivation: love.

Precious Heavenly Father, I have no excuse not to love as You demand, because You first loved me. Oh, how that love would change the slide under my life's microscope; not one etched with my *needs, but with things that break the heart of Jesus. Amen.*

February 20

WOMAN AT THE WELL

Jesus answered and said to her, "If you knew the gift of God, and who it is who says to you, 'Give Me a drink,' you would have asked Him, and He would have given you living water." John 4:10

Trudging wearily; intent upon her daily duty to fill the water jug, the woman nears the well. Today a stranger awaits, requests a drink. How was she to know her life was about to be changed?

Sometimes the stories in the Bible have such glaring applications to my own life that I am left standing amazed. I see that I am like the woman at the well. Wearied by cares and burdens, the duties I've assumed, I trudge obediently to the village, as it were, to perform yet another chore. How am I to know my life is about to change?

I am unknowingly dry and thirsty, yet I dutifully offer whatever I have. When promise is made of water for my own thirst, I wonder how a stranger can provide for my deepest needs. He doesn't even have a bucket to put the water in! Oh, how blind I've become…

To perceive Jesus as a *stranger* when He's offering living water to be poured from Himself into the depths of me! No need for a bucket—He *is* the water jar; and I become partaker, opening my needy heart. Living Water fills me, quenching my yearning thirst.

Lord Jesus, newly filled with You, and rejoicing I turn for home. May I never again allow myself to become so thirsty, having failed to drink of Your living water. Amen.

February 21

REFRESHMENT

For we have great joy and consolation in your love because the hearts of the saints have been refreshed by you, brother. Yes, brother let me have joy from you in the Lord; refresh my heart in the Lord.
Philemon 7,20

Refreshment: a sweet, consoling word. *Refreshments will be served* is a sure-fire way to induce someone to respond positively to an invitation! At least to me it promises something enjoyable.

I picked up on that word this morning while reading the Apostle Paul's letter to his friend Philemon. Twice in this short letter he mentions how Philemon's love brings joy, comfort, and yes, *refreshment,* to all the saints. What a commendation!

So, I wonder, do I have a love for others that brings joy to their hearts? I have been refreshed so many times by the love shown to me; unexpectedly, surprised by joy. That joy makes me smile, long to burst into song, to jump and shout; it is, as well, comfort that soothes my soul.

Joy and consolation are gifts to be received, coming from God on high, carried by the love of His people, and distributed as a source of refreshment in the Lord.

Father, may I always be conscious and grateful for the refreshment offered to me, and may I seek to be a refreshment to others, a promise of something delicious! Amen.

February 22

COMFORT

Let us therefore come boldly to the throne of grace that we may obtain mercy and find grace to help in time of need. Hebrews 4:16

In the middle of a busy week my husband remarked that it's "feast or famine": either nothing is going on, or everything happens at once! It is true; a lot of pleasurable events tend to come up in the midst of trials and duties. With that in mind, I recently went through my Bible looking at passages about grace, and I was so blessed to read the words that I've quoted above from Scripture. Before that day was over I had received four telephone calls from friends whose lives were in turmoil.

We were all in need of the above comforting words from Scripture. It was so good to share with hurting ones that God, who sits on the Throne of Grace, has an abundant supply of mercy and grace, and gives it freely. We need only to come.

When you find a need for this comfort, I pray you will come boldly and avail yourself of the limitless resources from a heavenly Father who longs to touch your life with a new realization of what He offers you—mercy and grace to help in time of need. Just come.

Dear God. I pray rich blessings on all of us today! From Your storehouse of comfort and mercy pour Your love into our hearts. We gratefully acknowledge that You are the Source of grace. And we boldly claim the limitless supply. Amen.

February 23

DEEPER PLACES

Can a woman forget her nursing child, and not have compassion on the son of her womb? Yet I will not forget you. See, I have inscribed you on the palms of my hands; your walls are ever before Me.
Isaiah 49:15-16

Isn't this a tender picture, a poignant promise? I cannot read it without a sense of peace. *This* is how we are loved by God, like a mother loves her child. We mothers understand this at a deep level, I think. No matter what her children may do, no matter how far they may run, the tenacious love of a mother follows them.

Absorbing and accepting the truth that God's love is like that can be difficult. At least it was for me. I tried to perform well enough to earn His love. I had a huge problem realizing that my name was already engraved on His hands by a hammer and nails. It is not what I do, how I look, or who I know that gives meaning to my life. That contentment comes from the deep knowledge of being entirely, sweetly loved.

I remember the way I felt when our son, who had been estranged from us for years, wrapped his arms around me and announced, "I love you, Mom." Love for him had filled me through those sad years, and could now burst into bloom! He was there; he was my son for whom my love had never slackened.

My dear Heavenly Father, what beautiful visual experiences You give us as illustrations! I have a hint from my own life how your tender love for me gives a settled calmness. I know my name is written on the palms of Your hands. May I never forget. Amen.

February 24

BEDROCK

And you shall know the truth, and the truth shall make you free.
John 8:32

Bedrock, solid rock beneath the soil and stones; a foundation. God's bedrock is truth, and He calls me to know it, stand upon it, and to walk in it. But in our society today, truth is a misty concept, becoming fuzzy and fudged; and, in fact, easy to ignore.

Jesus said knowing the truth would set me free. Maybe the fact that I sometimes feel bound and stifled is that the chains are of my own making. Have I indulged in some deceitful behavior, some dishonesty, not told the whole truth, not walked entirely upright, excusing myself because it seemed to be just a little deviation, a small sidestep?

I want to be free; what is the truth that I need to know? It is that I am *loved*. Loved by the God of the Universe… my Creator Who IS truth. When that fact becomes burned into my brain, into the very core of me, there comes a freedom to live and love; a willingness to trust, a longing to walk with the One Who holds my hand and will never let it go. And everything else falls into place.

Dear Father, teach me Your truth; its reality and infallibility. Even a small sidestep wounds You and causes me to slip, opening the door to a deeper loss. I want to know the freedom that walking in truth provides. I want to know *Your love. Thank you. Amen.*

February 25

MARGINS

There was not a word of all that Moses had commanded which Joshua did not read before all the assembly of Israel with the women, the little ones, and the strangers who lived among them. Joshua 8:35

When the children of Israel were delivered by God, many Egyptians followed. Several times the scriptures mention these "aliens." They lived among the Israelites, although they were sort of in the margins of the culture. But God didn't forget them.

What about those people in the margins of my life? Operating my computer provided an illustration of this for me.

When I meticulously set the margins of a document, I am careful to make sure the finished product will be neat and tidy. Making these adjustments is as easy as pushing a button! I wonder if perhaps I try to make the same easy adjustments in dealing with people in my life. Is any relationship that might be messy or destroy the symmetry of my carefully constructed life, rearranged and thus ignored by the push of a button in my heart.

In my stubborn insistence on keeping my margins tidy, I am effectively pushing aside the whisper of God, the Creator. The God whose heart bleeds for His creation. Who does not marginalize those who I might consider an alien. He pleads for me to do the same!

Father, forgive my callous indifference to those who may not be like me, who may not seem to enhance my selfish life. May I open my eyes to Your vision of caring for the aliens living beside me. Amen.

February 26

ONLY BUSY

Be still and know that I am God.
Psalm 46:10

Desiring to hear God's approving voice, I placed myself where I thought He wanted me and began to do all the right things. I thought by being useful I'd sense His pleasure in me. But it is becoming more and more evident I've been spinning my wheels all this while; not really useful, only busy.

Someone shared with me an acronym for the word "busy." It is convicting: "Buried Under Satan's Yoke". Being busy does not make me important in God's eyes; in fact it tears me away from Him in many ways. This is a lesson I must learn. A goal of the enemy is to keep me from growing in intimacy with God, so he points me to a list of tasks to be completed—with its accompanying guilt.

Some time ago, mired in frustration and undone duties, I somehow heard my Father say, "It's you I want not what you do." And it brought me up short, stripping away all my self-serving whining. Brought to my knees in my need, His voice continued, "I don't need you to do more for Me. I just long to love you better."

Oh my Father, when the urge to perform pulls me out of Your arms and I fill all my time with chores, instead of a whisper, please shout to remind me to choose to simply BE Yours. Then perhaps I will be useful and not simply busy. Amen.

February 27

THE REPAIR SHOP

Behold, I make all things new. Revelation 21:5

We have recently been watching a Discovery Channel program titled "The Repair Shop". It is fascinating, showing the restoration of precious items that have seen better days. Owners bring their treasures to the shop where creative, talented crafters breathe new life into memories.

It is so rewarding to observe the way the experts listen to the stories, examine the object and begin to take it apart and apply all their knowledge and skill and return the possessions to smiling or weeping owners.

I always look for a spiritual application when something touches my heart. When a tattered, rusty, damaged toy or piece of furniture is made like new it is expressive of hope, and possibility!

What is possible when we turn over our tattered and damaged hearts and rusty lives to the Master Craftsman and yield to His skill? Restoration! God's Repair Shop is open; its doors never close and He waits there to rebuild us, His treasures, and breathe new life into us.

Oh, Father, what a lovely illustration of Your ability to take what appears to be ruined and give it life. May I say, with the hymn writer, "Take my life, and let it be consecrated, Lord, to Thee."[13] *Amen.*

---

[13] Take My Life and Let It Be Frances R. Havergal (1836-1879)

February 28

JOY

This day is holy to our Lord. Do not grieve, for the joy of the LORD is your strength. Nehemiah 8:10

Joy is worth fighting for. Would you not agree? But sometimes we have to struggle against despair and anxiety. The enemy of our souls most definitely does not want us to possess the joy that God brings. I have taken Nehemiah 8:10 as one of my life verses, because I am discovering the truth that it IS joy—the joy of the LORD—that serves as the weapon that best fights the enemy's efforts to steal from me.

I once read a book titled "If Satan Can't Steal Your Joy."[14] It pointed out that, though it seems Satan is determined to steal our joy, he's really after our *strength.* He's not simply out to make us have a bad day, he's out to weaken our faith, and ruin our effectiveness as followers of Jesus.

It isn't always easy to be joyful; and, truthfully joy requires all-out war. But we are not fighting this war by ourselves! We have the giant-killing, mighty warrior God standing with us and His Word is Truth—the best and only offensive weapon we will ever need. We must stay in the Word, meditating on it to counteract Satan's tactics.

Heavenly Father, I so easily get discouraged when my enemy suggests that I am not enough. Help me to realize that I am not a weakling when I live in your joy. I am a warrior! Help me stand firm and raise the Sword of truth. The battle ultimately belongs to You. Amen.

---

[14] © 2004 Jerry Savelle

February 29

THE CALLING

For the Word of God is living and powerful and sharper than any two-edged sword, piercing even to the division of soul and spirit, and is a discerner of the thoughts and intents of the heart.
Hebrews 4:12

My Heavenly Father's *piercing* Word…I used to be so afraid of it because my deeds didn't bear scrutiny, particularly His scrutiny. I was running from Him—knowing I was running, and too stubborn to return. I feared the judgment of His Word, fleeing as a criminal pursued by the law.

But now after I have come home to Him I ponder this verse with sweeter clarity. His Word pierces to the places where I really *live* in relationship with Him: my soul and my spirit. It probes and examines whether I am behaving as His, or am I living life on my own terms?

God has wrought a difference in me. Instead of blinding panic and a desire to hide, there arises within me a sense of poignancy, a questioning, not of my deeds, but of how I am doing in my intimacy with Him.

So I ask my Savior, "Do I love You, Lord, really love You? Only You know." I want to know, too, in the depths of my soul. I want to hear His heart more loudly and clearly than I hear the gavel of judgment against me."

Dear Father, it is with a grateful heart, I affirm to You, I don't want to run from You *anymore. Amen*

March 1

CLOTHED IN GRACE

I will greatly rejoice in the LORD; my soul shall be joyful in my God; for He has clothed me with the garments of salvation, He has covered me with the robe of righteousness… Isaiah 61:10a

Covered. That is what this scripture is telling me. I am covered and clothed with salvation and righteousness! His all-encompassing grace is beyond my comprehension—this garment that I wear as His child. I constantly wiggle to unwrap myself from its folds to try life on my own. I wallow helplessly in self-inflicted misery while this lovely wrapping lies by the side of the road discarded. How I need to understand that this robe is to *enable*, not to *hamper*, and that without it I am wrapped in self.

You see, I have always dressed my heart in lovely, caring deeds, preening its *appearance* to be pleasing to God. Evil lurking there was not something I cared to consider; that would not be acceptable. But as I read this verse I look under that robe and see my naked heart, undressed of its pious works. Shivering at the sight of my sin, I am finally aware that in my flesh dwells no good thing.

So this morning I stand repenting, sensing with my spirit the power of God's perfect grace draping my naked heart with His robe of righteousness. My heart is clothed.

God, may your grace be the hat I wear that my thoughts are loving; the cloak draped over my body to cover my movements; the gloves for my hands, that my touch be tender; and the shoes for my feet, that my steps be always on Your path. Amen.

March 2

BLING!

I will greatly rejoice in the LORD; my soul shall be joyful in my God; for He has clothed me with the garments of salvation, He has covered me with the robe of righteousness… as a bridegroom decks himself with ornaments and as a bride adorns herself with jewels.
Isaiah 61:10b

This is a precious verse. I have spoken my gratitude to God for His provision, His covering; yes, I have rejoiced in them. As I look closer at the progression here, I notice that the joy and rejoicing come *because* of the covering of salvation and righteousness, which is the costume I am wearing.

There is, however, a little word here that I have missed somehow… It is *As. As* the bridegroom decks himself with ornaments and *as* a bride adorns herself with jewels.

BLING. I have a lot of friends and family who love to cover themselves with jewels, sequins and shiny stuff. Just the other day I remarked to someone that I am not comfortable wearing a lot of bling! "It is not me," I said. Imagine, then, my delight this morning to read this very familiar verse and discover that there is such a thing as spiritual BLING! But it only shines from the depth of a person's joy and gratitude.

It is enabled because God has made it possible. We are to shine like the joy of a bride on her wedding day and with the anticipation and thrill of the bridegroom.

Dear Father, there is nothing wrong with sequins, or rhinestones; sometimes it is fun to wear them. But I want to be sure that the BLING that I wear is like that of a bride on her special day, jewels of joy reflecting in my eyes! Amen.

March 3

BODY ARMOR

But let all those rejoice who put their trust in You; let them shout for joy, because You defend them; let also those who love Your name be joyful in You. For You, O LORD, will bless the righteous; with favor You will surround him as with a shield. Psalm 5:11-12

Righteous. That's me. It is so hard for me to say, but God says He sees me that way. Only however, because of Jesus. Not by any righteous acts I have done, but according to His mercy, I am surrounded by favor. That is the approval and acceptance for which I have so longed, and it is available to me from the Creator of the Universe! Why is it so difficult to comprehend that I am already surrounded by it?

That favor is a shield, the psalmist says: protection against the enemy of my soul. It wraps me, holds me so that I won't go looking for human favor. It is armor, body armor, to enable me to lay down the unholy desire for man's approval, and to soak, instead, in the truth that I am beloved. And then, I can truly rejoice!

Father, I see clearly that the enemy wants me to focus on the approval of men. I so need to pull Your defensive protection close to me and brandish that shield of Your favor in the face of him who would destroy me. Please help me to remember this. Amen.

March 4

BRIDAL GOWN

Let us be glad and rejoice and give Him glory; for the marriage of the Lamb is come, and his bride has made herself ready. And to her was granted that she should be arrayed in fine linen, clean and bright, for the fine linen is the righteousness of saints.
Revelation 19:7-8

It fascinates me to ponder on the analogies that clarify and endear a passage of Scripture to my heart. So often the Bible speaks of us believers, the church, as the Bride of Christ.

Personally I have never attended a wedding that didn't touch me deeply—I am a hopeless romantic! So perhaps I need to consider just what I'm to be wearing when Jesus returns.

I've been working on my wedding dress with great excitement! I know the day is nearing and my gown must be ready. My pattern (the radiant Christ) is beautiful, and I'm endeavoring to cut the fabric of clean white linen to His design. The walk down the aisle, I know, is only a twinkling of an eye, so I'm not sewing this gown for the admiration of the guests, I will be wearing it only for my Bridegroom

Jesus, as I stitch this gown of my life, Your righteousness covering me, my entire being throbs in anticipation for the moment when You lift the veil and I will see Your face. Amen.

March 5

THE SCAR

Praise the LORD. How good it is to sing praises to our God, how pleasant and fitting to praise him! He heals the brokenhearted and binds up their wounds. Psalm 147:1, 3 NIV

He himself bore our sins in his body on the cross, so that we might die to sins and live for righteousness; by his wounds you have been healed. 1 Peter 2:24 NIV

I've been thinking about scars lately. Some time ago I had open heart surgery and as a result, carry a lot of scars on my body. The worst one is on my forearm that marks the wound where they removed my radial artery to repair my heart. It is an ugly scar. But I never look at it without being grateful for my life. Though it has healed now, it does remind me of the many times I've brought my wounded soul, broken, sore and bleeding, to God; knowing He's the one whose written word promises my healing. Every time, my cuts were stitched and salve applied, but it wasn't long before I disobeyed and loosed the scab; sin tore it open wide.

My contrite heart reveals the need of soothing balm—forgiveness. As it cleans the gash, tender skin begins to grow and mending starts once more. I claim His healing now, although I'm aware it's more a process than a one-time deed and I will fall, unclose the wound, again to hurt and bleed. One day it will only be a mark to remind me of His healing mercy, evidenced in the scars Jesus bears eternally. By those wounds I am healed.

O Great Physician, every time you touch the pain cleansing the festering scar, help me remember the stripes by which I am healed. I lift my heart in praise and gratitude when I view my scar. Amen.

March 6

THIS TEMPLE

But will God indeed dwell on the earth? Behold, heaven and the heaven of heavens cannot contain You. How much less this temple which I have built! Yet regard the prayer of Your servant and his supplication, O LORD my God, and listen to the cry and the prayer which Your servant is praying before You today: that Your eyes may be open toward this temple night and day, toward the place of which You said, "My name shall be there"... 1 Kings 8:27-29

A favorite story example in the Old Testament is recorded in 1 Kings. I have included a few verses here, telling of King Solomon's dedication of the temple he had built for God. He was a good king, in ancient times, and he had built a home for the Most High where He could dwell among His own. Solomon, with his God-given wisdom, followed the plan he and his father, King David, had devised. He built it true to Heavenly blueprint and covered it with gold.

Though beautiful to earthly eyes, he called it humble and lowly. It was for the worship of his God, a house to bear His name. In earnest prayer Solomon asked the Lord to fill this "humble house". God heard the plea; His glory filled its sanctuary.

I have an earthly temple, this body where I live. God has heard my earnest prayer and now He lives in me. It's a humble house, but the Father is pleased to settle in. His Spirit fills me, gilds me with His love and lets me be His sanctuary.

Lord, in all my deeds may I be aware and mindful of your presence in me. With all I am let me show that this house bears your Name. Amen.

March 7

CLOAKS

"Go to the village ahead of you, and as you enter it, you will find a colt tied there, which no one has ever ridden. Untie it and bring it here." They brought it to Jesus, threw their cloaks on the colt and put Jesus on it. As he went along, people spread their cloaks on the road.
Luke 19:30, 36 (NIV)

Jesus, in triumph, rides on a colt covered with the cloaks of His followers. And as He nears His destination, people fling their own cloaks on the roadway before Him. What is the symbolism here, the message for me?

Perhaps it was excitement, a sort of mob behavior. Perhaps it was all they owned, casting all they had to welcome and honor Him. Perhaps they saw in Him a hope, a promise, and they longed to shed their covering for His. Perhaps it is for us to see in hindsight—those who know the end of this story—that it is a foretelling of His eventual victory…making ours possible.

The book of Isaiah explains what our response should be: *"I delight greatly in the LORD; my soul rejoices in my God. For He has clothed me with garments of salvation and arrayed me in a robe of righteousness…*[15] So I join the ancient prophet with my own words of joy:

Jesus, please take my cloak of pride. I cast it down before you now, that I may wear instead the white robe woven for me by Your sacrifice, provided by Your love and grace. What a glorious exchange! Hallelujah!

---

15 Isaiah 61:10a

March 8

GLADNESS

Hear, O Lord, and have mercy on me; LORD, be my helper! You have turned for me my mourning into dancing; You have put off my sackcloth and clothed me with gladness, to the end that my glory may sing praise to You and not be silent. O LORD, my God I will give thanks to You forever. Psalm 30:10-12

So many times inn scripture I've noticed verses that, when we read them, are very familiar. We quote them, memorize them, develop ideas or philosophies in relation to them; often not noticing the context or the words following. I confess I have done this with the verses above from Psalm 30.

Yes. God *has* turned my mourning into dancing, exchanged the miserable scratchy sackcloth of grief for a garment of gladness and joy. And this certainly IS a cause for gratitude and rejoicing; but the next verse tells us why! What is the intended end for what God has done? Is it simply to make me feel special to Him, something to cling to for myself? No! It is so that I will bring glory to Him, to praise Him! That my voice rise in song to Him. Forever.

Oh Heavenly Father! What I wear often reflects what is going on inside me, and being clothed, covered, in gladness indicates a joy that cannot be kept silent. Flying from the dimness of mourning into the light of your glory sets my feet to dancing. How can I not praise You? And I do. Amen.

March 9

THE HIGH WIRE

...you know how we exhorted, and comforted and charged every one of you, as a father does his own children, that you would walk worthy of God who calls you into His own kingdom and glory.
1 Thessalonians 2:11-12

Some time ago I watched Nik Wallenda's stupendous walk across the Grand Canyon on a wire strung 1500 feet above the canyon floor—without a net! I watched, thinking it was just another stunt. It was spine-tingling; he captivated me with his dialogue—each step was accompanied with a "Thank You, Jesus," "Thank You, Father." It was a praise-filled journey that fostered awe within me as well. I found myself praying out loud for him as winds whipped across the canyon in gusts.

And I thought of what a picture he was painting. We too are walking on a precarious wire in this world, held by God's love and grace. With each step, each moment, our focus should be on reaching our goal. No matter how deep the chasm of hurt or pain or fear we might be walking across right now, we must not only be conscious of our steps, but also filled with joy and gratitude all across our journey's vast expanse. I don't think I would have been as impacted if he had been praising himself, his skill and abilities. But he rather spoke his gratitude and praise to God.

His statement at the end stayed with me, "It's in my blood. It is who I am," he said. "It's my heritage."

Father, this event speaks to me and I want to apply it to my own life. I have accepted Jesus's sacrifice for me; I am Your child. The Holy Spirit has entered, infusing my spiritual bloodstream with His presence. Yes, I see... it's in my blood...the ability to walk the high wire of holiness: it's who I am! Amen.

March 10

THE NECKLACE

My son (daughter!) do not forget my law, but let your heart keep my commands; for length of days and long life and peace they will add to you. Let not mercy and truth forsake you. Bind them around your neck, write them on the tablet of your heart, and so find favor and high esteem in the sight of God and man. Proverbs 3:3-4

When looking into scripture often I find it helpful to look at lists. In these verses I discovered a list of instructions, and following that, a list of results of following those instructions.

Peace and length of days are the results of obedience. Taking hold of mercy and truth brings the result of high esteem and favor of **both** God and man. The wisdom of obedience is the thrust of this passage.

What is so fascinating to me is the instruction to take mercy and truth and wear them as a necklace, in a sense—an *outward* reminder of how to live. Then we are to write them on the tablet of our hearts—an *inward* motivation, so that we would live in a way that brings us high esteem and favor from both God and man. *That* is the longing of my heart.

Maybe I should have a necklace that has "Mercy" and "Truth" engraved on it! Of course, it's an inner attitude and awareness more than a real piece of jewelry. But how great it would be to have a constant reminder of the way a wise woman lives, reacts, and is motivated

Dear Father, I see that there are sweet results for obedience to your commands. My heart longs to see and celebrate those results, peace and long life, in my own behavior. Thank You for the clarity of Your words that constantly nudge me toward obedience. Amen.

March 11

PAIN

Then He said to Thomas, "Reach your finger here, and look at My hands, and reach your hand here, and put it into My side. Do not be unbelieving, but believing." John 20:27

My body carries a lot of surgery scars. Not very pretty. One day I was told by the doctor that if I would trust him, he would operate and relieve my pain, perhaps even take it away. I should have been leaping with delight. Instead I was swallowing panic.

Why? Could it be that I love my pain? Was it possible that it had become such a familiar companion that I dared not let it go lest I no longer have it to define me? Had I used my pain as an excuse? What if my hope was high and it *didn't* work? I agreed, however and now have a scar. But the pain is gone.

How about the pain of sin in my life? Hurt, anguish, betrayal, and disappointment caused physical, chronic pain, to which I clung in spite of myself. I will know the actuality of being sin-free someday, when my earthly life is over. Until then, however, I will carry scars: physical, emotional, spiritual scars. I am afraid to apply the soothing balm that will heal my soul. What would it be like to live sin free? Can I have the courage to let God perform some surgery in my life? Because I know there will be scars.

Jesus's scars made amazing grace available, reminding me of His work on the cross and His faithfulness to me.

Jesus, You died to heal my wounds. If I accept Your healing work, will You take my scars and turn them into beauty marks? I want to be free to reflect Your beauty. Amen.

March 12

SUN AND SHIELD

For a day in Your courts is better than a thousand. I would rather be a doorkeeper in the house of my God than dwell in the tents of wickedness. For the LORD God is a sun and shield; The LORD will give grace and glory; No good thing will He withhold from those who walk uprightly. Psalm 84:10-12

We often sing a worship chorus that goes like this: *How lovely is Your dwelling place, O Lord God Almighty…Better is one day in Your courts; better is one day in Your house, better is one day in Your house than thousands elsewhere.*[16] It is based on this scripture.

Some thoughts from my pondering of these verses: the psalmist longs to be even a gatekeeper in God's house in comparison to living in the tents of wickedness. Often the "tents of wickedness" offer an appeal, as we know, and we wander in and out. Or at least I do. But the next verse tells why God's courts have so much more for us!

Because God is a sun and a shield…shining and protecting with grace and glory. Grace He gives; glory expresses His worth. He is our sun, our Light; our shield. From His high realm He extends grace to us. What an amazing place to dwell: where light opens our way, amazing power shields us, and grace surrounds our every move! All because of Who God is, and how He operates under the weight of His glory, not denying *one good thing* to those who walk uprightly.

Oh Father, how promise-fulfilling the thought of dwelling in Your presence! No wonder the writer of this Psalm has a preference, as we also should. Show us Your glory. Amen.

---

[16] Better Is One Day ©1995 Matt Redman

March 13

INTERIOR DESIGN

Keep your lives free from the love of money and be content with what you have, because God has said, "Never will I leave you; never will I forsake you." Hebrews 13:5 (NIV)

Discontent with the familiar—the color on the walls, the same old furniture, dreary tedium, I look around my house and decide it is time to redecorate. How can I take what I have and make something new and different to perk up my spirit of unease? Why am I feeling this way, when God speaks to me of contentment?

And even as I begin tugging at the furniture, pasting up paint chips and imagining new window coverings I wonder if there isn't a need for redecorating in my *heart.* I know God in the person of the Holy Spirit dwells in me. How comfortable is He with the way I have everything arranged? Is it a warm, cozy place for Him? Does He feel welcome and cherished in the same way I would desire for my family or beloved guest to feel in my home?

Perhaps I am spending more time, effort and money looking to my comfort and sensory pleasure than in ensuring my heart is a place that suits *His* lifestyle.

O, Lord, please redesign my heart into a fit and beautiful dwelling place for You! Amen.

March 14

DIFFUSER

Now thanks be to God who always leads us in triumph in Christ, and through us diffuses the fragrance of His knowledge in every place. For we are to God the fragrance of Christ among those who are being saved and among those who are perishing. 2 Corinthians 2:14-15

Sticks in a bottle, immersed in perfumed oil; remember them? I was cleaning out a cabinet the other day and found an old set, unused, probably dried up. Called by an elegant name—diffusers—they are designed to spread fragrance throughout a home. We don't like unpleasant odors and therefore use every means possible to dispel them: scented candles, sprays, plug-ins, potpourri.

So as I read this beautiful description from the apostle Paul, it occurs to me that much of our purpose as believers is to be diffusers. The world around us reeks with the unpleasant aroma of sin; and we are placed here in its midst. What am I diffusing?

With my feet immersed in the perfumed sweetness of Christ's love and mercy I am to spread the knowledge of Him wherever I go, whatever I do, thanking God as He leads in triumph in Christ. To those who believe, as well as those who do not yet know Him I must be the bearer of His aroma, redolent of faith and trust and peace.

Heavenly Father, I so want to be conscious, always, of the responsibility and joy that is mine as I move about my earthly life. May I spread the fragrance of Christ everywhere; a diffuser. Amen.

March 15

EXTREME MAKEOVER - HEART EDITION

I will give you a new heart and put a new spirit within you; I will take the heart of stone out of your flesh and give you a heart of flesh. I will put My Spirit within you and cause you to walk in My statutes…Then you shall dwell in the land that I gave to your fathers; and you shall be my people, and I will be your God. Ezekiel 36:26-28

Makeovers are big these days. From personal appearances to a new home, screen images entice scrutiny and invoke hope. We think that if someone would come along offering to rebuild our house, redo our makeup and hair, give us lovely clothes, that our lives would be so much better. Deep within each of us, even as we watch an extreme makeover that changes a person's life we secretly wish that somehow it could be us.

That longing, that yearning, is valid. But there is only One who can fulfill it, Who can truly do an extreme makeover where it counts. All else is fleeting without the new heart He has promised. New houses wear out; new clothes do, too. Makeup can be washed off, and upon waking up the next morning the same person looks back at us from the mirror.

I must admit I sometimes enjoy the programs that seemingly change a life for the better. I've even wept over the poignancy of the joy I see there. But I wonder, when the excitement fades, is there still a need for a new heart?

Father, how about me? Am I looking at the outside, desiring an external change when it's the inside that needs some work done? Thank You, Father, for your promise of a new heart. Please renew mine. Amen.

March 16

THE HELMET

...above all, taking the shield of faith with which you will be able to quench all the fiery darts on the wicked one. And take the helmet of salvation... Ephesians 6:16-17a

Studying the Armor of God, I think my favorite piece of armor, described in this passage, is the helmet of salvation. Here is the bottom-line truth: the soldier's helmet is designed to protect the head. Similarly, the helmet of salvation is designed by God to protect our minds from false thinking. Salvation is about our identity. It's who we are in Christ.

But the enemy of our souls does not want us to comprehend that. He wants us to believe we are not good enough, not worthy, unloved and hopeless. When in fact, we have the greatest hope, we have the covering of Jesus' blood and God says He delights in us. By taking the helmet of salvation and placing it securely on our heads, we are defending against the poisonous barbs of negative thought that the enemy tries to foist upon us.

While watching a baseball game, I noticed a handsome young pitcher, standing on the mound waiting. I asked myself if I would recognize him if he wasn't wearing the cap that identified him as a member of our team. We all wear a hat of some sort. Our hats show loyalty to a place, a product, a memory. So, how are we wearing the helmet of salvation? Does it identify us as integral believers, those who trust in God?

Dear Father, it is so important that the helmet of salvation, the truth of who I am in You, is a definite part of what I wear daily. Help it to be so in my life. Amen.

March 17

SHOES

...having shod your feet with the preparation of the gospel of peace.
Ephesians 6:15

As I tied my shoes this morning I was remembering a time not so long ago when I was struggling with gout and could barely walk across the room. The diagnosis hadn't yet been confirmed and I thought the pain was coming from wearing shoes that pinched my toes and cramped my feet. Which led to thinking...the kind of shoes I wear determine how I walk, don't they?

If I have my walking shoes on I stride, without worrying so much about what is under my foot. If I wear thin-soled shoes I tread tentatively, mindful of stones and sharp objects, or water puddles. If I have slides on or slip-ons or sandals, I am barely limping...afraid they will slip off, make my ankles turn, causing me to stumble.

Is there a lesson for me here? I am impatient and don't want to bother with tying and untying, so I grab the easy ones, pretty ones that have the chance to trip me or hurt me. It pleases my vanity and saves me trouble, but they don't help my walk. In my spiritual walk, just like in my physical, I need to take the time to lace up my walking shoes, prepared with the gospel; or I may stumble because I've taken the easy way and worn the pretty sandals.

Heavenly Father, You call beautiful the feet of those who carry the gospel of peace. For You to see my feet as beautiful, my feet must be shod in sturdy, supporting gospel-laced shoes! Please help me be sure I have tied them securely! Amen.

March 18

RUBBER BAND

His lord said unto him, "Well done, good and faithful servant; you were faithful over a few things. I will make you ruler over many things. Enter into the joy of your lord." Matthew 25:21

I've been so busy seeking out the praise of man that the thought of waiting for and receiving God's affirmation is a rather foreign concept. I so want to reach that point where the thought of His hand resting on my head in approval and His words "Thank you, you've done well" is quite enough for me.

The irony is that striving will never gain it; it is the "Be still and know"[17] obedience that speaks to God's heart. Trying for man's approval may feel good temporarily, but I am beginning to realize, it does not satisfy the deep longings of my soul.

My real longing is to KNOW God's word of affirmation. That it is not a result of my labors but simply because He loves me. All the *struggling* to please Him never did until my *heart* was yielded. I held it back from Him, imagining I could control and protect it.

Oh, Heavenly Father, what a rubber band my life has been…pulling, stretching, snapping back and forth! Can You use a broken elastic? I don't want to pull anymore. Amen.

[17] Psalm 46:10

March 19

REARRANGED

He heals the brokenhearted and binds up their wounds.
Psalm 147:3.

I have never suffered a dislocated joint, although I have had a total hip replacement. I understand, however from those who have had it, that dislocation is incredibly painful. A joint out of place causes unbelievable pain, and immobility as well. It takes an expert to pull, press, and restore the injury. Indescribable relief follows the agony of correction.

What about a disordered life; a life dislocated, out of joint with God? There is pain in the separation, especially for those who have known close communion with Him. We in our human desires tend to pull away from Him and this dislocation immobilizes us from growing and serving. But the Great Physician can press and pull and restore a dislocated soul. There will likely be pain involved; often confession and repentance are painful. How wonderful to realize that He stands ready and willing to put it all back together when we yield to Him for His correction.

My Dear Father, sometimes the most hurt comes from the injury, sometimes from the fixing; but oh what joy to know there'll be relief when all is back in place. Thank You for Your promise of healing and restoration, as You rearrange my heart, my life. Amen.

March 20

MY NAME IN VAIN

Thou shall not take the name of the Lord thy God in vain for the LORD will not hold him guiltless who takes His name in vain.
Exodus 20:7

Some time ago my purse was taken from our car. I became a victim. A thief stole my identity and took with it my feelings of safety and invincibility. I have had to struggle to make real in my heart the truth that my safety is in God's hands, and find the promised peace in spite of what had occurred.

Working with the police and various agencies to get my documents replaced was an "adventure!" It has changed my life, in that I am more careful now, when I used to take too much for granted. I NEVER leave my purse in the car! The absolute worst moments were when I saw copies of *my* checks, signed with *my* name, but not by me. How violated I felt to think that someone used my name, my credentials and my reputation nefariously; how insulted and angry I was. My human heart wanted immediate revenge, not peace.

But a still, small Voice I recognized whispered in my soul and I was brought up short to think how God must shudder at the skewed use of *His* Name: the cursing; the false prophecies by which people attempt to use the majestic Name of the Most High to benefit themselves, thus defaming Him.

Heavenly Father, one day You will triumph, avenging Your Name, wreaking vengeance in my behalf because I am Your child. Until then, I need to learn to rest in Your provision, gathering strength from Your everlasting Source to deal with the myriad details of clearing my name, without tarnishing Yours. Amen.

March 21

THE LONELY CHURCH

These things says the First and the Last..."I know your works, tribulation, and poverty...do not fear any of those things which you are about to suffer...be faithful until death and I will give you the crown of life." Revelation 3:8-10

The countryside was brown, not green, and what I saw was heart-breaking. I had gone back to where I used to live and noticed there the little white church standing all alone, a relic of happy times long gone. It was only a little wood-frame building with no fancy trim or ornate gilding. There was such disrepair I could almost see through the cracks.

The boards were rotting and falling apart. I thought of the people who once worshiped there; how they came from all directions. The bell called all who would come bringing humble hearts and happy voices to praise and sing to our Savior and our Lord, and to offer petitions as they prayed.

I remembered happy times within that setting; baptisms, prayer meetings and beautiful weddings. There surely were times of sadness, too, memorials for loved ones who passed on.

Sermons were preached from God's Word. Hearts and lives were changed, mine was one included. Now sadly, the church has nobody in it. If I could, I'd buy it in a minute. I'd try to make it useful again; shore up those walls about to fall in. Some nails and paint to brighten it.

Father God, the little white church served Your purpose; now perhaps it's best to let time take its toll, and let it come to rest on Christ's promise; "My church always will be, not only in a building, but in fellowship with Me." Amen.

March 22

UNVEILING

But when it pleased God, who separated me from my mother's womb and called me through His grace, to reveal His Son in me that I might preach Him among the Gentiles… Galatians 1:15, 16a

Is Jesus revealed in me? Or am I so covered up with self-promotion that the clarity of His presence is hidden by smoked glass? Perhaps there is an outline of His shape, a glimmer of His light, but do I reveal *Him*; showing Him and His love to others? It is important that I consider this.

He called me, saved me, not only because of His great love, but so He could be seen *through* me. His purpose for me, just as it was for the Apostle Paul, is that I would shine for Him. I truly believe this is my purpose, my whole goal in life; to preach Him and reveal Him

I wonder, though, if I have not drawn the filmy curtains of self-gratification across the windows of my life, reveling in my deeds, rather than revealing His loveliness. I am sensing an instruction in these verses to be mindful of what is revealed through me.

Please, Lord God, my prayer is that You will draw me ever closer to You. Unveil Your glory in me. May You be revealed. Amen.

March 23

SOUL OASIS

For I will pour water upon him who is thirsty, and floods on the dry ground; I will pour My spirit upon your descendants, and My blessing on your offspring; they will spring up among the grass, like willows by the watercourses. Isaiah 44:3, 4

Often as I plod along in my daily walk I fail to acknowledge my thirst for God. Busy with my appointed tasks, I think I will get a drink of living water in a few minutes. Minutes turn into hours, and hours into days until the oasis beckons with its verdant beauty and my tongue, thick with thirst, croaks a dusty whisper, "Just a sip, just a sip of relief."

How generous is God! Instead of a sip, He *pours* water upon me. He cures the dangerous spiritual dehydration, not with drips but with buckets full. How refreshing this water is to my thirsty soul; this generous outpouring from a loving, caring God. I can go on now, filled and invigorated. I have been to the oasis.

Lord, I want to gulp the living waters of Your word, let it soak into the depths of my soul lest I dry up into chaff that the wind can blow away. Keep me camped beside the oasis, for in wandering the desert I may survive, but surely never will I thrive. Amen.

March 24

BLESSING BONES

Thus says the Lord GOD to these bones, "Surely I will cause breath to enter you and you shall live. I will put sinews on you and bring flesh upon you, cover you with skin, and put breath in you; and you shall live. Then and you shall know that I am the LORD." Ezekiel 37:5, 6

By the word of the Lord, by His spirit, dry bones will live again. The prophet speaks to *me,* as well as to His people Israel. My life was a rattle of dry bones, undone, piled in a useless heap.

I read somewhere that the reason God refurbished and replenished Israel was so that they may become, instead of dry bones, "blessing bones". I so connected with that truthful concept as I began my own journey back to intimacy with Him. I believe this is why He created and redeemed us: that we would take the new life and use it to bless others.

God's message is new life. Bones re-fleshed, tattered sinews renewed with strength, skin re-stretched to bind it all together, and breath—eternal holy breath—brought from the four winds by the Sovereign Lord restoring life You draw me from my self-dug grave; and now I know, my Father, You are the LORD!

Heavenly Father, I sense that fresh breath infusing me with Your purpose. Thank You for the renewal and the promise of usefulness to You. You are MY Lord. Amen.

March 25

FOUNTAIN OF LIFE

In the fear of the LORD there is strong confidence, and His children will have a place of refuge. The fear of the LORD is a fountain of life to turn one away from the snares of death. Proverbs 14:26-27

There is a fountain filled with blood drawn from Immanuel's veins, and sinners plunged beneath that flood lose all their guilty stains.[18]

This beautiful hymn always moves my heart to worship. The thought of the suffering Jesus endured to procure my salvation is enough to drop me to my knees. But I found the Proverbs verse above that tells me that there is a fountain of life that turns me from the snares of death.

We so need that strong confidence, the place of refuge. It comes by reverencing Him, fearing Him, hoping in Him. My acronym for this kind of fear is *Fully Experiencing Awe-filled Reverence*. Bowing in wonder before Him, considering all that He is, brings fulfilling life and light to my days. It turns me away from the snares of death, with all my guilty stains removed; the fountain of life IS the fountain filled with blood, drawn from Immanuel's veins.

Heavenly Father, Redeeming Savior, in our fear of You is found the place of refuge and the strong confidence in our future, eternal life in Your presence. Thank You for Your fountains. How grateful we are! Amen.

[18] There Is A Fountain, William Cowper (1731-1800)

March 26

CAIN, ABLE?

Then the LORD said to Cain, "Why are you angry? Why is your face downcast? If you do what is right, will you not be accepted? But if you do not do what is right, sin is crouching at your door; it desires to have you, but you must rule over it." Genesis 4:6-7 NIV

I read of Cain's sin, his rebellious sacrifice, one that was unacceptable to God. Refusing God's offer of a chance to repent, to do it right, he compounded his sin, and ignored the warning from God of a devouring enemy crouched outside his door. He committed the unthinkable, and Abel's blood cried out from the ground.

I set myself up with pride, never realizing that sin crouches at the door of my disobedience. Father, You come with outstretched arms to ask if I am willing to bring another offering, one of obedience. I am *able* to do what's right, but I have a choice: rebellion or compliance.

How often have I opened that door and allowed the crouching enemy in? Doing it my way brings only alienation, a mark of despair upon my forehead.

Father, I repent. Please accept my confession; forgive me as I turn away from the crouched serpent. Receive my humble offering, the one I am able to bring because of the sacrifice of Jesus. Amen

March 27

HIND'S FEET IN LOW PLACES

The LORD God is my strength; He will make my feet like deer's feet, and He will make me walk on my high hills. Habakkuk 3:19

My husband and I spent part of one summer entertaining a family of deer where we were living and working at a camp. A doe and her two young fawns felt very comfortable munching on our fallen apples and budding roses. It was enjoyable to watch them.

I read this verse in scripture and thought of our friendly forest guests; how delicately they walk upon the flatlands. Mincing steps and cautious tread carried them along until they were startled by an unfamiliar sound or perceived threat. Then they bounded with great leaps up the hills and into deep woods where safety beckoned.

Their feet are made for this, for the hills—not for the flat, even ground. They are at their best climbing and jumping, though often they must come down for food to survive.

And so I consider my own feet, created to be leaping upon the high hills of fellowship with God. He made my feet, not to scrabble for survival on the flatland of earth, to limp along its hot pavement, but to climb to the safety of His presence, to the deep woods of His protection. Instead I mince along with little steps, scrabbling, eating whatever I can find, while my soul longs for the heights.

Father, I pray that You will startle me with the scent of danger from the enemy of my soul, so I can use my feet as You made them to be…running, with no thought of what is underfoot, to You on Your high hills. Amen.

March 28

REMOVING THE PLANK

And why do you look at the speck in your brother's eye, but do not perceive the plank in your own eye? Or how can you say to your brother "Brother , let me remove the speck that is in your eye, when you yourself do not see the plank that is in your own eye?" Hypocrite! First remove the plank from your own eye, and then you will see clearly to remove the speck that is in your brother's eye. Luke 6:41-42

Oh, these verses always challenge me! I know I am quick to watch for specks in the eyes of other people, while willfully ignoring my own blocked vision. Blocked by a plank, the scripture says—something impossible to see around or through. Yet a teeny speck of a misdeed in someone else's life calls forth my righteous indignation.

I've no doubt that God sees the large board I'm attempting to see through and He calls me to look a bit more closely at myself; to break up the plank, letting it shoot splinters into my inflated ego. Yes, I am a hypocrite. I am critical, I am afraid of others, trying to make myself feel better by finding fault. This is convicting, for sure.

Jesus, You are telling me to remove that plank! And I know You are standing by to help me see my own issues and deal with them before I look around and pick on somebody else. Give me courage, I pray, for honesty. Amen."

March 29

NOT BY SIGHT

For we walk by faith and not by sight.
2 Corinthians 5:7

Do I need to have these words emblazoned across each window, each mirror, every direction I look? Because I tend to want to walk by sight! I am anxious to know what awaits. I wonder why? Maybe it's so I can plan my day, my own way.

My human nature pokes its nose into my thoughts and demands satisfaction, to know what to expect, and I get frightened when I can't see the future!

I'm discovering I trust the *illusion* that I am in control rather than God's sovereignty; the reality that it is *He* who rules, not I. Even though I have flashes of faith; truly walking in faith must be a life-style, not occasional wind sprints. It is a steady perseverance along the dusty road of life on earth, a willing obedience to trust.

So maybe it would actually be a good idea to paste the words of this verse wherever I look, to remind myself that I cannot see, not really. Faith means that I will not...but I must keep walking anyway. The only way I will be able to see is with eyes of faith, my spirit standing still before Him.

Heavenly Father, this brings me up short. To realize that I do not fully trust You but rather continue to be concerned with my own plans and how I can bring them to pass. Still my soul, and guide my steps. Amen.

March 30

18 WORDS

For God so loved the world that He gave His only Son, that whoever believes in Him shall not perish, but have everlasting life.
John 3:16

These precious words are so familiar that sometimes we pass over them without noticing, but the whole gospel is wrapped up in just these few words.

This pushes me to remember when I was a young Navy wife. My husband, a submarine sailor, would be gone for months at a time. In those days there was no way for us to communicate as we do today: with email, FaceTime and texting. We were, however, allowed a 20 word "family gram" three times per 100-day patrol, to try and express our love to our husbands. Of course, two of those words had to be his name and mine.

How to use 18 words to let him know all is well! To announce news, let him know how much he is loved? It involved a great deal of creativity and the conscious use of only necessary words. Our God is a very creative God! And in just a very few words, 25 to be exact, He tells His story.

It amazes me and brings me to a new appreciation of His truth, His grace, His love; and how to use words in the most effective way.

Heavenly Father, thank You for the gift of words. Let us be aware of their importance and power in our interactions…with You and with others. And may we ever find a way to simply and truly tell Your story. Amen.

March 31

SACKCLOTH

You have turned for me my mourning into dancing; You have put off my sackcloth and clothed me with gladness, to the end that my glory may sing praise to You and not be silent.
Psalm 30:11-12

This psalm is a song of gratitude, sung at the dedication of the house of David. This was an occasion, to be sure, of great joy and celebration! I have always identified with the joy and relief of the removal of sackcloth these verses announce.

This is aided by a memory! When I was a young girl, in the small town where I grew up, there was a high school tradition called "Freshman Initiation." The senior class would welcome the freshman into high school by making them wear silly costumes and appear absolutely ridiculous for a day. So the freshmen would be convinced of their lowly status, I guess. They don't do this anymore, probably for a good reason.

I will never forget my costume. I was told to wear a dress made out of a gunny sack and tie a chicken bone in my hair. That dress itched, and I was so happy to take it off when the day was over!

Here the psalmist is full of thanksgiving that God has removed his sackcloth (a symbol of mourning and/or repentance), and replaced it with gladness. It is a picture of our salvation, and it is beautiful! Our sin, when faced with God's love and forgiveness, can feel as itchy and uncomfortable as a gunnysack dress. The relief and joy that repenting brings turns our mourning into dancing!

Father, there is a reason for this exchange from mourning into joy, and it is so we can sing and praise You! Please lead me into the truth of what Your forgiveness provides for us, and may we dance with You to the music of Your love. Amen.

April 1

THE DAWN

But the path of the just is like the shining sun, that shines ever brighter unto the perfect day.
Proverbs 4:18

I love early morning! What is lovelier than dawn, the pearly purity of first light! Often I wake up early with a sweet anticipation, not quite knowing why. When it is not yet day, I sense the ever-so-faint lifting of the darkness. As I sit, I'm also sensing God's voice whispering in my heart. Did He stir me from sleep to show me Himself?

It is really peaceful in burgeoning daybreak as I think on Scripture. I am struck with wonder at the thought of this path, the one awaiting my next step, and I wonder if this does not illustrate the way I come to know God. It was dark earlier, the way life is before I came into relationship with Him. Perhaps I think I understand all about Him; but as I sit in darkness illumined only by my candle and His word, I see how little I do know.

Then the light begins to appear. Dawn breaks. In my home, in my heart, moment by moment, scripture by scripture, experience by experience. God is rolling back the curtain. The light gets brighter as morning approaches; someday my path will show His true brilliance the way I see the noonday sun now.

Father, how beautiful to greet the day with Your smile creating the dawn! I am here before You, sensing Your wonder; excitedly anticipating what is ahead as You open Yourself to me. My spirit swells the way my soul responds to this brightening day. It's not quite morning yet, but it is coming! Amen.

April 2

SPRING

While the earth remains, seedtime and harvest, cold and heat, winter and summer, and day and night shall not cease. Genesis 8:22.

Spring. Such a welcome thought. A transition, but not one that occurs in a moment. It is a process. After a long and bitter winter conversations often center on the question of when spring will arrive. We impatiently complain and wonder. No one, however—no matter how discouraged with winter—really doubts that it will come. Why? Because, long ago, God promised that the seasons of the earth will not cease! Spring is on its way; it is as sure as our next breath.

Spring begins, dispelling winter's final effort to thrust its tempestuous winds on the world. Winter leaves, replaced by gentle breezes of promise; which, in turn, transition to summer's renewal of the earth. Spring is a new beginning…as the ravages of the previous barren months are swept away. Tiny shoots of green erupt, thrusting bravely through cold crusty ground. Spring is *hope*—the hope of new life. It is *joy*—the joy of celebrating the truth of God's promises.

When the tempests of life begin to roar within us, and unending problems seem hard to bear; let us remember there is hope. Sprigs of new life are pushing up through the frozen despair to show the joy of living. God's promises remain.

Heavenly Father, thank You for hope. May we always remember that You are all about hope. Spring is on its way in nature—and in our hearts. Amen.

April 3

THE DEW

I will be like the dew to Israel; He shall grow like the lily, and lengthen his roots like Lebanon. His branches shall spread; His beauty shall be like an olive tree, and his fragrance like Lebanon.
Hosea 14:5, 6

The book of Hosea is a favorite of mine in that it tells a story that highlights God's tender pleading for His people to come back to Him. Throughout the book God remonstrates with the Israelites, detailing their idolatry and prophesying doom if they do not return. But in the last chapter He gives this lovely metaphor: He will be like the dew.

Drop by drop, the dew brings an early morning refreshment. Expected, needed and appreciated by every pore that drinks it, every eye that discerns it, every sense that absorbs its sweetness.

What a beautiful picture God gives us of Himself as the dew. Shimmering, it speaks of His presence: covering us, encouraging deep roots, strengthening the growth of our branches until our lives are like the spreading olive tree. We reach out to others, His fragrance emanating from us as sweet as cedar.

I bring my words of confession to You, my Father. I have wandered away, seeking selfish goals, constructing idols with my own hands. I come for Your refreshment, promised as the early morning dew sparkling like crystal in the sunlight. Amen.

April 4

NEWBORN

Jesus answered and said to him, "Most assuredly, I say to you, unless one is born again, he cannot see the kingdom of God." John 3:3

The other day I held an infant in my arms. I stroked the tender skin, delighted in the dimpled flesh, kissed the sweet spot behind the ear, smelled the freshness of new life, and exulted in the promise I was holding.

I was praising God for this tiny miracle, thinking of all that lay ahead… the first step, the first word, the thousands of other "firsts" that await. It seems that we lose our wonder so very easily! Why am I not as thrilled to be able to walk as this little one will be when he first moves across the room on his own? Why is it that the joy of eating delicious food isn't as exciting for me as the first taste at his mother's breast is for this little one?

Our eyes and senses become jaded and we take for granted the marvelous gifts of God that daily surround us. I know that I take my renewed spiritual life for granted and casually walk along in the way I first learned to do things. I should rather depend on the Spirit within me for renewal—for the freshness, sweetness and tenderness of a newborn in experiencing the kingdom of God.

Dear Father, I pray for new eyes, new challenges, new understanding of Your love. That is what. Forgive the way I blind myself to the beauty of You, and may I remember how it feels to be new born. Amen.

April 5

THE APPLE TREE

For there is hope for a tree, if it be cut down, that it will sprout again, and that its tender shoots will not cease. Job 14:7

My husband and I used to serve as caretakers at a camp. On the property was a small apple orchard. It was productive, but it needed to be pruned. The fruit wasn't really good, and the deer would eat it as soon as it hit the ground! This pruning was necessary. For years we had said, "We must prune the apple tree."

So, the apple tree was pruned today. The saw was wielded indiscriminately, it seemed, tossing to the ground useless, barren, moss-covered branches. It left only a bare-boned, skeleton divested of leaves and blossoms; and I feel a little sad. I regretted the chopping away, even though I comprehended it would produce good results.

I think my life is like the naked apple tree. All the beautiful branches I had grown, the fruit that I had produced was picked and gone. Gone – replaced by the realization that I have been too busy sprouting my *own* blossoms to let God prune me so I could bear the fruit that would glorify Him.

I feel stripped, lost and confused. There are tears in my eyes as I gaze on the apple tree – and on my life. But I hear His whisper, His loving whisper, "Inside the tree is everything needed to grow more fruit. Inside you is all I placed there from the beginning of time."

Heavenly Father, I am beginning to understand that sometimes there needs to be pruning in me. Although I feel shorn and emptied, I begin to thank You for the work You find necessary in me. And I know, because You've promised, the apple tree will bloom again, and so will I! Amen.

April 6

THE RIVER

But to each one of us grace was given according to the measure of Christ's gift. Ephesians 4:7

I have been seeing a lot of beautiful photos of nature lately, reminding me of a trip we took through the mountains of Montana. We had stopped to take some pictures beside a river, and as we pulled back on to the road I pondered how much I love rivers. If asked what body of water I like the most, I would say "a river." Musing to myself I am wondering why. The ocean is vast and fascinating, but it dwarfs me. Lakes and ponds are pretty, too...serene and peaceful. But a river! A river fills my soul, welcoming me. Always flowing, sparkling in sunlight; tumbling over rocks and impediments.

I was raised on the banks of the Madison River in Montana. That river rolls through my heart's recollections, part of the indelible memories from my earliest years. As for the ocean, it roars. Silent breezes riffle the surface of the lake, but I love the splashing constancy of the river.

So, I'm thinking of God's grace. Grace is like a river—filling me, welcoming me; constantly flowing over me, sparkling in the light of His Son's sacrifice that avails that grace for me. It tumbles over all the rocks and impediments of my old nature...it forms the base of all I am in Him. I am so grateful. My heart is at home.

Dear Father, as I look back and remember some of the experiences that have revealed the beauty of Your grace, I am filled with gratitude for the overwhelming, overflowing power that You make available to me. Thank You. May I accept, and extend, that grace. Amen.

April 7

DUGOUT BELIEVER

And whatever you do in word or deed, do all in the name of the Lord Jesus, giving thanks to God the Father through Him. Colossians 3:17

I have always loved baseball...warm summer evenings, green grass, the arguing with umpires, the crack of a bat extracting cheers from the crowd, the joy of victory and the disappointment of defeat. A sense of excitement begins each season-opening day.

It's interesting though, to watch the players in the dugout, sitting on the bench. They are part of the team, ready to be used at the coach's command. Prepared, exercised, with muscles stretched—just sitting on the bench. They may not be called to play today, or even tomorrow, but when the call comes they grab bat or glove and rush out to show what they can do.

There is a challenge for me as I watch. As a part of God's team, I belong to Him, He's my coach. Am I ready to go on to the field when He calls? Is my faith exercised, my heart ready to play ball with Him? I wonder.

Sometimes I think it's not enough, just sitting on the bench in the dugout. I want to go out and hit a home run; but maybe all He wants of me is to pinch hit, steal a base, or sacrifice another runner along. The point is: am I ready? And willing? Am I a dugout believer who is bouncing with eagerness to go out and play, or am I content to sit in the corner, hoping the coach won't call my name, satisfied simply to be on the team?

Father, is it possible I might need to go back to spring training? Help me to be ready for Your call. Amen.

April 8

WORDS

The words that I speak to you are spirit, and they are life. John 6:63b

I am a word person. That is, I am fascinated by the power of words; the comfort of words; indeed the communication of words. Over the ages the proper word at the right time has been the means of sweet communication. Jesus is called the Word of God, because He visibly expresses God.

The most incredible thing to me is how God speaks in my heart, especially when I am reading His written Word. I love to see my hand forming words as I write them in my journal while God is speaking them. The scripture above reassures us here that what we read in the Bible—Jesus' words—ARE spirit, and they are LIFE. This is true for me. It happens when I see words afresh as they become life, with Jesus "re-speaking" personally to me! An explanatory quote: "This is the way God speaks to us, not by visions and dreams, but by words. When a man gets to God it is by the simplest way—words."[19]

It is true that men can no longer write "inspired" things in the same way that the Bible is inspired. But we *can* write "illumined" things. It is true, then, that composition can be "guided"; our words can be so thoroughly under the mind of the Spirit that God can *own* them, and bless thousands by them. May that be true for me, as I daily wait before Him with my pen in hand!

Heavenly Father, I have heard you speak. And I ask that I may take seriously the truths that I discover when you do so. May Your Spirit train me to recognize Your voice as I read the words You have written. Amen.

---

[19] Oswald Chambers 1874-1917

April 9

GRACIOUS WORDS

A soft answer turns away wrath, but a harsh word stirs up anger. The tongue of the wise uses knowledge rightly, but the mouth of fools pours forth foolishness. Proverbs 15:1-2

I've been thinking a lot about words this week. I heard an interesting quote; "Words are free. It is using them that may cost us." How true that is! We are basically free to say anything that crosses our minds, aren't we? But it is also true that God has a lot of instruction and warning about how we use those free words.

I know I'm not alone when I have been angry and wanted to lash out and hurt someone who had hurt me. This causes more pain—not only for the one we intend to wound, but for *us*. The above passage notes that a harsh word makes us even angrier! The more we rail and holler, the madder we get, right? On the other side of the coin, I have been wounded by words from friends or family, building resentment. Words linger, long after they have been spoken!

Our words can be weapons...or a means of reconciliation. It is up to us. A soft answer, especially when we are seething inside, not only turns away wrath in the other person, it calms us as well. It takes grace to employ a soft answer, but we have that grace available to us, and only Jesus can truly tame our tongues, if we allow him. Indeed, as I once read, "Soft answers grow out of grace, and grace extinguishes anger."

Heavenly Father, may I learn to appropriate Your grace so that when anger or frustration tempts me to use harsh words, I will stop and claim that grace and watch my words! Amen.

April 10

TAKE AWAY THE STONE!

Then Jesus, again groaning in Himself, came to the tomb. It was a cave, and a stone lay against it. Jesus said, "Take away the stone."
John 11:38-39a

What is buried in the cave of my heart? I wonder this as I meditate on this incredible story of Jesus calling Lazarus back to life. I try to visualize the scene…Jesus, with tears on His cheeks, surrounded by a doubting, debating crowd, shows His compassionate humanity. Then with divine power He shouts, "Take away the stone!" Disbelief erupts, I imagine, as complaints are voiced, and heads shake ruefully. "He doesn't know what he's doing." "There will be a terrible odor." "Lazarus is DEAD!"

Then, in stunned amazement, the crowd hears shuffling footsteps in answer to Jesus' call. Lazarus leaves his grave, falling into the arms of loved ones, who frantically tore away his grave clothes. What a drama! What emotions must have filled all who were there! From doubt to incredulity, sadness to joy, as Jesus cements the truth of just Who He is—emotional humanity and powerful divinity in combination. Oh, there is such hope in Him.

So what can I take away from this? Is Jesus groaning in Himself over my refusal to hear His voice; my determined remaining inside the cave of my selfish ambition? I heard His command "Take away the stone!" loudly and clearly within me this morning.

Father, take away any stone that covers my heart and is keeping me from rejoicing in the hope You bring; may I look to You for my joy and strength, as You turn doubt and disbelief to amazement at the thought of what You have done for me! Amen.

April 11

EMANATION

Jesus said, "Take away the stone." Martha, the sister of him who was dead, said to Him, "Lord, by this time there is a stench, for he has been dead four days." John 11:39

As I have always been intrigued by this story in Scripture, I want to comment once more in its impact on my life. As Jesus approached the tomb of Lazarus, Martha, concerned about the stench of a dead body, remonstrates with Him. Seeing only with earthly eyes, and not aware of the miraculous sign she was about to behold, she attempts to thwart God's plan to glorify Himself. It seems a thoughtful thing to do…when we don't look beneath the surface.

I think we often are concerned about the stench of our sin being offensive to God. So we try to keep the stone over the opening, failing to believe in His merciful forgiveness; thus forfeiting a miracle of renewal in our lives. We are hindered by our fear of a reeking smell wafting on the air. The reality is that the stench of our sinfulness is already an offense in the nostrils of God, no matter how liberally we might spray air freshener. That stench is only sweetened by our confession, by repentance and by Christ's intercession for us through His blood.

My dear Father, trusting Jesus' sacrifice will release the fragrance of Your glory, an emanation that neutralizes the noxious odor of death and gives new life. May I ever avail myself of this process. I want the aroma of my life to be the fragrance of You. Amen.

April 12

AND THE ROOSTER CROWED

Immediately a rooster crowed. And Peter remembered the word of Jesus who had said to him, "Before the rooster crows you will deny Me three times." So he went out and wept bitterly.
Matthew 26:75

This is a poignant story, and it always makes me sad. Peter, whom we perceive to be strong and faithful, caved in when challenged about his relationship with Jesus. That he wept bitterly leaves us no doubt that he was disappointed in himself and fearful of lost love.

Reading a bit further it is sweet to notice that Jesus totally forgave Peter his lapse and the relationship was restored. It brings hope. I need to examine my own life: have I ever denied that I know Him? Have I let a challenge to speak for him slide past because I didn't want to be ridiculed? Yes, I have. And that is why this story makes me sad. I am too much like Peter. Thus I hear, in the distance, a new day breaking with the sound of a rooster crowing

Has the rooster crowed in your life? I believe we all need to check. Because otherwise we may never know the joy of Jesus' forgiveness. He knows; yet He loves us in such a perfect way that upon hearing our repentant weeping, He forgives.

Father, humbly I ask for strength and courage to stand for You, and not give in to the urge to deny You in deceptive self-protectiveness. May I keep that rooster from crowing in my life. Amen.

April 13

SILENCE

He was oppressed and He was afflicted, yet He opened not His mouth; He was led as a lamb to the slaughter, and as a sheep before its shearers is silent, so He opened not His mouth. Isaiah 53:7

Sitting in the darkened movie theater we were watching *The Passion of the Christ.* Actually I wasn't watching because I couldn't bear to do so. I was listening, my head in my hands!

It's what Jesus didn't say on that terrible day that moves me so. Jesus, the eternal Word, silent. How could He have sustained such agony without screaming "Stop?" Jesus, knowing Who He was, knowing His own power, closed His human lips, refusing to rise to His own defense.

His own creation spit at Him, whipped and taunted Him, yet He didn't say anything. I heard the whip striking flesh and my heart broke, my spirit screaming "Why?"

I understand now that it was in order that the prophecy be fulfilled. Knowing He was the only way of restoration, He participated in His beating by His submission to the torture, loving with unfathomable grace.

In His silence He said everything.

Heavenly Father, what a terrible, wonderful day it was when Jesus suffered and gave His life for me. Thank You for His silence. It shut the mouth of the enemy of our souls…forever. Amen.

April 14

I WONDER

And Jesus cried out with a loud voice, and breathed His last. Then the veil of the temple was torn in two from top to bottom. So when the centurion, who stood opposite Him, saw that he so cried out like this, and breathed His last, he said, "Truly this man was the Son of God."
Mark 15:37-39

I wonder…about the priests in the temple that day (the day the veil was torn). Did they rush headlong into the Holy of Holies which had so long been forbidden?

I wonder…as noon-time darkness enveloped the temple and quaking tossed them to the ground, did those priests peer fearfully inside at sights they'd never seen before

I wonder…was the light of the lampstand extinguished with the last human breath of the Light of the World? And did the showbread suddenly go stale as the true Bread of Life was broken?

I wonder…what really happened in the temple that day (the day the veil was torn). Did the priests realize their work was done when the perfect High Priest cried, *It is finished?*

I wonder…did they run into God's presence with a shout of thanksgiving? Or did they scurry about, trying to make everything function as before, not comprehending the sacrifice that brought about God's final satisfaction?

Heavenly Father, in the face of this wonder-filled day, I wonder…what would I have done? Fill me with joyful comprehension of the incomparable sacrifice that purchased my redemption, I pray. Amen.

April 15

COMMUNION

But their eyes were restrained, so that they did not know Him.
Luke 24:16

Now it came to pass, as He sat at the table with them, that He took bread, blessed and broke it, and gave it to them. Then their eyes were opened and they knew Him... Luke 24:30

And they told about the things that had happened on the road and how He was known to them in the breaking of bread. Luke 24:35

The Bread of Life was broken on Calvary. Torn beyond recognition, crumbled, that all might receive, that all might know Him. Two travelers on the road to Emmaus...eyes, formerly blinded as they walked with Him, were opened as the Bread of Life broke the loaf, and blessed it. The *revelation* does not come without the *breaking*.

And so it is in Jesus' *broken* body that *we* can know Him, experience Him. Eyes blinded by unbelief, sadness and grief are opened as He reveals Himself in our taking of communion. As I receive my own morsel of broken bread my heart opens and I am infused with a sweet knowledge of sacrifice and love, mercy and grace. It is Jesus, alive in me; this is the blessing...this *communion*.

My dear heavenly Father, my spirit fills with joy as I partake of the broken bread, seeing beyond myself to my Savior and His sacrifice. I am doing this, as He asked, in remembrance. Amen.

April 16

THE WAITING HOURS – A RETROSPECT

...there was a man named Joseph from Arimathea, who himself was also waiting for the kingdom of God. This man went to Pilate and asked for the body of Jesus. Then he took it down wrapped it in linen and laid it in a tomb that was hewn out of the rock...that day was the Preparation and the Sabbath drew near. Luke 23:50-54

I once had the distinct privilege of attending a retreat during Easter weekend called "The Waiting Hours." There was time for prayer, Bible reading and contemplation of just what Jesus's sacrifice meant to me. It was a precious experience in my life. I'm looking back at some of my journaled thoughts from that time:

"The waiting hours are the hours between Jesus's crucifixion and His resurrection. The concept of the waiting hours describes a time and place where I've dwelt so long: Tedious. Dry. Mediocre. Lackluster faith. Anticipation dulled by earth's banality. Longing for renewal and, yes, waiting. This weekend, though, I have been resting in my Father's arms, wrapped in tenderness and care. I have felt His nearness, heard His call; lifted my voice, and opened my soul."

The waiting hours...the work is done. The Savior waits to see the joy His appearing will bring to the ones He loves. In the words of a wise man in a message of hope..."It's Friday, but Sunday's coming!"[20]

Resurrection morning...The sun erupts in the sky, slicing the darkness, and the night is over. Hope, as dawn, breaks in my heart, and joy now overtakes the waiting hours.

Praise You, Heavenly Father, for the hope of resurrection we have. Because when the waiting hours are over, we too will be with You forever more. Amen.

---

[20] Tony Campolo (1935-)

April 17

SWEET SPICES

Now when the Sabbath was past, Mary Magdalene, and Mary the mother of James, and Salome, bought spices that they might come and anoint Him. Mark 16:1

How many times I've read the story of the resurrection morning! But somehow now I am struck by the fact that these women, loving disciples of Jesus, were bringing sweet spices to cover the stench of death. A sorrowful procession, completely unaware that He was not there. Long before they had gathered their packets of pungent herbs and begun their bitter trek to perform one last act of love, Jesus had shed His battered body and exploded in triumph from the dark tomb.

They didn't know, not yet.

And I, wondering if I truly comprehend the power of the Resurrection, trudge up the garden path carrying my own sweet spices, the carefully prepared good deeds, my efforts to *do* something nice for Jesus.

Should I not be running to the empty tomb with great freedom and joy, flinging the sweet spices of His fragrance everywhere, relying on His mighty power? That power that has freed me and forgiven me, enabling me to carry His precious aroma, the pleasing spicy scent of His love wherever He sends me.

Heavenly Father, You continue to challenge me with the truth of Your word: power that I scarcely can comprehend, is promised to me! May I avail myself of that Resurrection power and spread its joy everywhere. Amen.

April 18

MANIFESTATION

While they were still talking about this, Jesus himself ***stood*** *among them and* ***said*** *to them, "Peace be with you. Look at my hands and my feet. It is I myself!" When he had said this, he* ***showed*** *them his hands and feet…He asked them, "Do you have anything here to eat?" They gave him a piece of broiled fish and he took it and ate it in their presence. Luke 24:36-42 (NIV)*

Again Jesus said, "Peace be with you! As the Father has sent Me, so I am sending you. John 20:21 (NIV)

Concentrating on the passages of scripture surrounding Jesus' resurrection, I was struck by the many ways He manifested Himself!

He **S**tood—**P**hysical **P**resence;
He **S**poke—**P**eace be unto you;
He **S**howed—**P**ierced hands and side;
He **S**upped—**P**iece of fish;
He **S**ent—**P**ronounced His mission.

Heavenly Father, I find it extremely difficult to comprehend how anyone could ever doubt the truth of His resurrection! JESUS IS RISEN! HE IS RISEN INDEED! Hallelujah. Please open the eyes of those who do not desire to see. And may I go where You send me and show the way, bringing others to the place where they long to know You. Amen.

April 19

ARMOR OF LIGHT

Therefore let us cast off the works of darkness, and let us put on the armor of light. Romans 13:12

To me, this is a conundrum. How can something as nebulous and undefinable as *light* be a defense; or an offense, either, since armor is both preventive and proactive? I ponder on this.

Armor is made for warfare; its purpose is to protect the wearer. In the Psalms it says *The LORD wraps Himself with light, as with a garment.*[21] It is His light that provides protection against our enemy, because it reveals; it defends against falseness; and shatters clouds of doubt. And that covering is available to me!

Just what is this armor? I believe it is "the full armor of God" which is truth, righteousness, peace, salvation and faith.[22] The gift of His presence within me is my armor against the enemy of my soul. With Him is faithfulness, no shifting shadows. Light.

Unchangeable. It is God Who covers, shelters, and protects, me. Oh, gratitude rolls, as shadows flee. God reminds us: *Every good and perfect gift is from above, and comes down from the Father of lights, with whom is no variation or shadow of turning.*[23]

Father, thank You for arming Yourself with the Light that protects. Thank You that that there is no shadow of turning with You. I so need that armor and pray I let it continually surround me. Amen.

---

[21] Psalm 104:2
[22] Ephesians 6:14-17
[23] James 1:17

April 20

POLISH

For You, O God, have tested us; You have refined us as silver is refined. Psalm 66:10

Restore us to yourself, LORD, that we may return; renew our days as of old… Lamentations 5:21 (NIV)

As a believer in Jesus, I need to be conscious of how my life affects others. That is an awesome responsibility, and not to be taken lightly. However, I am finding that my human life can be compared to a silver vessel. Perhaps I was shiny and like new yesterday, fresh from an encounter with God, but today I am tarnished. I have allowed my fleshly nature to corrode it with an ugly dull stain. Today I don't give off a very good reflection of Jesus.

I don't have many things that belong to my mother. Somehow in all the confusion surrounding her death and the changes it made in our family, most of her belongings were lost. I do, though, have her set of silverware. I open the wooden chest and a flood of memories assaults me…along with a bite of regret that it is tarnished. Anyone who has been forced to polish silver knows, it has a habit of getting tarnished when it's not used regularly. I haven't used it enough to keep it pristine. So before it can be useful I must take polish and rub away the stains.

Father, so it is in my life. I must take care to keep the tarnish of the old me from spoiling my reflection of You. Won't you take a soft cloth in your mighty hand, dip it into the silver polish of your forgiveness and rub me 'til I shine again? Refine me and make me useful to You, please. Amen.

April 21

SHEEP-ISH

Thus says the Lord GOD, "Indeed I Myself will search for My sheep and seek them out. As a shepherd seeks out his flock…so will I seek out My sheep and deliver them from all the places where they were scattered on a cloudy and dark day…I will make a covenant of peace with them, and I will cause showers to come down in their season, there shall be showers of blessing." Ezekiel 34:11-12, 25a, 26

I collect sheep. For many years I have been gifted with hundreds of sheep collectibles. I enjoy them, constantly reminded as I look at them, how God uses the images of sheep and shepherd to teach us because we are so much like them!

Do you ever feel as though you have been "scattered on a cloudy and dark day?" I know I have; and so the promises God makes here are sweet to my soul. Promises to search for us, and deliver us. He then promises a covenant of peace with us; which He has done in sending Jesus as our Savior.

And then! *There shall be showers, showers of blessing*! I see in my mind's eye a verdant meadow, freshly washed by a cleansing rain, where we as God's children, His sheep, will be able to rest; reveling in being searched out, delivered, and restored. Sort of a Psalm 23 place, I guess! How wonderful, when life tosses us a curve, or things seem dismal, to call this picture to mind, and look to our Father as He seeks us.

Father, I am so grateful for the Scripture that declares the greatest love of all. When our lives are stuck in a cloudy and dark place, help us remember there is a nail-pierced hand reaching out, searching for us. May we grab hold and never let go. Amen.

April 22

THE SHEPHERD'S SHOULDERS

What man of you, having a hundred sheep, if he loses one of them, does not leave the ninety-nine in the wilderness, and go after that which was lost, until he finds it? And when he has found it, he lays it on his shoulders, rejoicing. Luke 15:3-5a

The next few days my meditations will make reference to Jesus as Shepherd and we as sheep. Often I have noticed that there are fascinating similarities between sheep and God's children. I collect sheep memorabilia and am reminded as I look at them how much like a sheep I am.

For so many years I wandered away from God, lost in a morass of rebellion and anger and bitterness. Of course I wallowed in guilt, especially when I would read in Scripture, a story from Jesus' lips about a lost sheep. But I would run further away, driven by pain and a reluctance to return.

The burden of His wandering sheep lies heavily on the Shepherd's shoulders. Shoulders that bore lash marks for His sheep, shoulders that sagged upon a cross under the weight of sin.

And so, He came looking for me, a lost sheep, wandering away, willfully leaving the Shepherd's arms. I was caught in the brambles far from the sheepfold. I know it was for me the Shepherd searched; and hearing my bleats of distress, He found me, laid me across those mighty shoulders and joyfully carried me home.

My Dear Shepherd, I am so grateful that You were willing to search for me and bring me back. Joyfully, the scripture says. And now I am rejoicing to tell everyone that I am that little lost sheep, back in the sheepfold, carried back in Your arms. Amen.

April 23

CAST DOWN

Why are you cast down O my soul? And why are you disquieted within me? Hope in God, for I shall yet praise Him for the help of His countenance. Psalm 42:5

I've said it before; I am always amazed at the many similarities between sheep and us as followers of God! Probably the reason the scriptures concentrate on God being our shepherd is because He knows how badly we need one!

For instance, sheep can easily become "cast down." Perhaps it has lain down to rest; then stretching on its side, it suddenly gets off balance. Heavy with fat or wool or with lamb, maybe even by lying on uneven ground, the poor thing finds itself on its back. As the sheep flails its legs frantically in the air trying to right itself, gases begin to build up in its stomach and cause circulation to be cut off, leaving the sheep prone to predators or to dying in the heat. The shepherd is the only hope for a cast sheep; it cannot right itself.

The word "disquieted" above has been translated "in despair," "depressed," or "down in the dumps." Mirroring, in a way, a sheep in crisis. Right now, I am in crisis, struggling with a cast-down soul. I heard a pastor say the other day, "Down time is prep time." Though I really do not understand how, I believe it is God working in my life, giving me some "down time". My hope is in God, for the help of His countenance.

Father, if You are preparing us for restoration and blessing,
please help us prepare our hearts to receive.
For You alone are our hope. Amen.

April 24

THE SHEPHERD'S SOVEREIGNTY

The LORD is my shepherd, I shall not want. Psalm 23:1

Shepherd and sheep. God and me! I am so grateful for the way God illustrates His care for us with an explanation of the relationship we share. When we say God is sovereign we mean that nothing can happen in this universe without God's permission. Even though man has free will and responsibilities, ultimately God has the final say. He is the supreme Ruler and nothing, no one, nor any circumstance of life, can thwart His desire or plan. This is who our Shepherd is, and why we do not *want.*

There is some misconception about the word "want." We often feel a bit resentful because we do not have everything we desire, but we are not really "in want"; we are incredibly blessed. We can become discouraged when we allow ourselves to yield to fleshly desires for pleasure or material gain. We fail to consider the provision our Sovereign Shepherd promises. The above verse sets the theme for Psalm 23. All we will ever need is laid out in front of us.

Heavenly Father, our Sovereign Shepherd! The more we know of You the more we realize Your care for us. Help us to learn to rely upon Your sweet sovereignty. We shall not want! Amen.

April 25

THE HIRELING

I am the good shepherd. The good shepherd gives His life for the sheep. But a hireling, he who is not the shepherd, one who does not own the sheep, sees the wolf coming and leaves the sheep and flees; and the wolf catches the sheep and scatters them. The hireling flees because he is a hireling and does not care about the sheep.
John 10:11-13

Here, Jesus identifies Himself as the Good Shepherd. He brings to us a picture of safety and protection; of His willingness to sacrifice Himself to save His sheep.

How vivid, then, is the contrast between a good, caring shepherd and a hireling! There's a level of care that a hireling—just a hired hand—simply lacks. For him it's just a job, working for a paycheck. But when he or the flock are threatened by danger, the hireling thinks only of himself and runs away.

Jesus assures us that He is the *Good* Shepherd. Sacrificing Himself, loving us. He owns us because He paid for us with His blood, and He will never leave nor forsake us, His sheep. It's not just a job for Him—His life is entwined with ours. This is purely and simply the greatest reassurance of a never-ending love and promise.

God, my heart swells with joy to read and ponder this truth. I pray I will never wander away from Your presence, forever welcoming Your shepherding. Amen.

April 26

FINDING PASTURE

I am the door. If anyone enters by Me, he will be saved, and will go in and out and find pasture. John *10:9*

Isn't this interesting? Jesus is saying He is the door…not that He opens or shuts the door, but that He IS the door. A little investigation found this little story…*A shepherd who knew nothing of God's Word was describing his sheepfold to a curious inquirer. As he pointed to the sheepfold the inquirer said, "But where is the door?" "I am the door," the shepherd replied. At night when the sheep enter the fold, I lie down in the opening. Nothing can enter or leave without going over me, because I am the door.*

As our Great Shepherd, Jesus is also the door that we must enter through. There's such beauty in this truth! And when we do enter, He promises that we will be saved—which is perfect *security*. We will be able to come in and go out—which is perfect *liberty*; and find pasture—which is perfect *sustenance*. All we need is in Him, through Him.

Speaking of pasture, I found a description that delights my heart: "A pasture is God's tender caring place; luscious, satisfying, nurturing, sustaining, refreshing, delighting me. It is free of dryness, emptiness, barrenness, hopelessness, despair, confusion, death."

Heavenly Father, in the pasture that is Your word, I can find all I need. I am so grateful that Jesus is the door. By Him I have entered in and found perfect security, perfect liberty and perfect sustenance Oh, how I thank You. Amen.

April 27

CHOOSE JOY

You will show me the path of life, in Your presence is fullness of joy, at your right are pleasures forevermore. Psalm 16:11

I think a lot about journeys. We are all on a journey called life. Life may seem burdensome and difficult sometimes; but there is *joy* to be found. I heard a quote about joy: *"Joy is a process, often muddled, sometimes detoured; a mystery in which we participate, not a product we can grasp."*[24] How interesting... joy isn't something we grab and hold on to, but a product of growth. We must not forget that it is a fruit of the Spirit, after all!

God is the Source of joy. Jesus, as He drew near to the cross, submitted to God's will because of *"the joy that was set before Him."*[25] Strength and joy are connected, especially in this context. Knowing the joy ahead was what gave Jesus the strength to endure the suffering. The process of joy-choosing (and it IS a choice) builds strength; our responsibility is to exercise it and let it grow.

So, where are you in this process? Seeking the Source of joy? Basking in the glow of His presence? Using faith muscles to build joy wherein you WILL find your strength? For myself, I am delighting in the process, attempting to choose to be joyful each and every day; chiefly because I know God loves me, and Jesus died for me.

Heavenly Father, with You My future is secure. Oh yes, I am filled this morning, and I pray I will be covered in joy, as I seek You and Your strength. Amen.

---

[24] Tim Hansel (1941-2009)

[25] Hebrews 12:2

April 28

CARVINGS

You shall not make for yourself a carved image, or any likeness of anything that is in heaven above, or that is in the earth beneath or that is in the water under the earth. You shall not bow down to them, nor serve them: for I the LORD your God am a jealous God…
Exodus 20:4, 5

We were vacationing in Mexico and doing some sightseeing. Visiting ruins and hearing the *oohs* and *aahs* of our companions on the tour. It *was* amazing.

High above the jungle the ruins rose, monuments to a past civilization, marveled upon, exclaimed over, and visited by millions. Incredible carvings on stone impact viewers with a sense of history lived, of gods worshiped. There is wonder expressed in the appreciation of intricate design and brilliant engineering.

But I pause and let my mind reflect on two tablets of stone I read about in Scripture. On these tablets were engraved words, the very words of the One who created the stone. Here God declared His Sovereignty, His design, His demand to be worshiped exclusively. Stones, carved by the finger of God, keep me mindful of His holiness—the standard I can never meet. His mercy took the words on those stones, carved by His hands, and fulfilled them in the flesh of His Son, the Word Himself.

Father, the high places, the historical ruins, are not for me.
My faith rests in You, my Creator, my Redeemer.
With joy I praise You. Amen.

April 29

BREAD IN THE WILDERNESS

In those days, the multitude being very great and having nothing to eat, Jesus called His disciples to Him and said, "I have compassion on the multitude...and they have nothing to eat." Then His disciples answered Him, "How can one satisfy these people with bread here in the wilderness?" Mark: 8:1-4

The disciples were stunned. Jesus ordered them to feed the multitude! Their question makes perfect sense; a wilderness is no place to buy bread, everybody knows that! But Jesus was not to be deterred from His purpose of feeding the hungry seekers. He discovered a paltry few loaves available; but a miracle of multiplication was about to occur.

I cannot help but think of another wilderness. God's people, recently delivered from slavery, stood complaining, begging for bread. *"And they tested God in their heart by asking for the food of their fancy...they said, "Can God prepare a table in the wilderness? Behold, He struck the rock, so that the waters gushed out, and the streams overflowed. Can He give bread also?*[26] God *always* sees His hungry children. He saw them then, and He provided manna from Heaven—a picture of Jesus, the Bread of Life.

As He prayed on Calvary, *It is finished. Father, into Your hands I commend my spirit,*[27] Jesus's wounded body suddenly became enough—enough to feed all those who come hungry to Him. It is He, Himself, broken on Calvary that feeds His people.

Father, sometimes in my wilderness of doubt and anxiety, I forget that You are enough. Stiff-necked and stubborn, I beg for bread, not making the effort to discover that it is readily available: I taste, and am satisfied, in awe of a miracle...bread in the wilderness. Amen.

---

[26] Psalm 78:18-20
[27] John 19:28

April 30

FACETS

The LORD their God will save them in that day, as the flock of His people. For they shall be like the jewels of a crown, lifted like a banner over His land – for how great is His goodness, and how great is His beauty! Zechariah 9:16-17

When asked one day what is the most thrilling thing about belonging to God, I responded, "It is simply the very fact of belonging." Yes. It is the truth of being accepted, known, loved. Also that Jesus died, paying the ultimate price for me. For me! I am looking forward to "that day": the day we will be lifted up like the gems in the crown that will proudly proclaim His glory. Shining like jewels!

Undoubtedly I don't feel very much like a jewel sometimes; I see only my rough-cut, unpolished state. He sees the facets of the gem He is cutting. The grinding and sanding, which are the trials and testing, all are designed to bring out the beauty in me only He can see. I cannot polish myself into a dazzling diamond, there is nothing innately sparkling about me. Living in this dark world, left to myself, I would shine no more brightly than a lump of coal.

But, oh, when *His* light shines the possibilities are endless! Because He combines the facets He's polishing in me with the facets He's perfecting in all those He loves; so that on "that day", that glorious day, we will join in His coronation, the miracle of His light refracting though us!

Dear God, You are the Stonecutter. I trust You; I know Your tools are sure and Your design is true. Oh, how great is Your goodness, and how great is Your beauty! Amen.

May 1

CALLED BY MY NAME

But now, thus says the LORD, who created you, O Jacob, and He who formed you, O Israel: "Fear not, for I have redeemed you; I have called you by your name; You are Mine." Isaiah 43:1

This verse has become so meaningful to me. Whenever or however I come across it, I am taken back to the day I began to absorb its truth. I never liked my name. I wanted a cuter name, like the popular girls had. But as I sat in front of the fireplace at the retreat center where we had been assigned the above passage and began to meditate on it, I realized that it wasn't the actual *sound* of my name that I didn't like; it was what it represented to me: self-loathing and failure.

But God formed me. He took His thought that connected to my name, and with firm and tender hands, squeezed that formlessness through His fingers, shaping and molding a unique person crafted by His touch. Then, determining the frame and structure of my days, He set them in motion with His breath. He placed me here, birthed into a fallen world, then gently began calling my name.

I have learned that I must not only accept that I am uniquely crafted and named, but embrace that fact and rest in it. Thus I am respecting and loving myself as God's beloved child—created, formed and fallen, yet redeemed. What does it mean to me that God knows me by my name? Everything!

Heavenly Father, I want to rejoice in the woman You have called me to be, and not complain because I don't like who I am. Help me to embrace Your calling on my life to become all You want me to be. Amen.

May 2

THE COOL OF THE DAY

And they heard the sound of the Lord God walking in the garden in the cool of the day, and Adam and his wife hid themselves from the presence of the LORD God among the trees of the garden.
Genesis 3:8

Long ago, God approached His beloved creation, continuing a custom of meeting personally in the cool of the day. I find such poignancy in this passage, sensing their regret at the cause of their shame: disobedience. Imagine the sad faces on Adam and Eve as they crept from their hiding place to face their Creator! They were just beginning to realize the magnitude of their loss. They hid; ashamed. They had disobeyed.

I, too, have had sweet and intimate times with God in the cool of my days. He longs for those precious times to continue. But sometimes I hide like my ancient parents did. I am ashamed of the way I have failed. Oh, yes, I readily blame other things—circumstances, time, weariness—but I know in my soul that I have turned my face from Him. The sound of His beckoning voice fills me with a deep sense of loss.

The consequences of Adam and Eve's disobedience have passed down to me. I am a sinner. My God, though, has provided a way so that fellowship in the cool of the day can be mine once again. No need of a fig leaf to cover my shame! I am covered by the redeeming blood of Jesus. I can rest in His presence. A simple repentant confession restores to me the joy of intimacy in the cool of my day.

Heavenly Father, how precious is the cool of the day when You are present with me. May I treasure that time and let it shape my life. Amen.

May 3

BAREFOOT

Then Joshua fell facedown to the ground in reverence, and asked him, "What message does my Lord have for his servant?'" The Commander of the LORD's army replied, "Take off your sandals, for the place where you are standing is holy." And Joshua did so. Joshua 5:14-15 (NIV)

What an incredible experience it must have been for Joshua, when a Man identifying himself as the *Commander of the LORD's army* suddenly appeared before him. I am sure that Joshua had seen many amazing things in his life and somehow recognized this appearance as a miracle, because he dropped immediately to the ground. It was holy, where he stood – holy because of the Presence of the Lord.

Pondering on this passage I was thinking of times when His Presence impacts me. Often when I am speaking before a group I, too, feel the presence of God so vividly that I am compelled to take off my own shoes.

I began to list in my heart the ways He manifests Himself: I hear Him in the whispering wind; in the voice of my husband and sons, in the cries of the lost and broken. I feel Him as the sun kisses my cheek; feel Him when I am worshipping, and in the wrenching reality of pain. I see Him in the rushing river. I see Him in the eyes of a hungry child, and in acts of love by His people.

Oh Heavenly Father, let me fully sense Your nearness; knowing that all around is holy ground, And I will stand before you – barefoot. Amen

May 4

SHALOM!

Peace **I** *leave with you, My peace I give to you, not as the world gives do I give to you. Let not your heart be troubled, neither let it be afraid. John 14:27*

Not too long ago my husband and I had the opportunity of being at a mountain camp retreat. It was amazing! We sat on the deck of our cabin, pondering the beauty of the place, thinking that God had done such a wonderful job of creating it. We heard children laughing and watched families coming together. Our hearts were full! I tried, unsuccessfully, to describe that feeling. But when I got home, a dear friend described it perfectly! That feeling is *Shalom.*

My heart echoed "yes!" to the word Shalom. It just felt right! So I looked it up. "Shalom" is a Hebrew word that means peace, harmony, wholeness, completeness, prosperity, welfare and tranquility. It is something only the presence of God can bring, and I believe it takes a knowledge of Him to recognize and experience it. Peace, as in absence of war, only describes part of "shalom"!

It's much more than a simple greeting or farewell, it is a prayer, a blessing, a deep desire, and a benediction. The word is packed full of the full blessing of God; and my heart still resonates with the joyful experience. I pray you, too, will find Shalom.

Heavenly Father, may Your Shalom be our covering, our hearts know Your fullness; may we find in You the greatest measure of contentment, and the deepest satisfaction that our hearts can possibly know. Amen.

May 5

HANDS

In His hand are the deep places of the earth; the heights of the hills are His also. The sea is His, for He made it; and His hands formed the dry land. For He is our God and we are the people of His pasture, and the sheep of His hand. *Psalm* 95:4-5. 7

I was having dinner with two of my high school classmates. These friends are both single, having lost their mates; and both are running ranches in Wyoming. Strong, resilient and independent; they have accomplished so much and I am always amazed at their tales of herding cattle and sheep, fixing fences, harvesting, and all the accompanying challenges. I so admire them. One of us suggested we lay our hands on the table. Their hands showed the effects of the work they do: sturdy and worn; as compared with my own, smooth and white.

I've pondered since about our hands and how we use them. Bringing comfort and tenderness, lovingly touching our children. The results of hard work: hundreds of dishes washed, meals prepared, floors scrubbed, beds made. So powerful, our hands; created by God to accomplish a multitude of tasks!

Reading this scripture with the picture it paints I sensed a new wonder and comprehension for God's hands; how mighty they are, how marvelous! In them He holds the deep places of the earth. By them He made the sea and formed the dry land. But what truly ignites my heart with praise is that in His hand—mighty, powerful and sustaining—He shelters *me*, a sheep of His hand.

Thank You, Awesome Creator, for the gift of my hands, I ask You to continue to make them useful. You made me, formed me, gave me life. Now You hold me…in Your sovereign, eternal, merciful hand. Amen.

May 6

EMBRACE

The voice of the LORD is powerful; the voice of the LORD is majestic.
Psalm 29:4 (NIV)

The might and power of God's voice are vividly described in this incredible psalm. Thundering, striking with lightning, it is capable of shaking the desert and twisting huge oak trees.

When I was a small child, still reeling from my mother's death, we heard the news that my father, returning from a conference, had been in an automobile accident. Without the communications systems we have today, there was no news of his condition.

In bed for the night, lying stiff with terror, I suddenly heard voices. I sat up to listen, frightened at what might be ahead, and I heard Daddy's voice. Instantly I was at rest. He was home, safe. I could sleep!

I remember this as I read of the majesty, the power, the force of His voice; and I, with the psalmist, cry "Glory!" Because, after portraying the terror of a storm more majestic than any I have ever seen, the psalmist closes with a beautiful declaration of God's provision for His children: *The Lord will give strength to His people; the Lord will bless His people with peace.*[28] Hearing God's voice, whatever the circumstances, reminds us that He is God, and we are His children; safe, Surrounded by with His strength and peace.

Oh, God, may we listen for Your voice and learn to rest in the comfort of the knowledge of Your embrace and Your peace. Amen.

---

[28] Psalm 29:11

May 7

TRUE REST

And God said to Moses, "My presence will go with you and I will give you rest." Exodus 33:14

This verse in Exodus is a favorite of mine and has been for many years, carrying me through many trials and doubts. There is a sweet assurance here, one that we can depend on.

I remember some time ago I was sitting with my Bible on my lap, feeling used up, discouraged, and oh so tired. Having returned from a trip and packing for another one, I was slammed by duties and a long to-do list. When my eyes spied this tender reminder, I bowed my head and wept.

What a gift we find in rest, true rest. Rest that can come only from God's presence. Whether we acknowledge Him or not; He is with us, as He promised. We strive to arrive at a place we actually are if we but yield to this truth.

As I shed tears of repentance for trying to walk in my own strength I sensed His presence. I realized that even my to-do list must be surrendered to His control, so that I can heed His voice, and separate the urgent from the important. This is an ongoing struggle for me. Because even in the midst of busyness, He is there. Peace descended on me.

Dear Father, I am tired of struggle. I wish to yield to Your presence with me; surrender my exhausted spirit to the sweet repose of Yours. And rest. Amen.

May 8

BREAD OF SORROWS

It is vain for you to rise up early, to sit up late, to eat the bread of sorrows; for so He gives His beloved sleep. Psalm 127:2

This phrase, bread of sorrows, has grabbed my attention. As I studied it a bit more I discovered that it refers to those who work very hard, day and night, for the emptiness of reaching for worldly success and material gain; thus robbing themselves of the true refreshment that comes from time spent in communion with God.

The bread of sorrows: tasteless bread, baked upon the coals of frustration, pride and envy; unsatisfying due to the imbalance between working and striving…and trusting. It is not that laboring is wrong; we are told in scripture that if we don't work, we don't eat! However, it is true that spending all our waking hours in labor for that which does not satisfy brings to the table loaves of the bread of sorrows.

Busy days, rushing to complete tasks before day's end…this is how we tend to spend our time. I think it has to do with balance. Instead of sleepless nights with anxiety, wouldn't it be better to enjoy the sleep He promises His beloved? Then, filled with the nourishment of balance we might not have any desire to taste the bread of sorrows.

Heavenly Father, I see that struggling and scrambling does not feed my soul. It only gives me tasteless, flat loaves of dissatisfaction. I need rest. I am tired. Show me the path of sweet communion with You. Nourish me with Your Word, as I turn my face to You and open my heart. Amen.

May 9

YOUR LOVE REMAINS

Hear my cry, O God, listen to my prayer. From the ends of the earth I call to you. I call as my heart grows faint; lead me to the Rock that is higher than I. For you have been my refuge, a strong tower against the foe. I long to dwell in your tent forever and take refuge in the shelter of your wings. Psalm 61:1-4 (NIV)

These verses express my deep longing. I've been trying to learn about intimacy, especially with God. I find it's a result of intense focus; concentration, not on myself, but on the One I desire. Look at all He is to me...refuge, defense, shelter. But as tenderly supportive as those roles are, I often find myself moving to the tune of my own music, thus changing the focus of my eyes, drawing my heart away. I can sense it happening. The things of the old life begin again to have a more definite appeal; stress and worry increase and the mantle of selfishness drapes itself over my shoulders.

Then a word of scripture, or a verse of song penetrates my mind. I sense Him whisper my name and my heart begins to ache with loss. So I wrench my gaze from myself to the face of God and let His loving forgiveness begin to close the distance I have allowed, bringing me home.

Oh, Heavenly Father, You haven't moved. Your love remains. As I focus on You I am restored, once more, to the delight of intimacy. I thank You with all of my heart. Amen.

May 10

LACKING NOTHING

For in Him dwells all the fullness of the Godhead bodily; and you are complete in Him, who is the head of all principality and power. Colossians 2:9-10

Complete. It seems impossible to be needy or to feel inadequate in the face of this scripture. Instead we often feel unsatisfied with ourselves, incomplete and sensing a lack of something necessary to be okay. So we read this verse with some skepticism, asking ourselves, "If this this true, why is my automatic response a nagging loss? Undone, and somehow unacceptable?"

I have come to realize that this feeling is accurate, because in our *own* strength it is true. We ARE incomplete. We are created to comprehend our own unworthiness so that in seeking to be full, we would find Jesus and become a yokefellow with Him. Our completeness is only found in Him, and His loving acceptance.

Father, I praise You because You made me to long for You. And You then fulfilled that longing through sending Your Son to die to redeem my incompleteness. Powered by Your love, His sacrifice embraces all that is me and encircles it with His acceptance. I am loved, accepted, and thus, complete, lacking nothing. Amen.

May 11

SILVER AND VELVET

His divine power has given to us all things that pertain to life and godliness, through the knowledge of Him who called us by glory and virtue, by which have been given to us his exceedingly great and precious promises, that through these you may participate in the divine nature having escaped the corruption in the world through lust. 2 Peter 1:4

Often our night times seem bleak with trouble and struggle, and fear triumphs. In light of the trials that we face, we feel inadequate to defend against what life has tossed against us. We have all experienced it.

But I recall an evening not long ago that shed beauty into the worry and darkness. We were on vacation, staying in a rural community in Arizona. That evening, I stepped into a desert nightfall pulsing with beauty.

Velvety darkness surrounded me, soothing my soul. Brilliant crystal stars and the rising moon were enchanting. Standing there, my heart turned toward God, the One who created the glory I was seeing. Wrapped in the softness of His care as though enfolded in a velvet cloak, the brightness of His promises glowed with a silver intensity; sharper and clearer than when I tend to view them against the lights of this world.

My problems seemed puny in comparison and I felt a new sense of trust forming deep inside me. Snuggling into the strengthening velvetiness, my eyes opened to the promises that shine more brightly in the dark. Fear receded, and hope returned.

Heavenly Father, Creator of all, I thank You for the promises You have given. Bring to our remembrance these displays of Your marvels which tell us of Your power available to those who trust You. Increase my trust as I worship You. Amen

May 12

STILLNESS

LORD, my heart is not proud; my eyes are not haughty, I don't concern myself with matters too great or awesome for me. But I have stilled and quieted myself, just as a small child is quiet with its mother. Yes, like a small child is my soul within me. Psalm 131

I fuss. I fret. I get concerned over the state of the world, my surroundings, and my family. That is not trust! I cannot fix the world. I may be able to affect my surroundings. I can be concerned and involved with my family; offering loving support and assistance when possible.

I have known the stillness of soul that God provides as a by-product of time alone with Him. In the words of Judy Gordon Morrow, "The sweetness of His presence defies words. The space of silence is God's gift to me, one that I will seek and treasure the rest of my days."[29] Yes, that is true—each word; but I find myself right now in the "seeking" phase. Attempting to rest in stillness. Stillness allows me to hear God's voice and leading. It is possible to know a stillness inside even when life clamors outside.

My mind is very aware of these truths, yet the clamor seems to win out too often. I want to find that stillness and dwell there, hearing God's voice. When He says "Still yourself", I will be obedient and cease this awful fretting and worry. It delights Him and feeds my soul when I choose to spend time with Him.

Father God, I must rest from my fretting about things that are too weighty and awesome for me while I nestle in Your arms like I used to do with my mother. May I place my hope in You. Amen.

---

[29] The Listening Heart © 2013, by Judy Gordon Morrow

May 13

NIGHT SONG

By day the LORD directs his love, at night his song is with me – a prayer to the God of my life. Psalm 42:8 (NIV)

Sometimes, in the dark stillness after midnight, I will awaken with a song of praise playing in my thoughts. I wonder, when I hear a snippet of a hymn strummed in my heart or words of worship pouring through my mind what God has just done in me. Because He must have spoken, or I wouldn't be so filled with His presence.

Perhaps He's unsnarled a tangled skein of concern…or shown my heart a new concept of Himself that my conscious mind could not conceive. Yet, deep at the core of my being He's revealed His heart to me and I am restored and awash in His love.

That love carries me in the daytime when I am awake and responding on a cognizant level. But with the night song, His tender lullaby wraps my soul in joy.

Father, I lift my prayer to You: sing on! Amen.

May 14

ASSURANCE

The righteous cry out and the LORD hears, and delivers them out of all their troubles. The LORD is near to those who have a broken heart, and saves such as have a contrite spirit. Psalm 34:17-18

Everyone wants to live to get old, but it seems we don't want to admit it when we reach it! I am grateful for life and health, yet I often let "reality" tear holes in my peace. So, I've been searching through scripture to get myself centered in the truth of God and His presence. There is nothing better for a bad mood than going to the Psalms!

So often we find ourselves with ragged, raw edges; and we need the assurance of His presence. "God promises to be there for the ragged edges of our souls," I heard someone say. Another place in Scripture we find these words: *Deliver me from my enemies; in You I take shelter.*[30] The study notes in my Bible say that its original meaning is "To You I flee".

When trouble or danger comes, we have a fight or flight response. Let us become confident that the direction of our flight be straight into God's arms. It is from that place that we fight—not alone, but wrapped in the fortification of the One Who loves us supremely. Isn't that precious? I find myself warmed and filled with joy and yes, hope! My ragged edges are healed.

To You I flee, my Father, my shelter. Hounded by enemies of fear and doubt, there's no safety, no peace, outside the walls of Your Presence. Let me be engulfed in the refuge of Your arms. Hide me, cover me, with Your very self, and let the hope You promise be my anchor. Amen.

---

[30] Psalm 143:9

May 15

DWELLING PLACE

He that dwells in the secret place of the Most High shall abide under the shadow of the Almighty. I will say of the LORD, He is my refuge and my fortress, my God, in Him will I trust. Psalm 91:1-2

I was contemplating Psalm 91 while writing in my journal, thinking of how beautiful it is. In my Bible it is titled *Safety of Abiding In the Presence of God.* I often quote it glibly, proud of myself for having memorized it. But I want to explore a few things here.

"Dwell," "Abide." This is saying when I live (dwell) in the presence of God, I will abide under His shadow. This implies a conscious decision. We decide where we are going to dwell. Circumstances may have some influence, but ultimately, we decide.

Is there a difference between *dwell* and *abide*? *Dwelling* is a variable; while *abiding* indicates permanence. Interesting. My Bible also uses *habitation* in Psalm 91:9 and that has the idea of retreat or asylum. A place of comfort and safety. Words like *refuge* and *fortress* also highlight the protection of God over those who trust in Him. The secret place—under the shadow of the Almighty—oh, it is so precious to be there! Because that's where I choose to be! I've prayed this psalm over my sons for years, even though they were far away. And I still do. But today I apply it to my own life.

Father God. I am so grateful to be able to dwell, to abide; to find a retreat in Your secret place, protected by all that You are, and to be the recipient of Your promises. Amen.

May 16

CRADLED

For in him we live and move and have our being. Acts 17:28

Do we really comprehend the depth of this truth? I know I always feel a sense of joy and purpose whenever I read it because there is a wealth of meaning in that one little preposition *in*. All we are, all we have, is wrapped into this. God is our Creator, Sustainer, Redeemer, Companion, Father, and we are lost without Him. He invites us to rest in Him; His rest yields peace, and in Him our very being is able to move freely and without strain.

Judy Gordon Morrow, in her book *The Listening Heart*[31] expands this thought with words that totally captivate me. God tells us to rest in Him and He will cradle us in His arms. I have such a desire to be cradled, as Webster defines it… *held gently and protectively*. Is that not a heart longing for each of us? Power sheathed in gentleness bringing safety, security and rest,

Let everything go but trust. That's all it takes. It's a simple truth, but often difficult to do, as we tend to leap out of His embrace and attempt to handle things in our own strength and timing. I've found it so much better to rest in Him.

Oh Heavenly Father, hold me, please. Cradle me within Your mighty arms. Let all I am begin and end with You. I know You will never let me go. Amen.

---

[31] The Listening Heart, © 2013 by Judy Gordon Morrow

May 17

HIS FACE

When You said, "Seek My face," my heart said to You, "Your face, LORD, I will seek." Psalm 27:8

This reminds me of a story I heard not too long ago. A busy father was working in his office, while his little son played nearby, happy just to be with his dad. Wanting to get a bit of attention, he said, "Dad," to which his father replied, "Yes, Son, I'm here," without taking his attention from what he was doing. Again the little boy said, "Dad!" Twice more this happened, with no change in the father's absorption in his work. Finally frustrated, the little boy said very loudly, "Dad, I want you to listen to me with your face!"

Although this brings a chuckle, it behooves us to think about it with regard to our relationship with God. We want Him to listen to us with His face, His total attention. Is it not to be assumed that He, too, wants us to listen to Him with OUR face? Over and over in scripture He asks us to listen, to heed, and that can't happen unless we give Him our total attention.

Ponder the words of this hymn: "Turn your eyes upon Jesus, look full in His wonderful face, and the things of earth will grow strangely dim, in the light of His glory and grace."[32] Oh, yes. There is blessing found in gazing into His face.

Oh Father, please help me to make Your face my focal point; that beautiful, wonderful face that sees me with unfathomable love, longs for my willing focus. Amen

---

[32] Turn Your Eyes Upon Jesus, Helen H. Lemmel (1863-1961)

May 18

BATTLES

Do not be afraid nor dismayed because of this great multitude, for the battle is not yours but God's. 2 Chronicles 20:15b

Reading of some of the Old Testament battles put me in mind of other military matters. I was reflecting that May is the month we celebrate Armed Forces Day on the 3rd Saturday of the month, paying tribute to men and women currently serving. As a military wife, this has always been a poignant reminder of the role the armed services play in protecting and maintaining the freedom we enjoy as Americans. I always pause to remember the pride and joy that ran deep in my heart, having stood behind and beside my Navy husband as he lived out his commitment to our country for 23 years. Yes, it was his *career,* yet the patriotism that drove him continues, even though now it only lives in our memories.

Interestingly, Memorial Day comes on the heels of Armed Forces Day. Memorial Day is a day of remembering the men and women who died while serving in the United States Armed Forces. It is, of course important to remember those fallen heroes who "gave their last full measure of devotion," as Abraham Lincoln remarked in his Gettysburg tribute. It is fascinating that we celebrate those military who are still living and serving, and remember those fallen all in one short period of time.

And then I thought about the future day when wars will all be over and Jesus, the Victor, returns. Separated no more, our reunions will be filled with joy.

Father, thank You that the ultimate battle has been won by Jesus on the cross. But we still live with wars among us. One day you will return. Until then, we fight on – all of us who love and serve You. Amen.

May 19

CLINGING ARMS

That you put off, concerning the former conduct, the old man which grows corrupt according to the deceitful lusts, and be renewed in the spirit of your mind, and that you put on the new man, which was created according to God, in true righteousness and holiness.
Ephesians 4:22-24

The new man. It is something we must choose to don. New life is given to us when we say Yes to Jesus, but a willingness to "put on" a new way of living is also involved. I long for revival and renewal, but I have realized new life has no room to grow in a soul whose arms are embracing this world. It is inherent in this verse that putting on also entails putting off. Again, a decision. We must reject the old habits, old ways, old needs…putting them away and embracing the new.

An *embrace* embodies affection, longing and yearning; a desire to hold closely a loved one, an idea, or a belief. How often my behavior shouts a need for intimacy; yet, ignoring the outstretched arms of my Savior, my arms stubbornly continue their earthbound clinging. I find myself holding tightly to the old nature.

Dear Father, receiving Your embrace demands my own arms outstretched toward You; free to receive, to enfold and be enfolded in your clinging arms. How much better to be held in Your arms than to stay attached to this world! Amen.

May 20

CONNECTIONS

Why do you spend money for what is not bread, and your wages for what does not satisfy? Listen carefully to me and eat what is good, and let your soul delight itself in abundance. Incline your ear and come to Me. Hear, and your soul shall live. Isaiah 55:2-3a.

As I sat down for my quiet time the other day, the subject of connecting was on my mind. I was alert to that thought and here is the connection that grabbed my attention…a physical, bodily action results in a soul reaction. I have been using verse 2, the *eat what is good* part as my "diet" verse! But now I see that it really means that taking care of ourselves, our *bodies*, causes the *soul* to delight itself in abundance. Overindulgence in the physical apparently results in leanness in the soul.

I was then reminded from reading in the Psalms, the children of Israel *lusted exceedingly in the wilderness and tested God in the desert, and He gave them their request, but sent leanness into their soul.*[33] I had not noticed before the correlation between obedience and abundance in my soul. In verse 3, it says *"Incline your ear and come to Me. Hear and your soul shall live."* Again, a physical activity; leaning toward Him, coming to Him; brings life to the soul, and the sweetest moments of my life are when I really hear Him! Obedience to His voice is where the richness of life is stored.

Heavenly Father, this is a lesson I don't ever want to forget, so that when my physical appetite lusts for things that are not healthy for my body, I will be reminded that giving in to that desire can bring emptiness to my soul. May I always delight in Your spirit-filled abundance. Amen.

---

[33] Psalm 106:14-15

May 21

BROKEN VOWS

That which has gone from your lips you shall keep and perform, for you voluntarily vowed to the LORD your God what you have promised with your mouth. Deuteronomy 23:23

I broke a promise the other day. I caused pain, and now I am filled with regret and sorrow. I know I can ask for forgiveness, and no doubt receive it, from my loved one. But I am realizing that all the glue in the world cannot put back together a promise that is shattered.

I guess that's why God takes promises so seriously. He never breaks His. I think of all the times I have promised Him something and casually walked away, my broken vows trailing behind me.

The sickness I feel in the pit of my stomach now is nothing compared to the ache in my soul as I begin to comprehend how disappointed He must be when I don't set a guard on my tongue and carefully consider the promises I make. Because He loves me, He forgives me when I repent, but a broken promise cannot be mended.

But we are able to start over again.

Dear Father, I am so sorry that I was heedless and casual with a promise; that I hurt someone who is dear to me. As I ask for their forgiveness, it shows me how much You have forgiven me, and how often I need it. I am so grateful, and ask for Your nudges to keep a watch on the promises I make. Amen.

May 22

WATERFALL

Create in me a clean heart, O God; and renew a steadfast spirit within me. Do not cast me away from Your presence, and do not take your Holy Spirit from me. Restore to me the joy of Your salvation and uphold me by Your generous Spirit. Psalm 51:10-12

We spent some time vacationing in a tropical area and I remember how fascinated I was with the waterfalls we were fortunate enough to see. Often when I am touched by something beautiful, I look for a spiritual application, asking, "Why does what I am seeing make my heart swell with joy?"

The power of a waterfall is amazing. Over time it can reshape and wash away debris, all the while retaining its beauty.

I'm thinking today about His cleansing presence. I read the phrase, *Create in me a clean heart*, and it grabs my soul. It is His presence that cleanses simply by being there. He is the Living Water. His indwelling Spirit washes me constantly as a waterfall cascades over stones, flushing out soil and impediments; gaining strength, and in its flow, tossing crystal rainbows into the air.

O God, I long to be ever cleansed by Your presence – eroding my sinfulness, reshaping the rocks of my old nature with the waterfall of Yourself. Renew my life to show only the sparkling splashes of joy, the proof of Your flowing in my life. I know You will do this for me. So I surrender. Amen.

May 23

EARLY

O, God, You are my God; early will I seek You; my soul thirsts for You; my flesh longs for You in a dry and thirsty land where there is no water. Psalm 63:1.

David, the Psalmist, spent a lot of time in the desert. So do we; at least I know I do. The *proverbial* desert, I mean. Fortunately I am blessed to live where it is lush and green! But there can be nevertheless, a desert of the soul; a Saharan dryness that breeds longing. When I find myself there, thirsty for the refreshment I have neglected, this passage lifts my heart.

How eloquently David expresses not only his own wistful yearning, but mine as well, and I find my soul responding. *Early will I seek You.* I looked up early. It means "before a given time, or near the beginning." I sense the importance of speaking my heart before the thirst consumes me, at the beginning of my day.

Hearing David's awareness of God's loving acceptance, his commitment to seek *his* God; and knowing that his thirst and longing will be met kick-start my own response of joy. I don't belong here in this dry and dusty desert.

Father, my Father, I am seeking You. First things first! It is early in the morning. My flesh longs for You, my soul is thirsty. I can feel the precious Living Water of Your Word, washing me, filling me; and with the Psalmist I rejoice in Your Presence. Amen

May 24

OUTPOURING

For I will pour water on him who is thirsty; and floods on the dry ground; I will pour My Spirit on your descendants, and My blessing on your offspring. Isaiah 44:3

Thirst for God consumes me. I pick up my pen and words elude me. The air seems to be filtered through cotton; I cannot feel the whisper of my Heavenly Father's breath, the murmur that is my inspiration, the refreshment that is so necessary for my soul's well-being. I am dry. Why?

Turning to the comfort of His word I hear it, the sound of a waterfall waiting to pour water on my dryness; His promise… not only water to quench the thirst, but of pouring His Spirit and blessing as well. A generous, free outpouring.

I have limited Him, haven't opened myself up to receive. I allow the desert of perceived failure to hold me captive. I flip to another portion of my Bible. This time a story of a woman who broke a bottle of expensive perfume and poured it over Jesus a generous, free outpouring. My heart tightens.

It occurs to me I am dry because I don't allow God to pour Himself into me, nor do I generously, freely pour His love out on others. I've wanted to be a sponge, I think, selfishly absorbing His love, rather than to be a conduit. But I've been wrong. Will my willingness to be a channel make my drought disappear and my refreshment return? I will find out!

Father God, a life-changing question…a conduit or a sponge? It is my choice. I trust in Your direction; Your love overflowing in my heart, so that it cannot help but pour out. Amen.

May 25

GENTLE CORDS

When Israel was a child, I loved him, and out of Egypt I called My son…I drew them (Israelites) with gentle cords, with bands of love, and I was to them as those who take the yoke from their neck. I stooped and fed them. Hosea 11:1 & 4

Do you hear God's heart in these plaintive verses? His children, His chosen ones, had not chosen to follow Him, in spite of such vivid examples of His care and protection for them. The entire book of Hosea is a story of God's love for His wayward people, how He called them over and over and offered forgiveness. But they refused. In this passage God enumerates many things He has done for them, lamenting their disobedience.

Sometimes I am overwhelmed with His tenderness. Of course I realize there are times when God's justice may seem to supersede His tenderness. That makes me all the more grateful to hear the tender words He speaks to me and feel those gentle cords drawing me closer! I have run from Him, but never so far that I was unable to respond to the bands of love that prevented me from making huge mistakes, and brought me to the place of repentance. How grateful I am. How sorry that I spent so many years on the run. But that makes His welcome home even more precious.

My dear Father, with gentle cords and tenderness You recaptured my heart and now shelter it within Your loving arms. Thank You. I will ever praise You. Amen.

May 26

GLORY

"But let him who glories glory in this, that he understands and knows Me, that I am the LORD which exercises lovingkindness, judgment, and righteousness, in the earth; for in these things I delight," says the LORD, Jeremiah 9:24

I hate to admit it, but I am often tempted to find a way to connect with those whom I consider celebrities. Back in the day I used to try to get close to the stage and/or get an autograph. Feeling that somehow it would enhance my value if I could say in a casual way, "Guess who I met the other day?"

Well…not too long ago I saw a celebrity. Up close and personal, as they say, and found myself elbowing and jostling my way to get closer in the hope I'd be noticed for a moment!

But that Voice I'm coming to recognize chastised me by reminding me that I already know the Greatest Celebrity of all time. I need not elbow or jostle to get close, He's always by my side. The Creator of the stars (as well as celebrities) waits for me to drop His name, yearns that I pursue those things that delight Him, living in such a way that I reflect His glory.

My dear Father, how could I waste so much time and effort trying to get close to some earthly celebrity when You are by my side always? And Jesus far outshines any human idol whose name I think could impress others. It seems silly, yet I do it. Please forgive me. Amen.

May 27

STRANGE FIRE

Then Nadab and Abihu, the sons of Aaron, each took his censer, and put fire in it, and put incense on it, and offered profane fire before the LORD, which He had not commanded them. And there went out fire from the LORD, and devoured them, and they died before the LORD.
Leviticus 10:1, 2

God takes our obedience seriously! I read the story of Aaron's sons, honored priests, who thought themselves above obedience to God. Mankind so often stands in bold defiance against his Maker. Proudly, considering himself wise, He offers strange fire, burning incense to the idol he's created; forbidden incense, mixed with high sounding phrases of praise to himself. God is not pleased with strange fire of misplaced worship, pagan in desire, unholy in practice.

Once God brought the above passage to my attention. I had been severely wounded by the berating words of someone who felt he was speaking for God. I cried out to my Savior through tears and brokenness. These words He brought to me reveal His justice and show how He feels about those who offer strange fire. And then, with typical tenderness He also led me to these words of David the psalmist: *"How precious to me are your thoughts, O God! How great is the sum of them."*[34]

Oh, Lord God, my heart is fixed on You. May my sacrifice of praise be burned in your purifying fire, the sweet savor of a surrendered life; my acceptable worship. Purge me of anger, of centeredness in self. Sprinkle my tears as blood on Your altar. And as I rest there in Christ's sacrifice, kindle a flame that will never turn to strange fire. Amen.

---

[34] Psalm 139:17

May 28

PARDONED

Let the wicked forsake his way, and the unrighteous man his thoughts. Let him return to the LORD, and He will have mercy on him; and to our God, for He will abundantly pardon. Isaiah 55:7

I opened the back door to welcome my little granddaughter. She had been crying, I noticed. Her cheeks were tear-washed, her eyes puzzled; and her precious cat preened in her arms. It was then I discerned the cause of her grief: a sparrow's body at her feet.

Questions tumbled from her lips—she who loves all things living. "Why? How could my kitty kill this little bird?" Grief, anger, and love struggled within her and I knew I must offer comfort; try to explain the natural order of things.

Stooping to answer, I held her and wiped her tears. My heart lurched as God whispered truth; understanding dawned in me. Though heartbroken, her love pardons her pet. In the same way my Heavenly Father grieves like this child when I go the way of my natural human inclination, rebelling against Him.

God's love mingles with justice. His holiness exacts a fee for our disobedience, but love sent Jesus to the cross and applied mercy that paid my debt. Grateful for His promised abundant pardon, I jump into His arms to accept sweet forgiveness that cost Him His all.

Dear Father, everything within me cries my praise and gratitude for a new realization of the truth of Your pardon, Your abundant pardon. Thank You. Amen.

May 29

UNSEARCHABLE

Great is the LORD, and greatly to be praised; and His greatness is unsearchable. Psalm 145:3

How can we ever begin to describe the greatness of God? Oh, we have many words that tell about His character, His works, His plans and promises. But my mind boggles as I attempt to explain "greatness."

The dictionary gives us these words: "Vastness, splendor, magnificence, brilliance, larger than ordinary size or ability…higher in degree or importance. Greatness can also be attributed to individuals who possess a natural ability to do better than all others." Well, that sort of sums it up, doesn't it? God is above all others. His greatness is unsearchable; it cannot be comprehended.

Who can conceive or express how great God is? Our human minds can never plumb the depths, never come to the place where we will exhaust the greatness of God. Which makes Him all the more worthy of our praise! Have you heard the statement that the more we learn about God, the more there is to know! I have found that to be true.

Father God, I often trivialize You, take Your love for granted. I confess it, and ask for Your forgiveness. Help me to see a glimpse of Your unsearchable greatness, that my praise may reach Your gracious heart. Amen.

May 30

SHORTCUTS

Many are the afflictions of the righteous, but the LORD delivers him out of them all." Psalm 34:19

There was a period of time I suffered with gout in my feet and ankles. It was a very painful learning experience for me. First of all I was angry at the pain...having just completed my rehab from heart surgery. Now I could barely walk across the room. It went on for months.

I noticed that with hurting feet, I was constantly looking for shortcuts—how few steps I could take to accomplish something. I didn't want to cause more pain, so I did everything in my power to avoid it. When the painful condition finally disappeared I asked myself, "What did I learn through this?"

It can be true for us in our spiritual lives as well. There is pain in sacrifice and the effort to do what is right, but we don't want to do the painful things! No, we would rather waltz around them instead, taking shortcuts, as it were, to try and reach the healing and peace for which we all long.

How precious is God's tenderness with us, even in pain—especially in pain. The knowledge of His Presence, the truth of His word, the joy of our salvation, the sweetness of prayers of others; and the comprehension that He is working. All these help us focus on His tender mercy, rather than on the pain.

Heavenly Father, please forgive, the shortcuts I take. Impress on me the truth of Your work in my life, and the lessons learned during situations I have been through. I ask for sensitivity to Your leading and that I be willing to walk the path You have set before me. Amen.

May 31

LEANING

Trust in the LORD with all your heart and lean not on your own understanding. In all your ways acknowledge Him and He will direct your paths. Proverbs 3: 5-6

The eternal God is your refuge, and underneath are the everlasting arms. Deuteronomy 33:27

I was reading through the Psalms recently and came upon a descriptive phrase *...this leaning wall, this tottering fence.*[35] And I wondered, would one ever lean against a tottering fence? Or trust themselves to a wall that is leaning and unstable? I don't think I would; not knowingly, at least. One never leans expecting to fall; the very act of leaning indicates faith and trust.

In these scriptures above we are given some important instructions, as well as a promise. I can chuckle at the idea of leaning against a fence that fails in its purpose, or a wall that doesn't uphold. I *want* to lean on God; my head tells me He will not fail. But I don't seem to let go and *lean!*

From where comes my fear of falling? From where comes the tightness of the grip that says holding on to this world supports me more completely than God does? His instructions are to lean on Him, not on my own understanding, and to acknowledge Him. Give Him the trust He is so eager to receive and heed the direction He is so willing to provide.

Then, we find the tender promise of His everlasting arms, His refuge!

Heavenly Father, thanks for this picture that illustrates the importance of depending upon You. There is no other way to learn to lean than simply to do so. Please help me. Amen.

---

[35] Psalm 62:3

June 1

UPLIFTED

For in the time of trouble He shall hide me in His pavilion; in the secret place of His tabernacle He shall hide me; He shall set me high upon a rock. And now my head shall be lifted up above my enemies all around me; therefore I will offer sacrifices of joy in His tabernacle; I will sing, yes, I will sing praises to the LORD. Psalm 27:5, 6

I come to His Word this morning, feeling troubled by the enemies of discouragement, defeat and despair. Here I find this touch of His love to my heart! Even though I feel surrounded by my enemies, being hidden in God's secret place is a much cozier, intimate surrounding. It is also protection.

Set high upon a rock, He places my head above said enemies—uplifted which provides a totally different view. Several years ago I experienced serious heart surgery. Through the dark night of my hospitalization and the healing journey that followed, God held me, hid me, hoisted me up to the Rock. Using the prayers of so many people, when I have been unable to pray, I have felt the Presence of His surrounding care.

Therefore I will sing praises to Him with gratitude for the dedicated ones who have been my uplifting force of prayer. Because I know, now, how the psalmist could sing. What a ringing affirmation of incredible belief in God's promises!

Heavenly Father, may my heart ever echo this song of praise from the safety of the Rock! Amen.

June 2

RUSH TO PETITION

Sing joyfully to the LORD, you righteous; it is fitting for the upright to praise him.
Psalm 33:1. NIV

If we confess our sins, he is faithful and just to forgive us our sins and cleanse us from all unrighteousness.
1 John 1:9

Be anxious for nothing, but in everything by prayer and supplication, with thanksgiving, let your requests be made known unto God.
Philippians 4:6

I look at these verses and am challenged to examine my own prayer life. It's not a pretty sight! Because this is what I find: bypassing praise, I dash headlong into God's presence. "Where is the reverent awe?" I ask myself. I wonder if I truly sense His power and greatness. Next, I say a rather placating confession because I know I must. But would a mumbled "forgive me" be enough if I were to look deeply into His face and really see my sin?

Worst of all, I omit thanksgiving, because my tendency is to overlook His wonders as though the blessings in my life were my due. And, feeling sanctimonious, I rush to petition, finding my voice full and strong. The needs of others, the lost and hurting, receive only a cursory plea; importance dimmed by my strident demands for myself.

Heavenly Father, I know I have the freedom and confidence to approach You. But maybe if I would heed more seriously Your instructions on prayer in Scripture, I would find my petitions not quite so urgent as I bask in sweet fellowship with You. And then, I think I would not want to rush. Amen.

June 3

HIGH PLACES

You shall utterly destroy all the places, where the nations which you shall dispossess served their gods, on the high mountains and on the hills and under every green tree. Deuteronomy 12:2

God told His people, as they entered a new land, "Destroy the high places. Tear down the groves and smash the false idols. Worship me alone." But all through the story in the Old Testament, this sad litany recalls: *However the high places were not removed; the people still sacrificed and burned incense on the high places*[36]. Even during the reign of the 'good kings', the high places called people to forsake God and burn their ungodly incense on altars of foreign gods.

I see now there are high places in my life where I slink off to bow down before altars of envy, pride and greed. On top of the hill where my high places lie, I need to view God's plan for me. The victory has been won, God's word assures me. And I claim this victory as I offer my all to Him.

God, I gave you my heart, so now take my will, bend it to yours, I pray. You promise me the victory if I abandon those high places and make I offer You pure true worship. I think I need to find a wrecking ball. Amen.

---

[36] 2 Chronicles 20:33

June 4

THE FRUIT OF MY LIPS

Therefore by Him let us continually offer the sacrifice of praise to God, that is, the fruit of our lips, giving thanks to His name.
Hebrews 13:15

I find myself intrigued by the metaphor of fruit as a *sacrifice*. Fruit is the result of growth, an outflow of change; something that is produced. Another observation: praise should not need to be *manufactured*. I admit I say "Praise God," quite often. But truth be told, sometimes I say it rather grudgingly, in quasi obedience; because I know that we are told to lift our hearts in praise. But as I write "Praise God" this morning I feel *real* praise bubble up in inside me begging for release.

I'm wondering if my lips often express a heart of discontent and grumbling, which praises reluctantly—mere words, rather than reflecting a heart of joy. The Scripture tells us: *Out of the same mouth proceed blessing and cursing. My brethren, these things ought not to be so.*[37]

Yes, praise can be a sacrifice. But for it to be genuine, it must be offered from a repentant, clean heart. Then, instead of dutiful obedience, it becomes *fruit*, a harvest from a living, growing spirit. A joyful sacrifice.

Dear Father, I am chagrined to realize that my praise too often comes as a duty, or just something I say because it sounds good. Please forgive me, make me clean before You so that my lips will offer my gratitude as worship from pure lips. Amen.

---

[37] James 3:10

June 5

A SWEET AROMA

All who are native-born shall do these things in this manner,
in presenting an offering made by fire,
a sweet aroma to the LORD.
Numbers 15:13

I have been reading of God's instructions to His people. The details are astounding, so numerous it boggles my mind. How on earth do the priests remember them all? The laws they are to follow are amazing as well, and as I read I give my praise to God that, because of Jesus' sacrifice in our place, we need not be bound by the myriad of instructions.

But I did notice one thing that blesses me. The smoke from the burning brings a sweet aroma to God. It stretches my mind to consider how the stench of burning animal flesh can be described as a sweet aroma. But that is not what God smells; what is sweet in His nostrils is the perfume of obedience and repentance that signifies the sacrifice.

I love perfume, most of the time. And I long to be a sweet aroma to those around me, especially to my God. I have long behaved as though my good deeds and moral living constitute a pleasing scent. But looking deep inside, I think the aroma God longs to experience from me is the smoke from the burning of self—freely offered repentance on the altar of my heart. A sweet aroma.

Heavenly Father, my prayer today is that my life will be pleasing to You. That I will heed Your plea for obedience and surrender, and offer perfumed praise that truly will be sweet in Your nostrils. Amen.

EYES ONLY

To You,, O Lord, I lift up my soul. Psalm 25:1

In my professional life I worked as a secretary, often serving a CEO or other top official. I loved my jobs; loved serving and sitting, in a sense, in the seat of power! It was a heady feeling, even though it demanded a lot of responsibility.

In the course of my duties there often came across my desk a sealed envelope for my boss, marked *Eyes Only!* It was my job to see that he alone was able to open the envelope and see the message inside.

I have been pondering the Psalms, and finding how often David, or another writer, mentions the "lifting up" process. Here, he says he lifts up his *soul*. I think this is what God delights in: the conscious seeking of His face, so He can incline His ear to hear our prayer. I wonder what He sees in the depths of me... when I really stop to pray; and am still enough to know Him for Who He is.

I think back to *Eyes Only* envelopes and my responsibility of making sure they ended up where they were supposed to be. I want now to be sure that my attention is directed where it needs to be—to the One who created me, loves me and longs for my love in return.

Only your eyes, Father, can see my depths. Only eyes of faith can begin to penetrate Your heart. But when I pray, my eyes tend to dart here, there and everywhere; lighting for a moment on a need, a concern or a desire. Have I lost the secret of delight in Your presence? Please help me narrow my focus and widen my vision to receive the revelation of You, Yourself—personal and confidential. Amen.

June 7

A TASTE OF HONEY

How sweet are your words to my taste, sweeter than honey to my mouth! Through Your precepts I get understanding; therefore I hate every false way. Your word is a lamp to my feet and a light to my path. Psalm 119:103-105

Each morning I receive an invitation as I settle into a quiet spot in my living room to spend time with my heavenly Father. He beckons me with a simple menu: words sweeter than honey. I am hungry. It is an invitation that I delight to accept!

How could I refuse such an enticing atmosphere? Lamplight and intimacy with the One Who loves me, Who has a meal waiting for me to savor. A delectable feast, a candlelight dinner for two; my Heavenly Father and I in devoted communication

This is a meal that fills and satisfies—that illumines and guides—settles my mind and soothes my anxious heart. There is encouragement and understanding; promises and love that settles deeply into my heart, filling all empty spaces. Sweet it is, and I am anxious to see just what awaits each new sunrise!

Father, let's light the lamps; I am ready for a taste of honey. Fill me; make me sweet with Your presence. Amen.

June 8

ANTICIPATION

Since ancient times no one has heard, no ear has perceived, no eye has seen any God besides you, who acts on behalf of those who wait for him. Isaiah 64:4 (NIV)

In these times of technology, texting and email, it is rare to receive a handwritten letter or note. Still, every day I go for the mail with hope in my heart! And almost every day I walk back from the mailbox disappointed when there are no letters—only bills and solicitations. Friendly phone calls from real people—not computer-generated—are a rarity as well; so entering the house with no flashing light on the answering machine often makes me a little lonely as well. How anxious I am to hear from my family; my children far away, brothers and sisters distanced by miles and divergent lives.

I look at my own life, though, and wonder just how often *I* reach out in a tangible way? I fancy myself busy also, and many times I fail to keep in touch with those I love. I'm not blaming others; I am just longing to hear.

So when I rest with open Bible, head bowed to pray; my heart hears and understands His welcome: "I've been waiting to hear from you."

Heavenly Father, how easy it is to forget that You are longing to spend time with me; to speak, listen, and enjoy the intimacy of communication. Forgive me for ignoring the pull of Your voice; because You wait patiently to hear from me like I wait to hear from my loved ones. Understanding dawns! Amen.

June 10

UNDIVIDED

I will praise You, O LORD, with my whole heart; I will tell of all Your marvelous works. Psalm 9:1

With my whole heart. This phrase grabbed my attention! I was convicted that too often I find myself coming to God with a *divided* heart. Worries and concerns pull at my attention as does ripping a Band-Aid from my arm. I hear God calling my heart to worship so I come, and sit with His Word for a while. But it isn't long before my mind tears itself away from beholding Him to how I can make money, care for myself or fulfill my duties. I usually write my prayers so that I can keep focused, but even so, my thoughts take on a life of their own, and the heart who longs to worship is bound again in worry. A divided heart.

My *undivided* heart is what God desires—not torn away by my wants and wishes—just my worship. Once again I am challenged and chastened by His word, and I turn again to truly seek Him. He says: *Then I will give them a heart to know Me, that I am the LORD; and they shall be My people, and I will be their God, for they shall return to Me with their whole heart.*[38]

Dear Father, my prayer for my life is to learn the discipline of coming to the feet of Jesus with my whole heart. I realize it will take a lot of discipline and learning to lean on You. As I love You more, may my heart expand in the fullness of loving devotion that leads to true worship. Amen.

---

[38] Jeremiah 24:7

June 11

A JOYFUL NOISE

Make a joyful shout unto the LORD, all ye lands. Psalm 100:1

Many times we find in scripture the exhortation to make a joyful noise to the Lord. We usually say it to excuse our imperfect singing! However I think it is concerned just as much with the way we *talk* to the Lord. So I was just wondering if what God hears from me is a joyful noise. There is plenty of sound, to be sure, but I'm not certain He finds it joyful. Mostly I am pleading for help, begging for healing, or moaning in exasperation. Does that sound joyful to Him?

How I need to be reminded of His uncountable blessings; and voice my humble praise with a heart full of gratitude. Those are joyful noises to His ears.

So I pray that when pressed by the circumstances that come into my life, whether I consider them to be good or bad, the noise that I make will not be a mournful whine, but joyful effervescence of new wine.

Dear Father, I hope my grateful song reaches Your ears as a joyful noise! Because I really am filled with gratitude for all You have done. What a lesson for me! Amen.

June 12

CONSIDER YOUR WAYS

Now, therefore, thus says the LORD of hosts, "Consider your ways! You have sown much, and bring in little; you eat, but do not have enough; you drink, but you are not filled with drink; you clothe yourself but no one is warm; and he who earns wages, earns wages to put into a bag with holes." Haggai 1:5-6

Haggai is an interesting little book. Though he may be an obscure prophet in the Old Testament he has a lot to say about what we *consider* as we live the days of our lives. Webster defines the verb "consider" this way, "a directing of the mind to a subject in order to understand it, or to make a decision about it; to look at carefully; examine."

The prophet is chiding the Israelites about their laxity in rebuilding the temple. God is concerned that the rebuilding has lost its importance; that the people don't care that it lies in ruins. So He spoke through Haggai that they needed to *consider* their ways.

Haggai's words intrigue me and I ask myself just what it is I am considering. What is my mind dwelling on? A rather bleak picture is captured in God's word here. I presently am overly concerned with living in my comfortable paneled house and filling an unfillable holey bag than I am with building up the temple of God that lives within me. I am therefore challenged by God's reprimand here to consider my ways—to build up that temple and fill it with praise. May we all take up the challenge to "consider our ways."

Father, you command us to praise You. When we truly consider You, it is easy to do so! So help us to heed this very important prompting to worship You! Amen.

June 13

STOLEN JOY

Do not sorrow, for the joy of the LORD is your strength.
Nehemiah 8:10

We read this verse in the Bible, we hear about it in sermons and we even sing about it. But what does this really mean? No matter how bleak your problem looks or how awful your circumstances, if you can read your Bible, you can rejoice! And if you can rejoice, you are a candidate for victor! Are you discouraged in your walk with the Lord? Has your joy been left along the wayside somewhere? Satan wants your joy—and he wants it badly—but he cannot defeat a joyful believer.

So…how *does* the enemy try to steal our joy? Number one on the list is **worry**. Joy dims when anxiousness sets in. Here's another that nips at my heels: *criticism.* Feeling criticized for something I've done or not done, or for who I am, can start me on a cycle of self-doubt. As a result, joy flees. *Pride*, too, can devour joy! The last thing I notice in my life that destroys the joy God longs to give is *comparison.* Comparison is a joy-killer because it makes me dissatisfied and feeling that I am lacking somehow.

Heavenly Father, I know I'm not alone in poor responses to the enemy's efforts to steal. Please help me to keep the joy robbers out of my heart and to fix my mind on You. May my strength come from the joy that in turn comes from loving and serving You. Amen.

June 14

STORED JOY

Though the fig tree does not bud and there are no grapes on the vines, though the olive crop fails and the fields produce no food, though there are no sheep in the pen and no cattle in the stalls, YET I will rejoice in the LORD, I will be joyful in God my Savior.
Habakkuk 3:17-18 (NIV)

Can we actually *store up* joy in our hearts? Yes! However it has to be intentional in order to combat the traps the enemy sets. Being intentional goes a long way toward storing up joy. What a terrible scenario Habakkuk describes here! But he arrives at the word *yet.* In spite of circumstances I also am determined to_find that joy. Our salvation itself is more than enough to give us joy.

Secondly, expressing *gratitude* fills our joy reservoir! There is something rewarding and inspiring about being consciously grateful. It takes away discontent and disappointment, helping us to re-focus; and it pleases God.

Our inner dialogue, then, needs to be examined in the light of God's word. How are we speaking to ourselves? Are we meditating on the wonder of God and His loving mercy and provision—or complaining because we don't have more?

We all long for joy, and it can only truly be found in knowing God. Learning to know Him through His word is enough to keep a deep well of rejoicing at the ready. Even Job finds himself coming to know God is a special way through his trials. In the midst of his suffering Job states a wonderful promise. *He will YET fill your lips with laughing and your lips with rejoicing.*[39]

Heavenly Father, I want to be intentionally grateful, meditating on Your Word. Thus I will store up the joy that strengthens and upholds me. Your storehouse of joy is inexhaustible. Thank you. Amen.

---

[39] Job 8:21

June 15

STEADFAST JOY

If you keep My commandments, you will abide in My love, just as I have kept My Father's commandments and abide in His love. These things I have spoken to you, that My joy may remain in you, and that your joy may be full. John 15:10-11.

Steadfast joy. Which is the best kind actually, because it is the joy that only God provides.

I looked up the word "steadfast" in the dictionary and found, as I had expected, that it means firm, fixed, settled; not changing, fickle or wavering. Wow! Steadfast joy is something that we can hold on to that won't shift under our feet, whatever is going on. Steadfast joy cannot be manufactured, it must be received. We can make ourselves laugh, we can get giddy with excitement. But true joy, the joy of our salvation and intimate relationship with God can come only from His hand, accepted and absorbed through His Word and is energized by His Spirit.

So, you might ask, how does this come about? It happens as we spend time with God in His Word, making it a part of us. The key: Stay. Since I love alliteration, I have chosen to say *stay* instead of *abide* or *remain*. If we *stay* in His love, receiving His never-changing joy, we can experience steadfast joy. Long-lasting, life-changing. I close my thoughts on joy with a favorite verse: *You will show me the path of life; in Your presence is fullness of joy; at Your right hand are pleasures forevermore.*[40]

Dear Father, the originator of true joy, I am filled with praise as I consider the truth of Your word. Help me stay in Your word and keep Your commandments so that I will know the reality of that joy. Steadfast and unchanging joy is my goal. Amen.

---

[40] Psalm 16:11

June 16

PERFECT HEARING

For the eyes of the Lord are on the righteous and
His ears are attentive to their prayer.
I Peter 3:12

I am hard of hearing. And I so hate to admit it! My hearing aid is often left behind and I find myself straining to hear, to be part of a conversation, irritating others with the constant, "What did you say?" It's a sign of aging that I am loath to acknowledge.

So, I praise God for His ever-hearing ear. I know it is attuned to my cry. He hears me even when I'm not totally aware that I'm crying out because His ear hears much more than my words.

He hears the argument between the flesh and spirit: the desire to trust battling against the earthly need for control. He hears the excuses, the protests; He feels the hurt of my begging for His help alongside my pushing Him away.

Yet His ear never tunes me out. He promised! He never puts in ear-plugs. He hears and experiences the whole battle, so how sweet to His attentive ear must be my words as they come at long last, "I surrender. I will trust You."

Father, the more I contrast my inability to hear with Your attentive ears, the more I realize my need for dependence on You. How trustworthy Your perfect hearing! I'm growing to love you better each day. Amen.

June 17

THE HANDS OF A FATHER

Keep your lives free from the love of money and be content with what you have, because God has said, "Never will I leave you; never will I forsake you." Hebrews 13:5 (NIV)

I was watching a family today—father, mother, children—as they walked along the street. The youngest child, just learning to walk with tiny, stumbling steps, would never have been able to keep up with the rest of the family had not his daddy slowed his own steps, leaned down to clasp the hand of his son and chided the older children not to speed ahead.

I began to watch the crowd a bit more closely as it passed by. It was easy to discern an adult walking with a small child by the slow measured pace and slanting of the body to accommodate short legs and small steps.

I was moved to tears as I considered how sweetly it reminded me of the heavenly Father. When we first begin our walk within the family of God, our steps are small, our legs of faith short and stumbling. But God leans down, grips our hand, and with sweet encouragement measures His pace to ours.

Yes, some of us have stronger legs and we try to run ahead of Him; but He reminds us to wait for Him; that He is in control and His plan will allow all of us in the family to arrive together.

Dear God, whatever the pace we walk within Your family, how precious to remember we are kept in a circle of care. It is Your hands that hold us, guide us—because of Your love. Thank You. Amen.

June 18

CRY

The righteous cry out, and the LORD hears, and delivers them out of all their troubles. Psalm 34:17

In my distress I called upon the LORD, and cried out to my God; He heard my voice from His temple, and my cry entered His ears. 2 Samuel 22:7

How many times have we felt that we were just *finished*? That we couldn't go on? Just recently I wrote these words in my journal: "The end of my rope is close. So overwhelmed with upheaval in my life, it seems the ends of my rope are rapidly fraying and my spirit has begun to sink into despair." We've heard the saying, "When you get to the end of your rope, just tie a knot in it and hang on."[41]

Sounds nice. But easy? Not unless we know just what pulls the knot together. That would be God's presence. His message to the hurting soul, in essence, is: "Call, cry out to Me. I will hear. I will listen, and I will bring relief. I will restore your joy. Even though you may have to wait a while—until my timing allows the work in you to be completed."

Yes, I am struggling to hang on, but my Heavenly Father is aware of my battle. *Easy* was never promised. But help was—and is. "Cry," He says, "Call on Me."

Father, I will cry out, unashamed, because You encourage it. You don't intrude; You don't step in until You know that I know my need. Then You will hear my cry. Amen.

---

[41] Franklin D. Roosevelt (1882-1945)

June 19

SCULPTURE

Keep your heart with all diligence, for out of it spring the issues of life. Proverbs 4:23

My heart. The center of my very being. Scripture tells me it determines the course of my life. So I'm left asking, "In what shape is my heart? Is it leading me on the right course?" My God, the awesome Creator who initially formed my heart, is the One who knows it intimately. He is the Designer at work in me. I have heard that at the end of my life there is one of three things that will have happened to my heart: it will grow hard, it will be broken, *or* it will become tender. (Maybe, and probably at some point, all three!)

Although my Artist is Sovereign, it is how I choose to allow His carving to take place within me that determines the final sculpture. A famous preacher once said, "The same sun that melts wax hardens clay."[42] May I be soft beneath His hand. May I let brokenness make me tender, vulnerable and malleable.

May I guard my heart against complacency and keep my thoughts focused on His truth.

Dear God, may I in humility ask You to form a heart that resembles You? Please be the Sculptor of my heart. Amen.

---

[42] Charles H. Spurgeon (1834-1892)

June 20

ENSNARED

Come unto Me, all ye that labor and are heavy laden, and I will give you rest. Take my yoke upon you, and learn of me, for I am gentle and lowly in heart, and ye shall find rest unto your souls. For my yoke is easy and my burden is light. Matthew 11:28-30

"Too busy." It's my anguished cry. Too busy to pray, too busy to spend a quiet hour with God, too frantic to hear Him, too important to embrace Him. There are things I must do.

Have I fallen into the service trap? More and more I am ensnared, and sense the trap snapping shut. I'm unable to pull out of it for fear of cutting off my leg. I wonder, though, isn't a crippled leg more desirable than a frenetic, useless life?

The more I struggle, the tighter the trap closes and I long for release. I am so uncomfortable, ensnared by my stubbornness to let go of what I think I have to DO. I need to realize that my God awaits my surrender and capitulation to His will.

Please, God, if I jerk myself free, no matter what the pain, is there room on your lap for another wounded lamb? Jesus, I come. Amen.

June 21

QUIETNESS AND CONFIDENCE

For thus says the LORD God, the Holy One of Israel, "In returning and rest you shall be saved, in quietness and confidence shall be your strength." But you would not. Isaiah 30:15

My spirit has been disquieted. I feel adrift, as though my anchor has lifted. But in the hurried pace of daily living I spend only a fleeting moment wondering why.

I don't really have to look far for help...God speaks plainly through the scripture. My prayers have been mostly frantic appeals, panicky pleas; and while I am confident that God hears them, I'm realizing I want more. I hear His plaintive cry *But you would not,* and my heart breaks with regret. There is no doubt that He knows why I am disquieted.

I want a life-style of faith and trust; with a knowledge of God that doesn't need to rush screaming into His presence when crises occur; a confidence that is steadfast, and unflappable. Is that not what brings joy to God's heart? His child *leaning* a little harder into Him, *holding* on a bit tighter to Him, and drawing strength from closeness with Him?

Precious Father, as I learn to obediently sit in quietness before you, I know I will find the strength and courage I need to rest in you. Thank You for Your promises. Amen.

June 22

MELODY

Be still, and know that I am God. Psalm 46:10

Nursery duty—not really the place where I looked forward to doing my volunteering! I want to do my part, but it is almost beyond my physical ability (now that even my grandchildren are taller than I am)! But they asked me to sit with the babies. Surely I could rock a crying baby. Of course—I would be sitting down!

As I took the screaming, kicking little one into my arms I began to hum softly, hoping the vibration of my voice would begin to calm her. It had worked with other babies, my own children and grandchildren for example. So I held her closely to me, rocking, continuing to hum a sweet melody. She didn't want to calm down; fought every effort I made to settle her by flailing her arms and legs, sobbing hysterically. I wondered how much crying her little body could endure.

Sitting there in the rocking chair, humming, holding, praying; God spoke to me. He asked if I could see myself in this baby: in the fighting, the crying, the flailing of limbs that spoke my rebellion, in my insistence on doing my own thing. I heard Him!

"All the time you are pushing against Me, the same way this child is pushing against you, I am longing for you to calm down, and hear the sweet melody I am humming into your ear."

Dear Father, suddenly it is so clear to me. As she settles from screaming to relaxed snuffling, and then off to sleep, I feel Your arms holding me. In my confession and surrender, the noise of my striving ceases, and a sweet melody caresses my ear. Thank You. Amen.

June 23

VOWS

Vows made to You are binding upon me, O God; I will render praises to You, for You have delivered my soul from death. Have You not kept my feet from falling, that I may walk before God in the light of the living? Psalm 56:12-13

This is an important matter. God takes our vows seriously. A vow is a promise and a serious commitment we're making; an unflinching determination, and should not be taken lightly. Over and over scripture reminds us that it is better not to make a vow than to promise and not fulfill our vow.

Earlier in this psalm David writes that when he is afraid, he will trust in God. He now shares his thoughts as to how God had delivered him, and reiterates his promise not to be afraid. God is faithful. He does what He has promised.

In response to God's deliverance he repeats his vow, *I will praise His word,*[43] a vow to the Lord. Does he? Yes. Do I? Do I claim the promise of deliverance, yet neglect to pay my vow of praise to God for what He has done? Oh, this challenges me.

Heavenly Father, You are so faithful. And so must I be. I must trust You, pick up my strengthened feet, refusing to fear, and pay my vow of praise. It is the least I can do. May I watch my words and when I say "I will"...then do it. Amen.

---

[43] Psalm 56:10

June 24

MERCY

Therefore strengthen the hands which hang down, and the feeble knees, and make straight paths for your feet, so that what is lame may not be dislocated, but rather be healed. Hebrews 12:12

A few years ago I was diagnosed with gout. It took a long time and many doctor appointments to determine the source of the pain in my feet and ankles. Constant pain is debilitating and colors everything else in life. I was frustrated and discouraged. One day I read this Hebrews verse and I chuckled. I thought "God must have a sense of humor!" Of course the writer of Hebrews is speaking of spiritual vitality, but sitting in the chair with throbbing feet, the verse seemed appropriate.

A few moments earlier I had been reading Psalms, *Show me Your ways, O LORD; teach me Your paths, lead me in Your truth and teach me for You are the God of my salvation; on You I wait all the day.*[44] Was God trying to teach me something here? Did He have a purpose for my incapacitation? So I read on, and it was verse 6 that made my eyes sting with tears. It touched me because of the reminder of where I was to focus: His tender mercies—He who has always been there for me.

Perhaps the words "tender mercies" resonated with me that morning because I was feeling such pain and discouragement, and needed a loving touch. What could be more loving than the surety that in His mercy, His tender mercy, He cares for me: He always has, and He will continue to do so!

Heavenly Father, the touch of Your word is precious and its promises are salve for my hurting, I am so grateful for the lesson learned. Amen.

---

[44] Psalm 25:4-6

June 25

VIRTUOSO

...that the God of our Lord Jesus Christ, the Father of glory, may give unto you the spirit of wisdom and revelation in the knowledge of Him; the eyes of your understanding being enlightened; that ye may know what is the hope of His calling, and what is the riches of the glory of his inheritance in the saints. Ephesians 1:17, 18

I love music. When I was younger I played an instrument, was active in the band and reveled in making melody. But I had a family member who played a violin. That, to me, seemed so very difficult. Much more than blowing into a saxophone! Flying fingers expertly form chords which are made into music by the long slow drawing of the bow across the strings. Mesmerized, I watched the fascinating interplay, my spirit absorbing the beauty of the sound.

A talented trained violinist is a virtuoso. One evening I watched as a woman whom I knew to be in the throes of dementia sit in the seat of the orchestra concertmistress and proceed to play each selection flawlessly. Amazed, music filled my soul, and God spoke to my heart while I watched. I realized this is how God works in me. Just as the violinist makes music, His masterful omnipotent fingers arrange, move and situate; forming the chords that create melody as He draws His sovereign bow across the strings of my life.

Father, may my life ever be a song of praise to You. Thank You for the music You are making. May I never forget how to play the instrument that You created me to be. Amen.

June 26

THE EVENING SACRIFICE

Lord, I cry out to you; make haste to me! Give ear to my voice when I cry out to you. Let my prayer be set before you as incense; the lifting up of my hands be as the evening sacrifice. Psalm 141:1-2

Reading through the Psalms, I pondered this verse. What is the evening sacrifice? Looking it up, I discovered that some scholars say it points to Jesus, offered in the evening of the world—the final sacrifice—after all the observances required by the Law. He made atonement for us, that we might freely exalt God with our lips, our voices, our lives.

It is now evening, and I am coming to offer God my sacrifice of praise…for Jesus, who Himself was the evening sacrifice; after the Law, fulfilling the Law, making it possible for me to cease from my labors and rest in Him.

So as I look back over my day, I consider the heat of the trials that bring me to the burning of my will, my daily sacrifice. I realize that through those battling fires comes the peace that prompts the uplifting of my hands in praise—my evening sacrifice.

Dear God, may my prayer, my sacrifice of praise, rise to You to gladden Your heart with the fragrance of incense. But just as the aroma of incense is not released without heat or fire, my prayer does not ascend without the holy fire of Your Spirit.
And I thank You for that fire. Amen.

June 27

REPROOF

O LORD, I know the way of man is not in himself; it is not in man who walks to direct his own steps. O LORD, correct me, but with justice; not in Your anger, lest You bring me to nothing.
Jeremiah 10:23, 24

I have been directing my *own* steps. Suddenly, I am so aware of it; standing before God, desiring His blessing on *my* efforts. I've had this lesson before; that's what distresses me. Even though I *know* better, I haven't *learned*… evidently.

Here I am, again; these words from scripture jerking my head from complacency to chastening. But, oh, the reproof comes so tenderly; mercy's sweetness reawakening my heart to the truth that my life is not my own, I've laid it on the altar of the Master Planner of my days.

He has every right to reprove me, to remind me, to gently correct my path so I can live in freedom and in joy.

Oh, Father, how often I need Your merciful chastening hand. My tendency for self-direction causes me to take my eyes off You and that is the reason You tenderly correct my path. Thank You. Amen.

June 28

REPOSE

The LORD your God in your midst, the Mighty One, will save; He will rejoice over you with gladness, He will quiet you with His love, he will rejoice over you with singing.
Zephaniah 3:17

The picture this verse paints in my mind's eye is one of peace and tranquility. It draws me to God's side, yearning for Him to create this in my life. However, I too often find turbulence in my soul. There is a turmoil that rages, a struggle that stifles; and I realize it need not be so. God's love could bring calm, encircling me with all I need for quietness...if I allow myself to give it the proper place in my heart.

In that love I can find *safety* because He is mighty to save. In that love I can find *joy* because He delights in me. In that love I can find *rest* because He is with me. That's what this Scripture tells me. My soul longs for the promise of rest, the repose that stills my heart's frantic striving.

Heavenly Father, as I sit before You this morning, desiring to hear from You, I read the promises to me in Your word. You simply, joyfully, delight in me! I sense the sounds of Your singing over me. And my soul finds its repose in You. Amen.

June 29

WITHERED FRUIT

"Abide in me and I in you. As the branch cannot bear fruit of itself, unless it abides in the vine, neither can you, unless you abide in Me."
John 15:4

I took a long look at the fruit I'm bearing this morning when I soaked in the Word of God. And I realized that it is not inviting or tasty – much less nutritious. Instead, peering closely I see only dry and withered fruit… pride, envy, impatience, unkindness, frustration. And the place where my branch joins the vine is severed and drying up so it cannot receive the life-giving sap of the Vine.

It doesn't take long for fresh fruit to wither when it has fallen from the vine! Staying connected – joined – takes work and I find myself giving in to indolence more often than not.

Father, will you, the Vinedresser, bind my branch tightly against the Vine again? Re-graft me into Yourself so I might feel anew the pulsing flow of the Vine-life. May the withered fruit drop off by Your pruning, and blossoms of newly-forming fruit begin to appear. Amen

June 30

HEART'S DESIRE

One thing have I desired of the LORD, that will I seek after; that I may dwell in the house of the LORD all the days of my life, to behold the beauty of the LORD, and to enquire in His temple. Psalm 27:4

I know many of you are aware of the special joys of being a grandparent! I like to remember an incident long ago when our granddaughter was about three years old. We were enjoying a long-anticipated family visit, and it was so good to welcome our dear children and grandchildren to our home.

Small arms wrapped around my neck. Snuggling into my lap, my granddaughter announced, "Grandma, I'm finally here. I can hug you all I want, and that's all I came for."

No expectations, simply the desire to love and be loved. My heart swelled with joy! On the other hand, it nearly broke; for deep in my soul I saw how I often approach my Heavenly Father. His joy when I come to Him surely is quelled when I simply haul out my shopping list. Does He ever hear from me the tender words "I only came for Your hug?" I was chagrined, and I have never forgotten this lovely moment.

A friend once shared with me that she often steps inside her laundry room, closes the door and spends just a few moments with God, telling Him, "I'm just here to let You love me." Oh, what sweetness that must be in His ear!

Father, teach me to snuggle into Your lap and whisper, "Here I am. Let me hug You. My heart's desire is to feel Your nearness... and that's all I came for." Amen.

July 1

FREEDOM

If you abide in My word, you are My disciples indeed. And you shall know the truth and the truth shall make you free. John 8:31-32

At this time of the year our thoughts turn to freedom and the privilege of living in a country where we still have a great deal of that! How often we have heard this verse spoken; *You shall know the truth, and the truth shall make you free.* It sounds like a great vision.

But I'm realizing that the two verses can't be separated. Jesus says in Verse 31, *If you abide in My word, you are My disciples indeed.* Verse 32 follows: *And you shall know the truth and the truth shall make you free.* It's the "if/then" connection that caught my attention. The truth that can set us free comes from abiding in His word, from comprehending and absorbing it, and walking in obedience to it.

God loves us unconditionally. He offers freedom from the bondage of thinking we have to perform a certain way. Freedom to let go of our own desires. Freedom from the tyranny of the clock.

This familiar concept strikes my heart afresh with an awareness of just how liberating this freedom can be.

Heavenly Father, as I get older, I can't do a lot of the things I used to feel were so important, and the freedom not to feel guilty is beautiful. May my freedom come from Your word: abiding in it, living in it, soaking in it. Please burn this truth into my heart. Amen.

July 2

CADENCE

No one engaged in warfare entangles himself with the affairs of this life that he may please him who enlisted him as a soldier.
2 Timothy 2:4

Parades! What a wonderful way to celebrate America, and the ceremonies evoke deep pride and patriotism. The color guard marching in solemn cadence brings me to tears: unity, pride and precision mark their advance through the room. *Cadence* means matched movement. As I watch, I think of the hours of drilling; learning to hold their hands, weapons and flags, in a certain way—each motion significant. They drill and practice until it becomes second nature to follow the voice of the leader as he sounds the cadence. Discipline, order and obedience are necessary, in order to become a team.

The muffled sound of boots marching in unison echoes my heartbeat's pounding with pride, patriotism, and memories. I am grateful to God for giving me the privilege of being a Navy wife, doing what I could to support and build up my husband so that he could freely serve. In addition, I sense the challenge to listen to the cadence the God of the Universe is directing, and learn to march in precision with Him. How I want to join with others and help enable them as we all learn to match our movements to His cadence.

Heavenly Father, it is often difficult to walk in step with others, and with You. But you call us to unity and precision with You. May the drumbeat of Your voice calling the steps reverberate so clearly in my heart that I will march with purpose and hope, pleasing You with my cadence. Amen.

July 3

FRUIT

But the fruit of the Spirit is love, joy, peace, longsuffering, kindness, goodness, faithfulness, gentleness, self-control. Against such there is no law." Galatians 5:22-23

Such a familiar passage! However as I looked more closely and tried to find how it applied to my own life, I noticed the word *fruit*! Food! Never far from my mind these days, as I struggle to eat healthy. Soon I was ruminating about the word *diet,* and the contrast between a restrictive diet and a balanced diet. With the first kind of diet I'm hungry, and angry at being told what to eat—and what not to eat. I get irritated and cranky, feeling deprived. But on the balanced diet I feel healthy and able to have some control with the ability to make my own choices. Since I am free to eat what I want, I can feel pleased with myself when I don't eat what I'm learning is not good for me.

Which brings another contrast to mind...that between legalism and grace! When told constantly "*thou shalt not,*" as I have been most of my life; I'm miserable, rebellious and wanting to do the forbidden. When I appropriate God's *grace,* it changes everything and I usually make the right choices because I can. I choose.

God is teaching me so much as I work at navigating a new normal...the importance of a healthy diet. I am very grateful to be discovering the joy of being yielded—and free! They *can* go hand-in-hand!

Heavenly Father, I pray You bring me the willingness to make the best choices, choices that will benefit both my health and my relationship with You. Thus there will be the fruit of Your Holy Spirit. And that fruit will honor You. Amen.

July 4

THE PICCOLO

Set your mind on things above, not on things on the earth.
For you died and your life is hidden with Christ in God.
Colossians 3:2, 3

The army band came to play, and stirring martial music filled the air. I felt like marching up and down the street, patriotism burning deep inside. Coming closer I observed a poignant sight…a soldier held a piccolo, nearly invisible in his giant hands.

"Stars and Stripes Forever", as always, brought tears of gratitude and love for my country to my eyes as the melody played high and sweet. Such intricate fingerings! I thought, how incredible to see these hands, trained also to hold a weapon, coaxing such delicate sweetness from this tiny instrument.

I watched, enchanted by the contrast, my soul alive to the music. I thought of how God holds us in His massive fingers, gripping us securely while He plays His tune. The piccolo could barely be seen in itself, but it most definitely was heard, because of the skill of the player.

Dear Father, the irony doesn't escape me…trained for battle against the enemy of our soul, we are at the same time, held hidden in Your mighty hands. May we be yielded to Your skill, because as Your breath blows through us we, too, can play a trilling tune. When You are the Artist, the melody is always sweet. Amen.

July 5

TRUE VALUE

Fear not, for I have redeemed you, I have called you by your name; you are Mine. Isaiah 43:1b

This tender portion of Scripture reassures us of our worth in the heart of God. It opens a litany of promises that is filled with pledges of His nearness, His protection and His plan for us. It is comforting to read this verse, which has been so precious to me for a long time.

I remember a day when I apprehended the meaning of the word *redeemed* in a very personal way. I discovered I had lost my 25th anniversary gift from my husband, a beautiful topaz ring. Frantically I searched everywhere I could think. Not finding it at home, we headed back to all the places we had been shopping that afternoon. Feeling hopeless, we entered the last store and asked about the lost and found. We approached the jewelry counter where we had been directed and, even before we could ask, we noticed my topaz lying amidst the tray of costume rings! I had thoughtlessly slipped it off to try on a cheap ring and left it behind. "Whatever it costs," my loving husband assured me, "I will buy it back for you."

God says that we are *precious in His sight.*[45] A great cost was willingly paid for our redemption because we are loved by God, precious in His sight.

God, please keep us aware of our worth to You. Thank You for paying such a dear price for our ransom. Amen.

---

[45] Isaiah 43:4

July 6

OUT OF THE NET

My eyes are ever toward the LORD, for He shall pluck my feet out of the net. Psalm 25:15

Have you ever tried to climb a cargo net? I had the opportunity to explore this activity as I led my cabin full of young girls on a ropes course at a mountain camp. I remember being terrified all night before the day we were slated to do the course.

The whole thing was daunting for me—a much older woman—leading these girls. I was to be an example of faith, but I was a quivering mass of fear, and they knew it! Somehow, by sheer faith and stubbornness, I did it! I was so proud of myself—and so relieved!

I read the above verse this morning and my thoughts veered back to that day and I remembered how very difficult it was to climb up that net. It seemed there was no stability, no place to hold firmly or to give purchase to my feet. The net swayed and moved with a mind of its own.

So many times I find myself entangled in a net of despair, sadness or disappointment. It seems there is no place firm enough to stand, no way to climb; my feet are wound in ropes that grab at every attempt to pull myself out.

There is hope, however! I find it in this verse: keep my eyes on God. Only He can pluck my stubborn feet out of whatever has snared me, and continue to hold me. It is a personal thing He does, reaching down to grab and release the rope. And all of a sudden I reach the end of my climb. Freedom!

Dear Father, help me to remember this example in my daily life; to consistently turn my eyes to You, so that my feet may stay free. Amen.

July 7

FLIGHT

...that by two immutable things, in which it is impossible for God to lie, we might have strong consolation, who have fled for refuge to lay hold of the hope set before us. This hope we have as an anchor of the soul, both sure and steadfast.
Hebrews 6:18-19a

Deliver me, O LORD, from my enemies; in You I take shelter.
Psalm 143:9

Sometimes we have a need for consolation. Sometimes the burdens of our lives here on earth feel too heavy to bear, and we restlessly look about, searching to find relief from the load of care we are carrying.

Which is why these verses so often soothe my troubled heart. There *is* hope; there *is* help. So I flee to my Heavenly Father to grab hold of the anchor He promises. When hounded by enemies of fear and doubt, I'm realizing there's no safety, no peace outside the enclosure of His Presence. Consolation comes from being held in the refuge of His arms. There we are anchored in hope.

God cannot lie; He is steadfast, immovable. So it behooves me to use wings of faith to fly to Him. He waits. He will deliver and shelter me.

Precious Father, please hide me – cover me – with Your very self, and let the hope You promise be my anchor. Amen.

July 8

DEEP STILLNESS

As the deer pants for the water brooks, so pants my soul for You, O God. Psalm 42:1

Deep calls to deep in the roar of your waterfalls; all your waves and breakers have swept over me.
Psalm 42:7 (NIV)

There is a picture of water three times in this psalm. From a *brook* to an *ocean* to a still, quiet *pond*, the psalmist illustrates the importance of God's movement in our lives. My spirit responds to all three pictures, but it's the deep pond that intrigues me most. One day I was pondering these scriptures, tramping in my thoughts as though hiking in the woods, my mind imagining an inviting pond. Clear, calm and deep, it beckoned my soul. Sensing its tug in the center of my being, I longed to slip into its cool depths. It was the very heart of God seeking me, drawing me into poignant communion. It was very appealing!

Yet had I plunged in, encumbered as I was with earthly trappings, I would have been unable to stay afloat. To be caressed by the silken waters of the pond I could not dive in and simply splash across its surface. To be immersed in the stillness of His Spirit, I must be stripped of self-righteous garments, pride and incessant striving. So, I throw off those encumbrances and surrender.

Dear Father, the depths of my heart answer the call of Your deep stillness. I will submit, and rest in the buoyancy of Your love that wraps and cleanses and renews my soul. Amen.

July 9

ACCEPTED IN THE BELOVED

So it shall be on Aaron's forehead that Aaron (the High Priest) may bear the iniquity of the holy things which the children of Israel hallow in all their holy gifts; and it shall always be on his forehead that they may be accepted before the LORD. Exodus 28:38

...to the praise of the glory of His grace, by which He has made us accepted in the Beloved. Ephesians 1:6

There's a longing in a soul so deep it can never be verbalized, yet it motivates behavior and attitudes. It is an urge to be accepted, to be an acknowledged part of something that defines and identifies and affirms who we are. For most of my life that desire has filled my heart with an abject fear that I would never be enough, never be acceptable. It has carried me to the depths of despair and imparted a sense of guilt that nearly paralyzed me.

But (I love the Biblical *buts*). I've learned that longing is a part of the way we are created, placed there by God to impel us to find our completion in Him. We try and try, however, just as I did, to find contentment everywhere else. Until one day, His whisper reached the depths of my soul. "You are Mine. I am your High Priest. Jesus Christ, bearing your guilt upon Himself, ensures that, in the Beloved—in Him, my Son—you are accepted."

Heavenly Father, You remind me in Psalm 5:12 that You will bless the righteous, and with favor You will surround him as though with a shield. May I ever be conscious of Your surrounding acceptance, as I trust in Jesus. Free at last! Amen.

July 10

BITTER WATERS

Now when they came to Marah, they could not drink the waters, for they were bitter. And the people complained against Moses saying "What shall we drink?" The LORD showed him a tree…When Moses cast the tree into the waters, the waters were made sweet.
Exodus 15:23-2

Marah was a place—a place of bitterness—the kind of place we will all probably come at some point in our lives. The name Marah means *bitter.* Thirsty they came, trekking across the desert, only to find undrinkable water. No wonder they grumbled! I grumble, too, when I arrive at a place that spreads bitterness in my heart. Marah was just a place on their journey; a place to camp, not a place to dwell. Because there was a resolution provided by God for them.

This beautiful Old Testament story holds a truth we would do well to remember. Moses obediently tossed the indicated tree into the waters; and immediately they turned sweet, slaking the thirst of the weary travelers. Bitterness dissolved into sweetness.

For us, too, when camped by bitter waters, there is a resolution. How often we need that miracle in our own lives. Our Savior, Jesus Christ, hung on a tree—a cross made of wood, giving His life to turn our bitter pain into the sweetness of joy and healing. We do not need to live in Marah; not when Calvary's tree holds our Redemption. Love's refreshment cures the bitter, rules in our hearts and satisfies the thirst; enabling our journey to continue.

Heavenly Father, how I love the picture You have provided here. My Savior's sacrifice on the tree has brought to me the miracle of redemption and turned my bitter years into sweet memories. I thank You and bring You my praise. Amen.

July 11

PREPARATION

For by grace you are saved, through faith, and that not of yourselves it is the gift of God, not of works, lest any man should boast. For we are His workmanship, created in Christ Jesus for good works, which God prepared beforehand that we should walk in them.
Ephesians 2:8-10

Preparation. It would seem to be a foreign concept to me. I don't practice it! My tendency is to wait until the very last minute and rush to make ready for what I should have been preparing all along. I have always defended myself with an "It's just the way I am" excuse. But I have recently been convicted by some words I read: "Preparation eliminates the need for scrambling… it is the framework for order, and God designed us to be orderly, because He is a God of order."[46]

So I have been striving to use this advice and make myself begin to do some preparing prior to a deadline! Here's the contrast…serenity and peace versus disorder, stress, wasted time, restlessness and disarray. Seems an easy choice, doesn't it? Frantic rushing brings panic, preparation brings peace. You know what? Though it's not easy, I'm finding it works. It is freedom!

Heavenly Father, You created us for good works, but those good works were all prepared for us beforehand. Your gift of grace prepares us to do them; strengthens and upholds. It's all Your plan, one of preparation and order. May I apply this truth to all I do, and thus bring the peace of thoughtful preparation into my life. Amen.

---

[46] The Listening Heart, © 2013 by Judy Gordon Morrow

July 12

DESOLATION

...because you have not heard my words...I will take from them the voice of mirth, and the voice of gladness, the voice of the bridegroom, and the voice of the bride, the sound of the millstones and the light of the lamp. And the whole land shall be a desolation...
Jeremiah 25:8a, 10-11a

Desolation. It came to the Beautiful Land when the Old Testament kingdoms refused to obey the Lord. No more mirth or gladness—no reason for it; no more wheat to grind for food; the candle's light extinguished; their liberty turned to slavery. Darkness, sadness, uselessness and captivity were the price of disobedience. It is not a pretty picture!

But how often do we find ourselves mired in just such a scenario? With no joy to express nor anything to celebrate. Desolation is miserable, hopeless. All because we "have not heard God's words."

When I am taken captive by the selfishness of my flesh, my joy is diminished, my service damaged; the light of His love in my life dims and I taste bitter regret, the price of my disobedience. It is a price I don't really want to pay, so it is up to me to take care that I am obedient.

Please, God, may I hear, and heed, Your words that I never again allow into my life the agony of desolation. Amen.

July 13

SHINING

Restore us, O God; cause Your face to shine, and we shall be saved! O LORD God of hosts, how long will You be angry against the prayer of Your people? Psalm 80:3-4

I find such comfort in this verse; in this whole Psalm, actually. It is full of questions the psalmist is asking God. And I suspect that cry rings down through the ages, echoing our frustrations today. "How long, O Lord?"

Where do I find its comfort here? I believe it is in the *hope* that surges through the words of petition for God to cause to shine His face so that we might be saved. In Scripture the shining of the face of God refers to God's favor. The psalmist is asking for God's favor to rest upon the land once more, for he knows that is the only hope of salvation. Here God is being asked to return, revive and restore.

What is so important to note is that God did cause His face to shine when He sent Jesus to the cross of Calvary. In that act was all of His favor, all of His love, all of His power, and we who believe are the beneficiaries! We are told, today, to look forward to the *shining*, the shining that promises Jesus' return...when all will be restored. In this rests our hope.

Dear Father, I read the question "How long?" and find myself wondering, too, when we will see Your shining face. We read Your words and rejoice in what's ahead, but sometimes we find frustration in the waiting. Revive my heart, Father, that my hope finds its home in the certainty of Your favor. I will comfort myself in that knowledge, until that day when all will be restored by the shining of Your face.
Amen.

July 14

KEYS

So Jesus answered and said to him, "What do you want Me to do for you?" The blind man said to Him,," that I may receive my sight." Then Jesus said to him, "Go your way; your faith mas made you well." Mark 10: 51-52a

This story of restored sight is a prime example of faith. Hearing that Jesus was passing by, the blind beggar called out to Him. What faith…*throwing aside his garment, he rose and came to Jesus.*[47] His garment was probably all he owned, but he heard Jesus calling. Leaving all his only possession he rose and came to Jesus. In that moment the blind man was healed.

My husband and I had a ritual. When he was on active duty aboard a submarine and out on patrol I had the responsibility of keeping everything together. As I would drop him off at the pier, he would place the car keys into my hand; in effect saying to me, "I am trusting you to care for yourself and our boys, handle problems that are sure to arise and meet me here when this separation is over." It was an example of faith in me, to me. At the end of the patrol I would gratefully drop the keys into his hand, saying, "I've done the best I could, it's all yours!" Faith, to me, is virtually dropping the keys into God's hand.

Heavenly Father, may I always trust You to take care of me, turning the keys of my life over to You in pure faith. Amen.

---

[47] Mark 10:50

July 15

DELIVERANCE

And there you will serve gods, the work of men's hands, wood and stone, which neither see nor hear nor eat nor smell. But from there you will seek the LORD your God, and you will find Him if you search for Him with all your heart and with all your soul.
Deuteronomy 4:28, 29

Moses had strong words for the children of Israel; warning them of consequences for disobedience. They would be scattered, conquered, worshipers of idols and out of fellowship with God. However, in the midst of the verse, the word "but" introduces a promise to them...and to me. Scattered among ruins, my hardened heart expels me from God's side. I stubbornly refuse to capitulate to the Voice that rules the universe. Yet His pleading whisper brushes across my soul: "Seek Me."

He does not give up, does not retreat, even while I worship at the shrine of self and the work of my own hands. He calls simply, and I begin to hear His promise: "But from there, out there where you are struggling, you will look for me and I will be found. Bring your heart, your seeking soul to me and I will carry you back to Canaan, the place of intimacy and rest."

The longing and the desire, build and swell and break this stubborn heart. And I pray....

My compassionate Lord, my covenant God, receive me, revive me, restore me. Because You are Jehovah and only You can satisfy my seeking soul in the circle of Your loving arms. Amen.

July 16

CATARACTS

And immediately there fell from his eyes something like scales, and he received sight…
Acts 9:18

Many of us have had cataracts removed. I'll never forget the emotional moment my eye patch came off. I shouted, "I can see!" I certainly identified with the Apostle Paul above. Having been blinded by the great light on the road to Damascus, he was suddenly granted sight by the obedient touch of a stranger heeding God's command. Paul's life was forever changed.

In my case, the scales were cataracts, milky cloudiness that comes with age, I'm told. So I submitted to the touch of the surgeon, and experienced a miracle. Everything was brighter! The colors were stunning, compared to the dimness to which I had become accustomed as the cataracts formed, slowly making my vision out of focus. Signs and lines became suddenly visible and squinting unnecessary. To me, it was a miracle!

Often, I'm thinking, our lives become beige, colorless and dim. Spiritual cataracts form over the lenses through which we view our existence. We live in dimness, unaware of the beauty that awaits. When the scales fall from our eyes we see Jesus revealed in all His loveliness and truth through the Holy Spirit's touch. "Miracle" is not too strong a word for this!

Dear Father, thank You for what I consider a miracle in my life. I can see…without my glasses! May I allow You to remove the spiritual cataracts and restore my vision so I can truly appreciate the beauty of Jesus. Amen.

July 17

FREEDOM FLIGHT

Stand fast therefore in the liberty by which Christ has made us free, and do not be entangled again with a yoke of bondage.
Galatians 5:1

Fear of flying is a term I've heard a lot. Fear of turning one's life over to a frail metal frame and its even more frail human operators. I have been guilty of scoffing at such fear, thinking I am not afraid. After all, don't I trust God with my life? But a thought tugs at the edges of my mind and I look at my timid trust with a new lens. I am not genuinely free from fear. Even though I would gladly climb aboard an airplane, I am dominated by a fear which is the opposite of freedom: fear of letting go and giving up control; clinging to it like a security blanket.

No wonder I don't experience freedom's promise. I'm still shrouded in the tomb of fear that insulates me from taking risks and truly trusting. Freedom can never be known until fear is cast upon God along with my other burdens. Author Brennan Manning calls it *ruthless trust.*

Heavenly Father, ruthless trust releases true freedom to be experienced by the soul. Tossing my security blanket aside to rest in a heap at Your throne will grant me the ability to leap from earth's bondage and soar on the air currents of Your mercy and grace. Oh, how I want to soar! Please lift my heart to You. Amen.

July 18

WISTFUL JOURNEY

Do not say, "Why were the former days better than these?" For you do not inquire wisely concerning this. Ecclesiastes 7:10

Because I have lived in so many places, I have often enjoyed going back to some of the locations that endure in my memory. Some time ago I went back to a place that lives as shining in my cache of recollections. I found it old and dusty and forlorn! What was once a highlight, a milepost of childhood adventure is now trampled by neglect, the ravages of weather and the passage of years.

As I stared at peeling paint and sagging doors, looking through empty spaces to perceive what used to be, I wondered why it had seemed so vital for me to return; to try to touch once more the places of my youth.

Kicking wistfully at the broken sidewalk, I think of times I have gazed back at my old life…my life before Jesus…and it beckons with gilded memories. When I look more closely, however, I see the sagging doors of pain. Peering through the lonely spaces, I wonder why I would ever desire to revisit.

The pull of the past is often strong, and events in hindsight appear to be gilded. It is conflicting to find them tarnished instead! I learned a lesson, though, from going back. Home is where I *am,* not where I used to be. Allowing reality to settle over the memories, I can still hold their sweetness even as I embrace the *now.* And I gaze into the future where Heaven awaits: my true and shining home.

Dear Father, the real lesson I need to absorb is that You were present with me there, You are here, and You will always be where I am. Thank You for that assurance! Amen.

July 19

HEART STEPS

You enlarged my path under me, so my feet did not slip.
Psalm 18:36

I will run the course of Your commandments, for You shall enlarge my heart. Psalm 119:32

Often I sit before God during a quiet time, contemplating His movement in my life. This verse seems to capsulize the truth of His protection, care and provision. So many times I could have slipped and caused ruin, but somehow didn't! And it mystifies me…until I read these verses! Looking back at moments when I could feel my ankles about to turn as danger approached, suddenly it seemed that my steps would strengthen, and I remained upright!

Now I am older, and physically I find this phenomenon occurring in a new way. I am literally unsteady. I have fallen, and am not always confident when walking unaided. Yet I know that He is holding me, steadying my steps as if on firm ground. I love it when the physical mirrors the spiritual.

This physical/spiritual connection is not lost on me here. I may walk a narrow path as God's child, but it is broadened by Him, enlarged to accommodate stumbling feet.

Dear Father, this is a beautiful assurance! Not only do You give me physical strength, but You enlarge my heart to walk the spiritual path, following You with heart steps. Amen.

July 20

VICTORY

The LORD is my strength and song, and He has become my salvation. Psalm 118:14

Okay, I admit it—I enjoy watching sports on TV! Especially baseball, but college basketball intrigues me as well. I clearly remember one vacation when where we stayed in our condo and watched almost every game of the March Madness tournament. Looking back it seems sort of silly, but we let ourselves get involved and didn't want to miss anything.

Nowadays, with DVRs and their recording ability, we have all sorts of advantages. How about fast forwarding through the commercials? So it would be very tempting to fast forward and find out who won! Had we had that technology back then, we might have recorded the games and done a few tourist activities.

How differently we watch when we are certain of a victory. There are no anxious heartbeats, no pulse-pounding encouragement offered verbally—virtually—to the officials or players through the TV screen. It's not needed: we already know the final score!

What about our spiritual lives? In the game of life we know who wins because God's Word tells us. Nothing we can do or say will sway the final score. Therefore we need not stress and struggle, but rather rest in the confidence that our team is victorious and walk relaxed toward the championship in touch with the heartbeats of the heart of God.

Dear Father, we win because You've won! Help us to live in that confidence; thus to enjoy the game! Amen.

July 21

GRACE ON MY LIPS

One who loves a pure heart and speaks with grace will have the king for a friend. Proverbs 22:11 (NIV)

This verse inspires me to be more aware of how I speak, and how things I hear affect my responses. I remember singing a familiar hymn one Sunday morning. I prayed that the words would truly be from my heart, these especially: *Take my lips and let them be, filled with messages from Thee.*[48] I was filled with resolve to watch my words.

Immediately the enemy struck. I received an email filled with anger and hurt from a family member. Thoughtless words brought me back to angry feelings of worthlessness and envy instead of the grace that I had resolved to emulate. I struggled with this, trying not to allow myself to descend to the defeat that paralyzes me and keeps me from enjoying my relationship with my heavenly Father.

God, however, showed me how I had let a few words, carelessly written, destroy all the gracious words I had received earlier. Words from His Word spoken into my heart: His love for me, His care of me, and His promises that wrap me in hope and delight.

Chagrined, I repented. And His words of grace reached me anew. Words of grace that I trust will stay on my lips and characterize my actions and reactions to those with whom I am in relationship.

Father, Your Word is true. It brings salve to wounded hearts and teaches us to guard our lips. Hear my prayer, Father, and grant me the power and peace to consciously speak with grace on my lips. Amen.

---

[48] Take My Life and Let It Be, Frances R. Havergal (1836-1879)

July 22

LOST!

All we like sheep have gone astray and have turned, every one, to his own way, and the LORD has laid on Him the iniquity of us all.
Isaiah 53:6

We got lost the other day trying to find the home of an old friend. To me, there is very little in life more frustrating than not knowing how to get where I want to go!

Tension was thick in the car; I felt guilty because apparently I had written the directions wrong (this happens a lot lately!) and we were getting more and more anxious as nothing appeared to be right. After a while we gave up and I asked a woman at a convenience store how to find the road we wanted. She actually volunteered to lead us to it, going far out of her way, so we did eventually arrive at the right place.

There is of course a spiritual application here in this story. We get grumpy and frustrated when making wrong turns, unwilling to ask God for the help He offers, and determine to do it all ourselves! I am learning I must humble myself and ask for the help God offers me constantly.

What joy when that sweet stranger took the time to lead us where we had been seeking! And what relief occurs when we submit to God's leading, finding once more the path He has laid out for us. It's challenging also to be sensitive to someone else who is lost and may need my help.

Heavenly Father, may I keep my eyes and heart open today…maybe I will find someone to whom You are leading me, and I can bring the sweet relief of Your presence, Your support or a hand to hold. May we all do that. I will be watchful. Amen.

July 23

BACKSLIDING

"Return, backsliding Israel," says the LORD; "I will not cause My anger to fall on you. For I am merciful," says the LORD; "I will not remain angry forever." Jeremiah 3:12

Backsliding. I used to hear this word a lot when I was a child. It came with a dire warning. We don't hear it much anymore, and I wonder why not? I think perhaps we esteem God's grace too lightly, unconcerned with the importance He attaches to obedience.

I woke up the other day with a heavy spirit and didn't even want to get out of bed. I actually said, "What's the point?" to myself and crawled deeper under the blanket. Later as I was looking into scripture I could feel my spirit lightening. As this passage in Jeremiah leaped out at me I was convicted by how many times God spoke through the prophets begging His children to return.

And me? I had been backsliding into despair and ennui and defeatism. Backsliding is nothing more than pulling away from the close obedient relationship we could be sharing with God. And I had backslidden, hence the heaviness. Joy exploded as I confessed my longing to return and receive the mercy He offered me.

Yes, Father, I am returning, finding my rest and spirit-healing in You. I am grateful that You use Your word to convict and convince my heart of Your love and forgiveness. Thank You. Amen.

July 24

DEMONSTRATION

But God demonstrates His own love toward us, in that while we were yet sinners, Christ died for us. Romans 5:8

Why is it that we feel a need to see and test before we buy? Why do we need a demonstration? As I ponder this question I think of consumers flocking to vendors offering a taste of a featured product. Consider the food demonstrators at places like Costco! Often the sample tastes so delicious we are moved to buy what we have tasted. I do it. It helps to know what we are getting, don't you think?

Scripture tells us that God has a very active demonstration going on! He offers us something that is free and of inestimable value. Why are we not urging people to flock to the counter to sample it: taste His goodness and love, to avail themselves of what He offered in the sacrifice of His Son?

After all, is not eternal, abundant, life something to be desired? And we who have answered God's invitation should be shouting from the rooftops! *Oh, taste and see that the LORD is good.*[49]

Dear God, help me to be always demonstrating just what it means to know You and to experience the joy and peace of Your salvation. Amen.

---

[49] Psalm 34:8

July 25

FENCES

For the message of the cross is foolishness to those who are perishing, but to us who are being saved, it is the power of God.
1 Corinthians 1:18

I was born and lived most of my childhood in Montana! Montana has such beautiful spaces! One of my memories has to do with the fences that striped the landscape; called buck-and-rail. Buck and rail is best described as a three-dimensional, A-frame, rail fence. A section of the fence consists of two A-frame "bucks", spaced an average of 12-16 feet apart, with 3 or 4 "rails" attached to the standing A-frames.

In the days of old on the western frontier ranchers used whatever means they had available to corral their livestock and keep them safe.

Many of those rustic fences are still standing, and as we drive along nowadays it brings me a sense of joy and sweet memory. These fences were sturdy, the cross bucks supporting the horizontal rails and vice versa. They did not fall down—even a heavy snow would *anchor* the fences rather than toppling them.

As *I* view what remains, my heart turns to the Cross of Jesus. The fences somehow resemble a cross, and I think of that precious cross that even now supports us. It is sturdy and rugged, and nothing can topple it. If we place our trust in the One Who died upon it, we rest in the security of His promise never to fail us, or buckle under us. We are safe in the corral of His love.

Heavenly Father, as ugly and painful as was Jesus's death on that Cross, may I always be reminded that it continues to keep me safe for eternity, Amen.

July 26

WAITING

Therefore the LORD will ***wait****, that He may be gracious to you; and therefore He will be exalted, that He may have mercy on you. For the LORD is a God of justice; blessed are all those who wait for Him.*
Isaiah 30:18

Waiting is tough, isn't it? Here in this scripture, it becomes evident that waiting is a mutual activity. God tells us that when we run off and do our own thing, He will wait so that He can be gracious to us. I think that means that when we are being rebellious and stubborn we can't receive His grace; so He waits. But then comes our part, we are blessed when we wait.

But what rings through here is His desire to bless and be gracious to His people. He waits to hear our cry. When we absorb this truth, our cries indicate that our hearts are waiting on Him—depending on Him for His mercy and grace—rather than our own efforts. So I am thinking that it's important to make sure I'm waiting on Him.

I went back a few verses and read, *For thus says the Lord GOD, the Holy One of Israel: "In returning and rest you shall be saved; in quietness and confidence shall be your strength." But you would not.*[50]

Therefore it seems God is saying, *Wait on Me. Rest, return and find your strength in being close to Me.*

Father I hear Your encouragement. I am so grateful that, along with this exhortation You remind us that You are standing by, waiting, May I heed Your voice. Amen.

---

[50] Isaiah 30:15

July 27

FOUNTAIN IN THE VALLEY

The poor and needy seek water, but there is none, their tongues fail for thirst. I the LORD will hear them; I the God of Israel will not forsake them. I will open rivers in desolate heights, and fountains in the midst of the valleys; I will make the wilderness a pool of water and the dry land springs of water. Isaiah 41:17-18

Dehydration. It has significantly influenced my wellness throughout the years. I find it hard to drink enough water and thus have ended up in the hospital with serious issues. Drinking plenty of water is an important role in keeping our bodies functioning well.

Plenty of water is needed for our spiritual health as well. Yet too often I stumble into the valley – soul-dry, thirsty and choking on dust kicked up by my rebellious heels. My spirit is parched. I have experienced mountain-top euphoria followed by the valley of perceived reality. Though I long to return to the mountain, strength is needed for the climb and I am dry. I have forsaken the delight; the joy of the Lord is eclipsed by selfish goals as I turned my face from His and I am dry. The prophet Jeremiah writes: *My people have committed two evils, they have forsaken Me, the fountain of living waters…*[51]

In the valley a fountain awaits, a waterspout for my parched heart. A pool in the wilderness to quench and cool. The pages of Your Word are life-giving rivers. I drink, and am no longer dry.

Heavenly Father, I am offering my empty cup up to You. Please fill it with Living Water and cure my dryness. Amen.

---

[51] Jeremiah 2:13

July 28

BID ME COME

But immediately Jesus spoke to them, saying, "Be of good cheer, it is I; be not afraid." And Peter answered him and said, "Lord, if it is You, command me to come to You on the water." Matthew 14:27-28

Captured in a storm-tossed craft, white-knuckled trembling men on the Sea of Galilee awaited their doom. Crying out with fear at the approach of a figure from out of nowhere, they hear the words, "It is I. Be not afraid."

Impulsive, stalwart Peter begs for assurance, "If it is really You, bid me come." "Come," his master says. Jumping out of the boat Peter obeys and does the impossible: he walks on the water. Sometimes I'm storm-tossed; waves of despair and fear crash upon me and, though a disciple I might be; white-knuckled, I clutch at my fragile craft. "Jesus," I cry, "if You're really there, bid me come." The invitation, "Come," rings in my heart as I step into the water.

It is often frightening to obey, to plunge out of what we perceive as safety into crashing waves. But just as Jesus, the Master of the Sea, did for Peter; I can trust Him to do for me. He who holds the waves, my boat and my life in omnipotent nail-pierced hands, will extend them to catch and steady me.

Heavenly Father, why does it seem so difficult to trust You sometimes? I do want simple trust in Your sufficiency to characterize my life. Help me grab Your hand, and hold on. Amen.

July 29

IT'S GREEN THEY SAY

A sound heart is life to the body,
but envy is rottenness to the bones.
Proverbs 14:30

Envy, grown lush and green, fertilized by constant tending, has burrowed its way into my heart. My face is twisted into a grimace that passes for a smile—which I know is forced because I begrudge. I want all the things—more and more. And while I know it's an unholy thing, I clutch and cling and won't let it go.

Webster defines envy as "a feeling of discontentment or resentful longing aroused by someone else's possessions, qualities, or luck." Most of my life has been filled with that, because I never felt I was worth very much; thus I desired what other people had. Actually sometimes it was just what I *thought* they had, but it didn't keep my spirit from twisting in jealousy and anger—the sense that I had not been dealt a fair hand. It was insidious, the way it tangled my motivations and ruined relationships.

But a new realization of God's love for me convicts my heart and brings me to my knees in sorrow. And over and over I am reminded, when envy knocks at the door, that I am loved. Loved as I am. So I can pray…

Jesus, please stroke my brow with Your gentle hand. Wipe away frustration, rage and envy. Make my smile real. Let me rest quietly in You, Who made me and loves me as I am. Uproot bitterness that it not take hold; and may caring love instead be the green growth in my life. Amen.

July 30

PLANTED

Those who are planted in the house of the LORD shall flourish in the courts of our God. They shall still bear fruit in old age; they shall be fresh and flourishing. Psalm 92:13-14

There's always hope! Even as the years pass and birthdays pile up, God still writes His encouragement to His beloveds. Too often we let ourselves feel useless and washed up. It's true that the energy levels dip and reactions lag behind the sharpness we used to have. But look: God says that we who are planted in His courts will flourish, even in old age.

Planted. Do we realize what expectation and anticipation that word suggests? Planting is never done without the hope of growth. It is our experiences that root, ground, water and fertilize our lives, and there is no expiration date for fruitfulness. It doesn't always look promising; "sometime when you're in a dark place, you think you've been buried, but you've actually been planted," says author Christine Caine.

The poet Longfellow, when he was up in years, with white hair, yet cheeks as red as a rose, was asked how he was able to keep so vigorous and write so beautifully. Pointing to a blooming apple tree nearby, he replied: "That apple tree is very old, but I never saw prettier blossoms upon it than those it now bears. The tree grows a little new wood every year, and I suppose it is out of that new wood that those blossoms come. Like the apple tree, I try to grow a little new wood every year."

Father, it's that "new wood" that provides the nourishment for growth. It is depending upon You for the development that enables a flourishing fruitfulness. May I ever lean on Your gracious tending as I age, and know You have p laced a message within me. Amen.

July 31

RECOGNITION

Wash me thoroughly from my iniquity, and cleanse me from my sin. For I acknowledge my transgressions, and my sin is always before me. Psalm 51:2-3

I noticed a transgression—or two—today. I sensed a displeasing attitude, rebellion against my God's clearly-spoken instructions. He brought it to my attention and I saw it for what it was…sin in my life. So I waved at it in recognition.

It occurred to me this is what I often do. Somewhat like seeing an acquaintance, perhaps at the grocery store, and I wave in recognition. If I desire to engage in conversation I will stop and make the effort to connect. But many times I'm guilty of ducking around a corner to avoid acknowledging them. Perhaps I'm in a hurry; perhaps I look a mess; perhaps I'm uncomfortable with that person. Perhaps there's strife between us. So I wave in recognition and move on without truly acknowledging their presence.

God wants me to *acknowledge* my sin. He knows there is no cleaning up or changing in me until I do. Am I in too much of a rush to meet with Him? Am I ashamed of the mess I'm in? Am I uncomfortable because of the strife between us due to my disobedience? Am I waving and ducking to keep from engaging with Him?

Forgive me, Father, for I have sinned. I acknowledge it to you and throw myself on Your mercy. Please cleanse me. Amen.

August 1

TODAY

This day *the LORD your God commands you to observe these statutes and judgments; therefore you shall be careful to observe them with all your heart and with all your soul. Today you have proclaimed the LORD to be your God and that you will keep His statutes and His judgments and that you will obey His voice. Also today the LORD has proclaimed you to be His special people, just as He promised you.*
Deuteronomy 26:16-18

This day, what will it hold for me, for you? God's commandment is always for obedience. We, His people, too often proclaim that we will be compliant, allowing Him to be our God, and before much time has elapsed in our day we wander off, seeking our own way. At least, I do.

So I am struck by the progression portrayed in this Scripture. God says "Obey." We say "Okay". Then He says, "I'll stay". He promised, you see, and He is faithful.

The Israelites declared Him as Lord and promised, as well, to obey. He kept His promise…they did not; and neither have I. God warns us about keeping the promises we have made to Him. I sit here rebuked, seeing the words "today" seeping into my consciousness.

It is early in the morning…a new opportunity awaits to make Him Lord. He asks me in the quiet of my heart, "What will you do with today?"

Oh God, I long to answer Your question with a promise to exalt You with my life today. Remind me of this when I'm tempted to make a decision that does not honor this goal. Amen.

August 2

DEATH IN THE POT

There was a famine in the region of Gilgal. While the company of the prophets was meeting with Elisha, he said to his servant, "Put on the large pot and cook some stew for these prophets." One of them went out into the fields to gather herbs and found a wild vine and picked as many of its gourds as his garment could hold. He cut them up into the pot of stew, though no one knew what they were.
2 Kings 4:38-39 (NIV)

Interesting little story! Hungry prophets, looking forward to a tasty meal. With a famine going on they were no doubt searching everywhere for edible food. Making the stew is not the end of the story however. When the stew was served they began to eat it and instantly knew something was wrong. They cried out, *Man of God, there is death in the pot!*[52] They could not eat it. Poison, it was, from the wild vine.

Have you ever cooked something that was totally inedible? I have, a time or two. I don't think it was poisonous, but it didn't taste very good. May I carry this a bit further? Let's look at what our lives are stewing up to feed those around us. We need to be aware of what we are putting into the pot. Is it healthy and life-giving, or are we pulling from the field something that may look tasty but would poison a life that tasted it? Something that could be poisonous to us as well.

Heavenly Father, may we ever be sensitive and aware of where we are seeking nourishment, that we keep our lives pure and free of the enemy's poison. Amen.

---

[52] 2 Kings 4:40

August 3

BACKWASH

Finally, all of you be of one mind, having compassion for one another; love as brothers, be tenderhearted, be courteous; not returning evil for evil or reviling for reviling, but on the contrary blessing, knowing that you were called to this, that you may inherit a blessing.
1 Peter 3:8, 9

I live in the Pacific Northwest. We sometimes need—or choose—to travel by ferry across Puget Sound. On a balmy day it is refreshing to go out on the deck to enjoy the scenery and the sweet breeze. On one occasion I was leaning over the rail as the ship pushed forward through the waves. I thought how determined was its progress because its destination was firmly fixed. It is fueled to perform its appointed task and programmed to complete the mission.

Standing at the stern, I was staring at the frothy wake churned by massive propellers, musing on the power creating such agitation. Suddenly a small boat crossed the wake, bouncing nearly out of control in the backwash of the ship.

It caused me to ponder my own journey. As I press unheeding toward my goals, do I churn up froth, making waves that embroil those about me in distress? And I, in determination to complete my mission, sail obliviously on?

Oh, God, may I look around for the smaller boats, and slow down in my passing so that crossing my wake will not cause them to be tossed about, frightened or lost. Amen.

August 4

FOUND!

Therefore we do not lose heart. Though outwardly we are wasting away, yet inwardly we are being renewed day by day.
2 Corinthians 4:16 (NIV)

Lately the mantra around our house is "I can't find..." As I get older and skills begin to decrease, or fade, it seems I constantly misplace things. Or perhaps immediately forget what I meant to do or where I put something I had just held in my hand a moment ago. It is a bit disconcerting! We make jokes about it, but the reality is that as time goes by, things change. Mental quickness slows down and we are caught in the clutches of what my sister describes as prompt forgetting! It is difficult to admit, because it reveals the truth that outwardly we are wasting away, as the Apostle Paul writes.

Today as I was fruitlessly searching for my crochet hook (I just had it!), I remembered something I had pondered some time ago. There is joy in being found; but in order to rejoice in being found, one must know he is lost. Being found is the result of a search. A search begins with the desire in a heart to find.

I was the object of a search and I didn't even know it—not until I was found by my loving Savior! Now I rejoice, because I know I *was* lost. In my search to discover who I am, I could never have found myself without first having been found by Him.

Heavenly Father, how can I ever thank you enough for seeking me, finding me and carrying me back to You. What joy to realize I am loved, and found! Amen.

August 5

VISTA

By faith, Abraham dwelt in the land of promise as in a foreign country, dwelling in tents with Isaac and Jacob... for he waited for the city which has foundations, whose builder and maker is God...For here we have no continuing city, but we seek the one to come.
Hebrews 11:9-10, 13:14

Several times we have been privileged, (at least it seemed so to us country people) to go to the big city for an overnight stay in a fancy hotel. On one particular visit I spent some time at the window, with swirling thoughts. Thirty floors up, I have a vantage point from which to peer at the city. Here I am surrounded by concrete, glass and steel; by people and things. That is the reality of the city which encircles me. Yet I am only a visitor here.

Situated here I can also see between the buildings across the water to the mountains where I live. It really is a lovely vista: the misty, pine-covered mountains; and my eyes are drawn away from the city to its peaceful pristine panorama.

Far below I watch the tiny people as they huddle beneath the skyscrapers, scurry along the sidewalks, intent upon survival amid the boundaries of the city.

I was thinking that's how it is with us. We are pilgrims on earth, caught in the web of this world, distracted by its pleasures and responsibilities. It dawns on me as I gaze at the mountains that even experiencing all the excitement of the city, my heart longs for my home.

My Father, just as I am often captured and captivated with my earthly life, You want to lift me up to look at Heaven's vista that beckons me and calls me to my eternal home. May I keep my eyes on that precious vista. Amen.

August 6

OBEDIENCE

I also will no longer drive out before them any of the nations which Joshua left when he died, so that through them I may test Israel, whether they will keep the ways of the LORD, to walk in them as their fathers kept them, or not. Judges 2:21-22

How very often our lives mirror those of the chosen people of God, the Israelites! I read the stories with amazement and a kind of rueful wonder...how God protected them, won their battles, and provided for them. All He wanted from them was obedience.

I notice here in the Book of Judges that God announces His choice to leave some of the nations, enemies of Israel, in the land so He could test them to see if they would obey His commandments. *Obedience* means compliance with a request or law; submission to a higher authority. It involves making a choice. And God allows us to be tested to see if we will follow His rules.

Thus, the lesson here—the key, if you will—is obedience. Obedience must be chosen. We *always* have a choice; we are not robots. God delights when we look at the "enemies" around us and choose to obey Him instead of allowing ourselves to become enmeshed in the selfish pleasures of earth. Obedience indicates our acknowledgement that God knows how to deal with the enemies of our soul better than we do. Without freedom of choice, our actions would be it is nothing but blind, mindless *acquiescence.*

Heavenly Father, sometimes I wonder why You have given us free will. But I see that our choice to obey means so much to You, and so I pray that You will guide our choices; may we stay attuned to Your Word, and heed it so we make wise choices, and please You with our obedience. Amen.

August 7

A VESSEL IN PROGRESS

Then I went down to the potter's house, and there he was, making something at the wheel. And the vessel that he made of clay was marred in the hand of the potter; so he made it again into another vessel, as it seemed good to the potter to make. Jeremiah 18:3-4

How many times have we gazed at a beautiful piece of pottery, admiring the skill of the potter? I have been thinking about the vessel God is making out of my life, thinking that unless I'm yielded to Him I am useless. Though I try with all my strength, my self-willed efforts just won't do. Pulling away from the Potter's hands puts His work on hold. I become misshapen and incomplete from refusing to let His plan unfold.

Am I to force the Potter's wheel to sit still and silent; with His eager hands poised above, waiting? He longs for me to yield to the molding of His love. I must turn back to the Potter, becoming again a shapeless lump of clay, so His hands can begin to redeem the marred vessel and make it anew into a vessel of His choosing. It will take willingness to abandon my own efforts and allow myself to become once again a piece of pottery in progress, being redeemed by the Master Potter.

Lord, take my bitter, lonely years and grind them into dust. I know I've messed up, but with Your consummate skill You can redeem the mistakes and brokenness. Blend the dust gently with your tender tears and make of that clay what you intended. I yield now, my Potter, and rest in the hands of the One Who created me. Spin the wheel, smooth and shape, and I'll be mended; gratefully whole. Amen.

August 8

GO. WASH. SEE.

And He said to him, "Go, wash at the pool of Siloam," (which is translated, Sent). So he went and washed, and came back seeing.
John 9:7

One day Jesus was passing by and saw a man born blind. He SAW him; not a passing glance, but a compassionate knowing. What a beautiful story, how Jesus used His own saliva mixed with earth, to anoint those unseeing eyes. How tender, how caring, He was. Breaking all the Pharisaical laws, He then instructs the man to go and wash in the pool of Siloam. Wonder of wonders, he came back, seeing!

The mud did not heal the blindness; it was his faith to be obedient: to go, to wash—and then, to see! I am amazed as I contemplate what might have been in the heart of the blind man; who for so long he had sat, unnoticed, by the side of the road, begging and hopeless. I wonder how he got to the pool. Did someone help him? Or did he make his own way? What a scene…muddied eyes and a beggar crying out for assistance. Somehow, though, he went, he washed…he had sight!

Jesus could have spoken a word and healed the man. Many times He did just that. But He was teaching, not only the blind beggar, but me, also. "Go." (Faith) "Wash." (Obedience) "See." (Blessing)

Jesus, do I really want to see You? I've spent a long time sitting blindly by the road. Your instructions are clear. Help me hear Your voice directing me to the pool of Yourself. Wash the mud from my eyes, so I will truly behold You! Amen.

August 9

MY CLOSET

Therefore we also, since we are surrounded by so great a cloud of witnesses, let us lay aside every weight, and the sin which so easily ensnares us, and let us run with endurance the race that is set before us. Hebrews 12:1

I don't know if any of you can claim a neat, organized closet, but I can't! Crammed with old and worn items, it's convenient for dumping unnecessary things I can't give up. I wish I had the gumption to dig in and clear it out. Possessions often weigh us down, don't they? "We might need it someday" is our mantra.

I was convicted that my hall closet is typical of my life—crammed as it is with old fears, guilt and hurts—it's a good place for dumping problems I've been unable to handle. We humans seem to have a grasping mentality. I know I do! I find myself saying so many times, "Today I will clean out that closet." Yet due to a cluttered day or undone tasks, by evening I find it still messy—with even more junk thrust inside.

These instructions in Hebrews encourage endurance. Often our minds and hearts are ensnared and entangled with many things that keep us from being our best. I'm trying to untangle some of those things that have me bound. I know God wants this for me—for you,—and will be beside us every step in keeping our "closets" clean!

Heavenly Father, give me courage, and energy to untangle possessions, to rid myself of worthless objects. I now give you permission to do the same with everything weighing down my life. Oh, what an adventure it's going to be, cleaning out that closet…and me! Amen

August 10

DARKNESS

Then the LORD said to Moses, "Stretch out your hand toward heaven that there may be darkness over the land of Egypt, darkness which may even be felt." So Moses stretched out his hand toward heaven, and there was thick darkness in all the land of Egypt three days. They did not see one another, nor did anyone rise from his place for three days. Exodus 10:21-23

I was musing on Psalm 105; reading verses 26-28, which were sub-titled *The Darkness of Disobedience*. The psalmist is recounting the plagues that God sent on Egypt when His people were in captivity there. The 9th plague was darkness...thick, concealing, debilitating. The Bible says *He sent darkness and made the land dark – for had they not rebelled against His words?*[53] Wow! I thought, "This is exactly what I feel rests over our land!" Is it not? So much anger, pain, and confusion. Darkness seems to be everywhere over our country.

As I pondered this I was reminded that only obedience brings light, the dawn of understanding. I went back to Exodus 10 and read the story of the 9th plague, I was fascinated to see that though Egypt was in total darkness, the land of Goshen, where the Israelites lived, was full of light.

Father God, You have challenged me to be a light, Your light, in the darkness of our land – in my small way. Please give me wisdom to discern Your words, and commit them to obedience that I will shine Your light. Amen

---

[53] Psalm 105:28

August 11

BROKEN CISTERN

For my people have committed two evils; they have forsaken me, the fountain of living waters, and hewed them out cisterns – broken cisterns, that can hold no water. Jeremiah 2:13

This is a poignant verse to me. I look at the words *broken cistern* and think of the way I—and many others I am sure—often go to an empty well, so to speak, and find no water. It never fails to disappoint. It reminds me of my friend who has been abused by her mother, and yet keeps trying for her approval. She is aware her mother is completely unable to connect or have any tenderness toward her daughter, because of her own past. But the need for just that connection is so deep it surpasses that awareness.

In the same way, we were created with that need for connection with our Heavenly Father. However, we tend to search for it everywhere except at His feet. Forsaking God, the fountain of living waters, I see I have dug a broken cistern, a leaky well filled over and over again, it would seem, with my good deeds. Yet I find it continually empty! I did not realize that, in the digging, it was Him I was forsaking.

God, please plug up that broken cistern, my disobedient creation, as I run returning into Your arms. Fill me from the fountain of Yourself so I overflow with Your love – Your life – instead of simply leaking the feeble efforts of my own making. Amen.

August 12

SECRETARY

My heart is overflowing with a good theme; I recite my composition concerning the King. My tongue is the pen of a ready writer.
Psalm 45:1

An ancient poet once penned these words: "Of all the creatures both in sea and land, only to man Thou hast made known Thy ways, and put the pen alone into his hand and made him secretary of Thy praise."[54]

Amazing! Of everything God has made, we humans alone have received His word, His story, so that we can know Him in a totally different way than the rest of creation. Since I was a secretary in my professional life, this struck a chord within me.

I am still a secretary! Now, though, I take dictation from my Heavenly Father, and do my best to be accurate in transcribing what I hear. What an honor! I'm a record keeper, one who is allowed into the inner sanctum of the holy place, to hear, in order to share the desire of His heart. I used to be so proud of my position, sitting in the place of secretary to the president. I made my employment my identity.

My identity is still in my position. The only difference is that now that responsibility is to kneel before Him in gratitude, knowing my job is secure in Him.

In a sense, we all hold a pen in our hands, as we write our story—one way or another. We are all part of God's story, privileged to be able to know Him and hear from Him. We shouldn't take our work lightly. This challenges my heart. Perhaps it will do the same for you.

Father, yes, I will work for You. I will transcribe Your words onto my heart. Thank You for the honor of being Your secretary. Amen.

---

[54] George Herbert (1593-1633)

August 13

CARPET

The LORD looks from heaven; He sees all the sons of men. From the place of His dwelling He looks down on all the inhabitants of the earth; He fashions their hearts individually; He considers all their works. Psalm 33:13-15

We were taking a drive one beautiful summer afternoon. I was fascinated, watching the countryside slide past, by the brilliant green fields. They appeared as an emerald carpet undulating, rolling toward hills rising dark with spruce and pine.

From our car window it seemed unbroken, solid, this living meadow. Yet if I were to kneel in the midst of it I would see that millions of sprouting plants, thrusting skyward, have created the carpet. I recalled the above Psalms verse and considered that from above, humanity must appear as a carpet laid around the earth. An unbroken mass rolling endlessly. Yet that is not how God sees it. He bends down, aware of each new tender shoot, each mature stalk. Delighting in His creation, providing for its growth.

How glad I am to know He gazes at us at me—at all of us—in our churning humanity, not from high atop the hill but crouched low, hovering. His nurturing love prunes tenderly, as it enriches the earth around each plant; designing a carpet of living souls that rolls toward His throne.

Heavenly Father, thank you for this lovely picture! Such a comfort to realize You are there, watching and cherishing your handiwork. May I always treasure Your Master Gardener touch on my life. Amen.

August 14

STALKS OF FLAX

But she had taken them up to the roof and hidden them under the stalks of flax she had laid out on the roof. Joshua 2:6 (NIV)

I have always enjoyed this story, Rahab outsmarting the guards searching for the two spies God had sent into Jericho. God so often prepares situations in advance so that His purpose can be fulfilled. Flax was a very important crop in those days, and in order that it becomes usable for making linen it must be laid flat to dry for the fibers to separate. Gathering and drying the flax was mainly the job of women.

Here are two spies under stalks of flax, hidden in God's mercy. Was this a chance encounter? No! It never is with God. But the prior preparations…a softened heart, an open door and a rooftop refuge…were God's work beneath a surface that breathed enmity toward Him. It is no accident that the spies were sent out at flax-harvest time, nor that they arrived at a home that was ready and waiting.

And me? Am I hiding under stalks of flax, in a sense, simply reveling in my salvation, His merciful covering? I have been sent out on a mission. Am I gratefully hiding out, or am I under the stalks of flax ready and waiting to hear the words, "Get up and go"? When the way was cleared, the spies obediently departed to complete their mission; after promising deliverance to the woman who had protected them.

Heavenly Father, I want to be obedient. I want to see the need, to be ready. I want to be alert to hear and follow as You lead. Just what am I doing under these stalks of flax? Show me what You have prepared for me. Amen.

August 15

ACROSS FROM JERICHO

These are the commands and regulations the LORD gave through Moses to the Israelites on the plains of Moab by the Jordan across from Jericho. Numbers 36:13 (NIV)

I often think of a child's plaintive question while traveling. "Are we there yet?" How never-ending to a small one's eyes must the trip seem—those who have a different concept of time and distance. My small nephew, on a trip to visit us, had asked his daddy that question many times. So many times that he was warned, "Do NOT ask me one more time if we are there yet! Or how many miles." Quiet ensued for a few minutes, then a small voice piped up from the back seat, "Daddy, how many feet?"

What must it have been like, across from Jericho? The Promised Land had been visible to them for forty years. Did they still look longingly at its verdant green slopes? Still yearn for it? Or had complacency set in? I wonder. Forty years is a long time!

Now, we ourselves are situated, across from Heaven. Only eyes enlightened by faith can see our Promised Land. A vision forms within, a glimmer of glory. Heaven is an intriguing mystery, which we anticipate. How acute is our longing? Are we still looking for it; yearning for it? We are not there yet, but we are not to become complacent. Rather we are to live ready to go, gazing at the horizon, trusting in the hands of our God Who will carry us safely across the river to the final splendor of the Promised Land.

Heavenly Father, I pray You will build a longing in me for heaven, a yearning that colors my motivation to live in anticipation and share You and Your hope with others. Amen.

August 16

FOLLOWING

Mercy and truth have met together; righteousness and peace have kissed. Truth shall spring out of the earth, and righteousness shall look down from heaven. Yes, the LORD will give what is good; and our land will yield its increase. Righteousness will go before Him, and shall make His footsteps our pathway. Psalm 85:10-13

Mercy, truth, righteousness and peace. Jesus. He is all that. And how grateful I am for that fact. I find it so fascinating that He is spoken of this way in the Psalms! Somehow it's easy to visualize Jesus in these verses because His footsteps literally did travel this earth.

I was thinking, when I read this verse, about when I was a little girl. We had winters where the snow was higher than my head. I remember so many times that my daddy would head out into the day, and I would follow him, intent on walking in his footsteps, my little feet struggling to keep me upright on the path he had created.

It's a sweet picture in my memory box. How beautiful, also, is the above picture of just what Jesus brings to us. In His mercy He has redeemed us, He surrounds us with His truth and shows us that righteousness and peace go hand in hand. He brings blessing and abundance. It is His righteousness that forms the steps in which He desires we walk.

Father, it is so true that Jesus is the pattern and I gratefully I accept the deep impressions His feet have made to forge my path. And I commit to being attentive to following in those footsteps that help me walk straight. Amen.

August 17

GIFTED ARTISANS

Then Moses called Bezalel and Aholiab and every gifted artisan in whose heart the LORD had put wisdom, everyone whose heart was stirred, to come and do the work.   Exodus 36:2

The tabernacle was God's dwelling place on earth. Its building process is a fascinating story, one I've read many times. Truthfully, more like glossed over, finding it a bit boring to read all the measurements and rules. Today, however, I noticed how the scripture uses the term "gifted artisans" over and over.

One might wonder how a band of former slaves who were only proficient in building for the Egyptians would have the knowledge and skill to create the beautiful structure God asked them to build. There is a progression here. God *prepared* those gifted artisans, by teaching them what they needed to know. Then He *called* them to the work. God *endowed* His chosen artisans with the instructions, then the vision, then wisdom straight from Himself. He added a passionate heart, with the desire to bring the vision into fulfillment.

We all have a gifting. Maybe it is not expressed in the arts, so to speak, but we have a responsibility to search out the avenue in which we have been gifted to serve. God provides His wisdom; yet it is up to us to be watchful for ways our gift can be used. One might be an artisan, having the talent to make beautiful things; but unless energized by God's wisdom and understanding, the gift is devoid of fruitfulness.

Heavenly Father, what a challenge I find in this passage! May I truly discover the wisdom from You that infuses the way You desire to use me. And then, as You beckon me to begin the work, may I obediently follow. Amen.

August 18

BIG PITCHER

Yet you, Lord, are our Father. We are the clay, you are the potter. We are all the work of your hand. Isaiah 64:8 (NIV)

I want to be a big pitcher—perhaps a giant crock or a huge bowl. I want to be used in a big way; be filled with great wisdom as well as a huge helping of compassion. I wonder why it isn't happening…at least not in the way I envisioned it when I began this odyssey of faith. It doesn't seem that God has yet made me into a beautiful vase, or a big vessel out of which to pour His love on all mankind.

I think a key to answering my question has to do with usable material. Knowing that He is the Potter, I ask myself, "How much clay have I yielded to Him? Can it be that I've only given Him is enough to fashion a small pitcher?" He who makes the vessels can use only what is tendered to Him for His workmanship.

Am I wrong to desire to be a big pitcher? Taking a look at the big picture would temper my complaint. Desiring to become a big pitcher could be all about me, I'm afraid, when I examine my motives. Perhaps a little creamer filled with richness is more what He has in mind! Big Pitcher or Little Creamer: the truth is that He fills whatever vessel He creates with *Himself,* and He provides the situations where I can pour Him out.

Heavenly Father, I see here that I should yield all I am to You and let You decide whether or not I become a big pitcher. In yielding, I must be content with what You make, willing to pour out whatever I can hold in an obedient sacrifice of surrender and joy. Amen.

August 19

REST

Hear my cry, O God; attend to my prayer. From the end of the earth I will cry to You, when my heart is overwhelmed; lead me to the rock that is higher than I. For you have been a shelter for me, a strong tower from the enemy. I will abide in Your tabernacle forever; I will trust in the shadow of Your wings. Selah. Psalm 61:1-4

So many times I have been counseled to rest; which, apparently, I have a problem doing! But I think that is because I haven't really comprehended exactly true rest is. I noticed I had written "REST" in the margin of my Bible next to these verses. Abiding and trusting constitute rest. Then I read the last verse which says, *So, I will sing praise to Your name forever, that I may daily perform my vows.*[55]

What got my attention was this: praise enables us, apparently. The words "perform" and "daily" also stood out. I wondered, "How does praise enable?" My conclusion: It re-establishes our minds on God—who we were made to focus upon. It relaxes—takes away the stresses that focusing on performance brings. Thus changing "*How am I doing*?" to "*Look what God is doing*." It reforms our thinking and it rests the soul.

Praise produces a proper performance. It doesn't produce a sluggard mentality, which I have often confused with rest! If I achieve a life full of praise and trust, it is worth so much more than completing my to-do list each day!

Dear Abba, I have pledged to learn to rest. In order to do that, it seems that I must include praise as a part of all I do; all I am. Daily then, by praising You and performing that pledge my heart and soul at rest. Amen

---

[55] Psalm 61:8

August 20

HARNESSED

I will instruct you and teach you in the way you should go; I will guide you with My eye. Do not be like the horse or like the mule, which have no understanding, which must be harnessed with bit and bridle, else they will not come near you. Psalm 32:8-9

At first read this passage seems amusing. Looking deeper, however, I feel a bit of vexation to consider He might be talking about ME! We hear the phrase, *Stubborn as a mule,* often implying a reluctance to do what one is instructed to do. Oh, yes. I see myself in this!

I admit there have been many times when I have heard God offer to lead me and I refused. Listen to the gentleness of His voice, above, as He explains His willingness to guide us. The horse and the mule may not be able to understand; but we can, and therefore should not need to be bridled or forced to draw near to Him. We should desire to do it, beckoned by the gentle call to His side and His loving eye upon us.

Earlier in this psalm, we find these words: *You are my hiding place; You shall preserve me from trouble; You shall surround me with songs of deliverance.*[56] That appeals to me! How about you?

Heavenly Father, I really don't want to have a bit placed in my mouth, but rather fill it with praise and thanksgiving. May I draw nearer and nearer to You. Please guide me with Your gentle eye. Amen.

---

[56] Psalm 32:7

August 21

MOUTH GUARD

Set a guard, O LORD, over my mouth,; keep watch over the door of my lips. Psalm 141:3

I read this verse and immediately my thoughts go back to a day when I didn't heed it—I did not set a guard over my mouth. We were vacationing with family and I made a snide hurtful comment to a dear sister. It didn't take long before I overflowed with regret. How ugly were my words playing back through my mind. Thoughtless, critical and harsh, they spewed forth; inflicting pain on my loved one. How small I felt as I crawled worm-like into my room and covered my head with the pillow.

Had I ruined everything with the verbal barbs I threw? Just that morning I had prayed, "Lord, may I keep a sweet spirit." But before nightfall, I'd let the dark underbelly of my sinful nature be ripped open; its contents spilling venom. I'll never forget the shock and hurt on her face, and wished with all my might that I could unsay the words. But we all know that those remarks linger in the air and cannot be taken back.

I apologized, and I was told I was forgiven. But I found forgiveness difficult to accept. Something was broken. I prayed for God's forgiveness and the chance to repair the relationship. He has been faithful to do that but an important lesson was learned that day.

Heavenly Father, I remember how sorry I was and You forgave me. Over the years the relationship with my sister has been restored. I am grateful; but may I never again speak with haste and meanness. Because I felt desolation, and I have no desire to feel that way again. Set a guard over my lips, please, God. Amen.

August 22

CAUSE AND EFFECT

Therefore my spirit is overwhelmed within me; my heart within me is distressed. I remember the days of old; I meditate on all Your works; I muse on the work of Your hands. I spread out my hands to You; My soul longs for You like a thirsty land. Psalm 143:4-6

Overwhelmed seems to describe my life most of the time. And that leads to disappointment, and then to discouragement and despair.

These verses above are some of my very favorite comforting ones, to be sure. I go to that part of my Bible often; because my spirit gets overwhelmed, and my heart tends to become distressed. Whatever the cause of distress, whether it is circumstances, lack of trust, or perhaps a sense of failure in my life, the effects are the same. So, recognizing them for what they are, I turn to this reminder.

Today, however, I found a new truth here. It is the work of His hands that causes me to spread out my own hands. It is the memory, the musing, on what He has done, that illuminates my need to trust. I lift my hands in surrender to Him, who alone can satisfy the thirst and longing within me.

Heavenly Father, I need this word today. I am overwhelmed, again, with thirsty desire that I have been working to satisfy. But only You can do that, so I yield to You with an open heart. Fill me with Yourself, please. Amen.

August 23

AIR QUALITY

Nor is He worshiped with men's hands, as though He needed anything, since He gives to all life, breath, and all things…for in Him we live and move and have our being. Acts 17:25, 28

These words remind me of something that happened recently. As I got out of bed one morning, I looked out of the window to check on the smoky air we'd been having. It had spread a yellow, brownish cast over everything. So often we hear the phrase "air quality", something we haven't often had to consider in the Pacific Northwest. I thought of those struggling with fires near and threatening, and of the air hazardous to breathe, and my heart was breaking for them.

As I began to pray I remembered lyrics to one of my favorite praise choruses. *This is the air I breathe, this is the air I breathe, Your holy presence living in me. This is my daily bread, this is my daily bread, Your very word spoken to me. And I, I'm desperate for You, and I, I'm lost without You.*[57]

In that melody and in those words God reminds me of the truth of His word: that air breathed in the presence and awareness of His spirit is sweet and pure; the breath of heaven. And though air on earth can be hazardous to health and safety, there is the breath of the Spirit of God available to us for our spiritual health and safety.

Father, with gratefulness I breathe deeply of Your peace, and kneel before You in praise. Amen.

---

[57] This Is The Air I Breathe - Marie Barnett

August 24

FALL RISK

Now to Him who is able to keep you from falling, and to prevent you faultless before the presence of His glory with exceeding joy, to God our Savior, who alone is wise, be glory and majesty; dominion and power, both now and forever. Amen. Jude 24, 25

During one of my recent hospitalizations they placed a bright yellow band on my wrist. It said *Fall Risk.* No going anywhere, even to the bathroom, without someone in attendance. Now that I am well, I believe that if any of us look honestly at our lives, we will see that we are all "fall risks". Because of the original Fall, we are sinners and fall when we aren't leaning on our attendant God.

At first I resented that wristband, but I began to feel some comfort in knowing that all I have to do was ring the call button and there would be help to keep me from falling.

Throughout Scripture we are told of the dangers of trying to do things on our own, that God has provided ways for us to hold on to His hand. But somehow we insist on doing things our way! And the insidious thought that we are capable of navigating our pathways alone, doing it "my way", pulls us away from the promises and warnings of our God. The Apostle Paul advises: *Therefore let him who thinks he stands, take heed lest he fall.*[58]

I am grateful for the promises, the provisions, the protection, that following and leaning on God brings. I AM a Fall Risk, both physically and spiritually! We all are.

Heavenly Father, you are able to keep us from falling. May I ever hold Your hand in trust. Amen.

---

[58] 1 Corinthians 10:12

August 25

THE NOTICER

Then they will see the Son of Man coming in a cloud with power and great glory. Now when these things begin to happen, look up and lift up your heads, because your redemption draws near. Luke 21:27-28

My husband notices everything! Especially anything that is out of order, like telephone wires in an old Western movie. He will ask me, "What is wrong with this picture?"

Recently we went out for breakfast. Three times people whom we knew walked past us and did not notice us! We looked at each other and chuckled. We are always looking around for someone we know, hopefully to make a connection. Of course we don't go as far as to wave our arms and jump up and down, but we hope!

That morning a gentleman we didn't know stopped at our table and asked, "Guess who I got to see today?" Intrigued, we said, "Who?" thinking it was a celebrity. He answered, "You!"

We had a conversation then; he congratulated us on our anniversary and shared some of his life. We totally enjoyed the encounter. What an interesting way to open up dialogue!

Later I opened my devotional for the day, the title being "Look Up"! Amazed at the way God gets my attention, I was fascinated to consider the truth of this Scripture.

We had been studying prophecy in our small group, so this explains, perhaps, why I noticed this passage, following on the heels of an earlier discussion. I believe that "these things" have begun to happen, and it behooves us to lift our heads and notice!

Heavenly Father, there is great hope here. Our Redemption is coming, and our destiny is set, if we believe in Jesus and His sacrifice for us. May we ever look up and look around, noticing, and see to what and where God is pointing. Amen.

August 26

WISDOM

Lord You have been our dwelling place in all generations. Before the mountains were brought forth, or ever You had formed the earth and the world, even from everlasting to everlasting, You are God. Psalm 90:1-2

The solidity of the above statement enthralls me and fills me with joy and comfort. I was reading this psalm the other day, pondering on the way it holds such sweet praise and promise. What incredible things God was able to do through Moses, the author of this psalm. Reading further I find: *So teach us to number our days that we may gain a heart of wisdom.*[59] From the eternality of creation to the numbering of our days, God remains. He maintains His presence as our dwelling place. !f we persevere, wisdom will be ours.

Thinking back, I remember that I chose the word "wisdom" as my "one perfect word" for the year 2020. Who knew what that year of pandemic and fear would hold, and how much I would need that promised heart of wisdom! Timothy Keller says, "Wisdom is not only for deep thinkers. It is how you get through daily life.[60] Our wisdom will guide us as we grow in the knowledge and image of God's Son Jesus, who is Wisdom itself. But it is up to us to seek Him and daily explore His wisdom and truth.

Oh, how we need to hear this! As time goes by it becomes more and more apparent that the knowledge of God we gain through the scriptures fuels good decisions and wise counsel.

Father God, I pray Your word back to you in Psalm 90:17. "And let the beauty of the LORD my God be upon me, and establish the work of my hands for me; yes, establish the work of my hands." Amen.

---

[59] Psalm 90:12

[60] Timothy J. Keller (1950-)

August 27

FASTENED

And now for a little while, grace has been shown from the LORD our God, to leave us a remnant to escape and to give us a peg in His holy place; that our God may enlighten our eyes and give us a measure of revival in our bondage. Ezra 9:8.

There are days when I feel like a leaf fluttering in the breeze; loose and barely tethered to the tree. As I was feeling lost and purposeless, this verse caught my eye. The metaphor *peg in His holy place* caught my attention. To me this means to be fastened and secure. I often find my thoughts in a downward spiral, but fortunately, God waits to catch me and be my security.

A brief background to the passage is helpful. Ezra's people (Israel) were in captivity, in bondage to a foreign nation. They were disobedient and yet Ezra,—teacher, scribe, man of God—was tasked with taking a remnant back to their homeland and begin to rebuilding the temple. Here is one of the rare mentions of grace in the Old Testament, so it captured my attention.

God is able to enlighten our eyes, to lift our thoughts, and—here is what I hang on to—*to give us a measure of revival in our bondage.* Let any of us feeling in bondage to disillusionment and disappointment claim that promised "measure of revival".

Heavenly Father, may our minds be fixed, as a peg in a sure place, fastened on the truth of Your grace extended to us. Draw us to Yourself no matter what is going on inside us; whether disappointment or defeat, and revive us, we pray. Amen.

August 28

JUST JESUS ONLY

"This is My beloved Son in whom I am well pleased. Hear Him!" And when the disciples heard it they fell on their faces and were greatly afraid. But Jesus came and touched them and said, "Arise, and do not be afraid." When they had lifted up their eyes, they saw no one but Jesus only. Matthew 17:8

There is a song with lyrics that clutch my heart and won't let go. "I'll worship only at the feet of Jesus. His cup alone my holy grail. There are no other gods before Him, just Jesus only will never fail."[61] This song draws my heart to the story of Jesus Christ's transfiguration on the mountain, which I've included above. The hearts of the disciples were filled with fear at the vision yet found their eyes truly opened, seeing only Jesus.

Do I see anything besides Jesus in my own worship? My mind scrambles and refuses to settle, which means I don't see only Jesus. I am blinded by the view of my goals, my self, sitting on the throne of my heart.

I am intrigued by the disciples who actually witnessed this phenomenon. Greatly afraid, they had fallen on their faces. But consider Jesus. He knew them, He came to them, touched them and spoke peace. How tender. How mind-shattering it must have been for them! Enough so that with new eyes all they could see was Jesus only.

Heavenly Father, how I want to be so in tune with You, so aware of who Jesus is that He is all I can see. And then I know that I could truly "worship only at the feet of Jesus." Amen.

---

[61] Bill and Gloria Gaither

August 29

WHAT ABOUT ISAAC?

And Abraham stretched out his hand and took the knife to slay his son. But the angel of the LORD called unto him from heaven, and said, "Abraham! Abraham!" So he said, "Here I am." And He said "Do not lay your hand on the lad, or do anything to him; for now I know that you fear God, since you have not withheld your son, your only son, from Me." Genesis 22:10-12

Faith, in the life of Abraham, is played out in obedience. Praised for generations for his willingness to sacrifice the one he loved, he is known for an act that seems almost inconceivable.

But what about Isaac, lying on the altar, his life threatened? Did he struggle against the ropes, or did he simply acquiesce to his father's will? Scripture is silent. The scene pictures the obedient Son of God nailed to a cross, the eternal sacrifice.

So I marvel at Isaac, his questions answered with only a promise of God's provision. He trusted in his father's love.

And what about me? Is my faith strong enough to obey God's voice when He asks me to sacrifice my self, my pride, my desires, my will? I want to offer my life upon His altar, bound by ropes of trust in His love—positioned for service, provisioned by His spirit, abandoned to His will. Just like Isaac.

Oh, Heavenly Father, You have given such an example of surrender in the person of Isaac. May I be faithful to follow that example, trusting in Your sovereign will, offering all I am to serve You. Amen."

August 30

CLUELESS

If I had not come and spoken to them, they would have no sin, but now they have no excuse for their sin. If I had not done among them the works which no one else did, they would have no sin; but now they have seen… John 15:22, 24

I happened upon this verse where Jesus explains to His disciples why some would not believe Him. I examined my own life. How many miserable rebellious years I spent pushing Him away, doing my own thing!

I knew better. I had heard the words of Jesus over and over. They were buried in my mind—there was no excuse for my sin. But the world would be clueless without Jesus' earthly ministry, the words He spoke, the miracles He performed.

How many people I meet every day are without hope because they haven't heard His words? I become impatient with people who don't believe in God or His Son. But maybe they really haven't heard His words…they are clueless!

But, can I justify looking down on them? I, who knew, who had heard, and yet refused to acknowledge Him as Lord? I've never been clueless; I've heard His voice, there is no excuse for my sin.

Heavenly Father, I stand now in awe of Your promised forgiveness, and claim it as my own in the words of Mark 9:24, "I believe, help my unbelief!" Amen."

August 31

JEREMIAH...AND ME

Then the word of the LORD came to me saying, "Before I formed you in the womb I knew you; before you were born I sanctified you; I ordained you a prophet to the nations." Jeremiah 1:4-5

Here is the story of Jeremiah, called by God before his birth; appointed, consecrated, set apart. It occurs to me that God actually says that of *me*. There's no difference, then, between us: I hold God's word of truth, my mouth and hands are touched by Him and the commandment still is sure. "But I'm afraid, I cannot speak," Jeremiah cried—like me.

Gently, yet insistent, God weaves His commands with promises, saying in effect: "Go, and speak, don't be afraid; my presence goes with you. Pluck up and plant, don't be dismayed; my protection stands as walls of brass. Men will oppose, but don't back down; I will preserve you, hold you fast."

We who believe in Jesus all have this same commission and its accompanying promises. We too offer excuses, just like Jeremiah did. So often, fears of rejection or ridicule, of not being enough, confound us and render us useless. Even strong Biblical characters like Jeremiah struggle in the same way. But, did Jeremiah really have a choice? Of course he did! He surrendered when he heard God speak. Though beaten, jailed and scorned, he stands today as an example of what God demands from all who tremble with the urgency of truth. God still says "Go"; He still says "Speak". Is there any other choice...for me? Yes. May I surrender.

Heavenly Father, I have heard Your call. Please help me, strengthen me. I want to be obedient and I want to trust Your promises. Yet I struggle. Only You are able to uphold and encourage me. Thank You for your Word. Amen.

September 1

IN THE STRUGGLE

But he gives more grace. Therefore he says, "God resists the proud, but gives grace to the humble." Therefore submit to God. Resist the devil and he will flee from you. James 4:6-7

So often I wonder why I fight so hard to bring about *my* goals, rather than submitting to the One who holds my future in His hands. It's rather like the condition of my bed after a sleepless night; sheets and blankets crumpled, twisted, evidence of struggle against the release of sleep. Or like my knitting after a series of mistakes; knotted and messy.

That's what I do to my life. God longs for me to rest in Him. He'll keep the sheets smooth if I lie still. And if I would knit more slowly, paying attention to the instructions, there wouldn't be tight knots or ruined yarn from frustrated pulling.

Yet, even as I learn His lessons, I realize, there is growth in the struggle, To both *survive* and *thrive,* I need the strength He provides as a by-product of our tussle; and I understand that inertia brings defeat but surrender brings victory.

Father, You know I want You to be pre-eminent in my life. But I seem to be a slow learner. Thank You for Your patience with me as I struggle. I do know You are faithful to teach me and help me. Amen.

September 2

CAREFUL

The Lord your God commands you this day to follow these decrees and laws; carefully observe them with all your heart and with all your soul. Deuteronomy 26:16 (NIV)

I have been reading in Deuteronomy lately. It's such a wonderful book, in which Moses speaks to the children of Israel just prior to his death, giving them instructions from God before they enter the long-awaited Promised Land. *Deuteronomy* means "second law", and sort of summarizes and emphasizes what is contained in the first four books of the Bible.

I have always enjoyed reading this book, but now I am noticing over and over the word "careful". Moses uses it a lot, along with "take heed", and "beware". I guess God knows well the tendency of His people to wander from His laws and become lazy and rebellious. It is so important for us to take heed, to be careful and to know the truth. It is a good exhortation for us.

I am reminded of a cute story. Our little grand-nephew, age three, was enthralled with his grandma's collection of porcelain carousel music boxes, which she displayed on the glass coffee table in her home. He was getting closer and closer to yielding to the temptation to touch them…a forbidden thing. His mother called out to him, "Don't touch. Remember, you have to be careful." To which he replied, "Don't worry, Mommy, I'm carefulling!"

I wonder, as I look at my life, am I carefulling? Am I paying heed, beware of the danger of yielding to temptation? It bears thinking about.

Dear Father, help me to remember always to be carefulling, obeying Your law, that You can bless me, just as You have promised. Amen.

September 3

GOLDEN IDOLS

So all the people broke off the golden earrings which were in their ears and brought them to Aaron! And he received the gold from their hand, and he fashioned it with an engraving tool, and made a molded calf. Then they said, "This is your god, O Israel..." Exodus 32:3, 4

Bored, and tired of waiting for Moses to come down from the mountain, God's children made mischief. Bringing their gold, they handed it over, let it be melted and formed into a golden calf—a worthless substitute. The gold they carried was a gift from God, spoils taken from Egyptian masters. God meant that it be used for building His tabernacle. Impatient, they grieved Him.

So I wonder about His lesson here for us. How many times is a gift from God tossed away by an impatient hand: rejected in the heat of the moment; an idol to self, raised from the fire. Oh, we must be aware of the treasures we carry, gifts showered down from His hand. May we not let them be turned into idols; but instead, be used to build up His kingdom on earth.

Lord, as I look into my own heart I ask: is there a golden calf in my life? Am I misusing the golden gift You've given me, molding an idol in my own impatience? I ask You, please melt my heart and form me into the person You've created me to be. Amen.

September 4

THE FORCE

Now on the day that the tabernacle was raised up, the cloud covered the tabernacle, the tent of the Testimony; from evening until morning it was above the tabernacle like the appearance of fire. Whenever the cloud was taken up from above the tabernacle, after that the children of Israel would journey; and in the place where the cloud settled, there the children of Israel would pitch their tents. Numbers 9:15, 17

I find the story of the cloud and fiery pillar fascinating, in that God's presence was within these supernatural signs. He covered, protected and led His children throughout the wandering years. As they began the life-changing journey to the Promised Land, they had no idea where to go or how to get there, save following God. Depending entirely upon the cloud by day and the fire by night, their focus remained on the movement of God's visible presence. How many times have I felt stuck, unsure of my direction…and wished God would send a definitive cloud or pillar to point out my next step?

In a flash of inspiration I realized that there's no need to look to the sky for a physical cloud or pillar of fire. Indeed not, because Jesus sent a parting gift to me, made possible by His sacrifice—the Holy Spirit. He is the driving force within me…and is sent to be my guide and much more. Instead of a *visible* manifestation to direct my path, I am guided by His very presence in my heart, no less real.

Father, Your Holy Spirit lives in me…a cloud of fragrance and a burning fire that motivates and enables me to follow You! In confidence and joy and power Your Spirit is the Force on which I depend. And upon that truth will I pitch my tent. Amen.

September 5

WALKING WORTHY

...as you know how we exhorted, and comforted, and charged every one of you, as a father does His own children, that you would walk worthy of God who calls you into His own kingdom and glory.
1 Thessalonians 2:11-12

The worthy walk. What is it? I believe it is a calling—high and holy. And it is for each child of God. This calling is a challenge, one that takes courage and boldness, because it's not a trouble-free walk. We are tasked to go where Jesus walked, and in the way He walked. It is a choice, and we can refuse or follow. Are we willing to live in the manner He asks—in obedience and trust? Or would we rather walk in our own way, hoping in vain for His direction and blessing.

Before our faces droop in despair at our failings, there is hope! We cannot *make* ourselves worthy, but we are *counted* worthy because of our position in Christ! His promises are our consolation when earthly cares oppress us; and in the comfort of His presence we can find rest. Ultimately there is the approval of a father, given with love as to a child and the certainty of His blessing, when the final step is taken. It IS possible to walk worthy. To answer the challenge, choose to lean on God and reap His commendation and consolation. He knows the way may seem hard...but He also promises it is easy when we are connected to Christ. For M*y yoke is easy and my burden is light.*[62]

Heavenly Father, I see that I have a new calling! A challenge, a choice. I do want to walk worthy of the sacrifice made by Jesus in my behalf. It's a new path, but You walk beside me, guiding and supporting. Help me to consider my steps, that I make wise decisions, and follow Your leading. Thank You. Amen.

---

[62] Matthew 11:30

September 6

ONE SONG

Blessed be the LORD God of Israel from everlasting to everlasting!
And let all the people say "Amen"! Praise the LORD!
Psalm 106:48

The phrase "all the people" captivates me. There is unity and joy in people praising together. How beautiful it was...an agreement with God as He reminds us of how He has moved in our lives.

I have the opportunity of singing in our community chorus. Some time ago we performed a selection entitled *One Song*.[63] The lyrics were very moving— "If we all sing one song, if we all learn the words, imagine what tomorrow would bring..." As I read this Psalms verse I was reminded of that song and how it had tugged at my heartstrings. All of us had felt a stirring of longing; there were tears among the singers. I believe the emotional impact is because the song speaks to our deep-seated desire for unity, togetherness and peace. I can't help but imagine that I hear God saying, "Oh, if My people could all say Amen and sing My song, imagine what tomorrow would bring!"

I know one day those of us who believe in and claim Jesus as our Savior will sing one song, which will be around God's throne. It is what we were made to do, and the longing rests deep inside us, a yearning created from His heart. Until that day, however, we sing praise and gratitude for the promise that sustains us...with voices united.

Heavenly Father, how we long for the day we will ALL sing one song, a song of praise and thanksgiving to You. We now have, though, the opportunity to sing praise, and may we raise our song in beautiful harmony. Amen.

---

[63] One Song, by Tevin Campbell

September 7

BRING ON THE BERRY PAIL

I press toward the mark for the prize of the high calling of God in Christ Jesus. Philippians 3:14

Blackberries...delicious scourge of the Northwest! When we moved to Washington from desert-like southern California, I was excited by our wild-growing blackberry vines. I couldn't wait until the berries ripened. So naïve was I! Though the vines teased with the promise of fruit, thorns rewarded me with vicious stabs each time I reached for a berry. Soon, wondering if it was worth fighting for the few berries I managed to pick, I became anxious to rid our yard of those stubborn, invading vines. Yet it appeared to be impossible! The roots go on forever, it seemed, and the vines grew back as fast as we cut them. An extremely frustrating endeavor. But I've made peace with the blackberry; accepting the fact of its prickly presence. I now consider the delicious pie and jam worth the cost of scratches and pokes.

I think that life is like picking blackberries. Reaching toward a goal, we are often stabbed painfully by the thorns of heartache and hardship. Is the prize worth the scratches? Are we willing to go deeper into the thicket, determined to come home with a pail of berries, even though we may become stained purple and stinging?

God is pleased when we say "Yes. I want to press on". The fruit we gather tastes sweeter when we accede to the fact of the thorns of adversity. Victory is all about determining to claim the promise, in spite of the brambles.

Dear Father, I want my berry pail to contain the prize of Your high calling. Help me to press on; through all adversity trusting You. Amen.

September 8

HARMONY

I, therefore, the prisoner of the Lord, beseech you to walk worthy of the calling with which you were called, with all lowliness and gentleness, with longsuffering, bearing with one another in love, endeavoring to keep the unity of the Spirit in the bond of peace. Ephesians 4:1-3

In addition to the large chorus, I am privileged to sing with a 16-member A Cappella group . We work very hard, because in A Cappella singing, the voices are the be-all and end-all: there is no accompaniment. Singing in this way lays our voices bare, and it has to be nearly perfect. It is hard work, and we bond together as into a family, going over and over a measure or two until the harmony kicks in and each part sounds like one voice. We strive for the moment when it all fits into that one chord that gives us goose bumps, that perfect harmony...and we KNOW that we have done it! It's pure joy to see our director's face and sense the fulfillment of his efforts as well.

So I was thinking about how God views our A Cappella efforts as we sing to Him with our lives. He stands with baton raised and asks us to praise Him. Some of us croak, some sing melodically. Some shout, some whisper. Unlike the directors of an earthly choir, He is not looking for any other sound than the harmony of unity between His children. That is the music He longs to hear. We need to work together and practice, bonding as a family. We do it over and over until He gives the downbeat and we respond with all we are in a tremendous melodious shout of pure, joyful praise. That is Harmony with a capital "H!"

Dear Father, harmony is a beautiful thing. It is so much more than just singing the right notes, it is a connection of our hearts, uniting with Yours. Please give us discerning ears and sweetness of spirit that results in the harmony that brings you joy. Amen."

September 9

CHASTENING

My child, do not make light of the Lord's discipline, and do not lose heart when he rebukes you, because the Lord disciplines those he loves… Hebrews 12:5-6 (NIV)

The other day I was enjoying lunch at a nearby restaurant. A family was doing the same and I was observing as their child, a beautiful little girl, misbehaved. She touched something forbidden, clutched in selfishness and caused some distress. I watched as her mother smacked her hands to redirect her attention. Startled, the child looked into her mother's face. For correction? For direction? To question "Why"? Her face crumpled in tears.

I turned away to hide my rueful smile, remembering my young-mothering days. But my smile faded soon as God spoke to me and made me aware that my own hands had reached out and touched things not pleasing to Him. I had grabbed at my life in my own puny strength instead of accessing the Holy Spirit's power placed at my disposal.

I felt my hands being smacked. And so I turned to look into His face. There I saw His compassion, His patience, His desire for me to do what is right. I stand rebuked.

Dear Father, I realize suddenly that I need correction, discipline. But I also see the love in Your eyes. I am chastened, so I ask You, please, to redirect my life. Thank You. Amen.

September 10

POSITIONED

Do not be afraid nor dismayed because of this great multitude, for the battle is not yours, but God's…You will not need to fight in this battle. Position yourselves, stand still and see the salvation of the LORD, who is with you… 2 Chronicles 20:15b, 17

Battles. They are ever with us, threatening our peace of mind, perhaps even our very lives. It has always been this way; life was not intended to be a cake walk. It is the *way* we fight those battles that determines the outcomes as well as our growth.

King Jehoshaphat faced a battle of gigantic proportions; an army of thousands was marching toward Jerusalem. Let's examine the heart of Jehoshaphat. First, the Bible tells us he was afraid…not so different from us when we face an enemy. In contrast to my usual reaction, this king sought God. I often try to find a way to win the battle in my own puny power. Jehoshaphat called for a nationwide fast to seek the Lord, and the people prayed: *For we have no power against this great multitude that is coming against us, nor do we know what to do, but our eyes are upon You.*[64]

Here is the formula for winning battles: Seek the LORD with a heart of praise; listen to His voice; position yourselves; stand still—and watch Him move!

What is my position when danger threatens? Bowed before God, my heart standing still, watching? *Or* brandishing my powerless sword hoping to win the victory that has in fact already been won?

Heavenly Father, I am challenged! I want to be in a position of worship, praise, and surrender where the vision of You fighting in my behalf is sweet to my soul. Please correct my battle stance. Amen.

---

[64] *2 Chronicles 20:12*

September 11

SELAH

I remember the days of old; I meditate on all your works; I muse on the work of Your hands. I spread out my hands to You; my soul longs for You like a thirsty land. Selah. Psalm 143:5-6

In scripture, there is a word used many times in the Psalms that we often ignore. It is "Selah". Intrigued, I wanted to discover what it means, why it is there. And what I learned brings me to a place of wonder and delight.

Most translators agree that it indicates a pause, a rest in a music score, while the notes just played linger in the ear and ready the senses to listen to the next. The Psalms are the songs of God's people. So it occurs to me that He has a reason to call for a lull, to ask us to ponder what we have just heard, and intensify our desire to hear the next notes of His composition.

How fitting, then, to read once again the above verses before the Selah, and hold those thoughts in abeyance; musing on His wonderful works—what His hands have done. In response, anticipation is heightened for what is ahead.

The rests—the pauses—in music are as integral to the composition as the notes themselves, adding intensity and drama to its whole. I am finding so much beauty in the "Selahs" God is placing in my life, thirsting times, respite and reflection times. I desire never to pass by this word in scripture without contemplating His message to me.

Heavenly Father, before You raise the Conductor's baton to begin again, my heart breathes, "Amen. So be it, Lord." Selah.

September 12

BACKGROUND MUSIC

Blessed are the people who know the joyful sound! They walk, O LORD, in the light of Your countenance. In Your name they rejoice all day long, and in Your righteousness they are exalted.
Psalm 89:15-16

I love music! Melodies, harmonies and beautiful lyrics. God created music, in part, that we may discover how He makes order out of chaos. There are only seven notes in a scale and yet from them the amount of chords and combinations are infinite! Only God could do that, and we have the benefit of hearing His love through the gift of music.

Our lives each sing to background music. We may be aware, or not, of its melody. We step lightly however, allowing its rhythm to beat a cadence. So as I ponder this, I ask God, "What is the background music of my life? What is the sound that surrounds and affects my spirit?" Is it subdued enough so I can hear His whispers? Is it truly joyful, or has the raucous confusion of the world crept in and encompassed my heart?

I remember the words of an old hymn: "We have heard the joyful sound! Jesus Saves!"[65] Oh, yes. I've heard *that*! Though I am immersed in its truth, it is also vital to determine that the melody in my spirit is so much more than simply noise. Are my ears and heart attuned to the melody God is playing?

Father, I so desire to ensure that the joyful sound of Your loving voice of guiding wisdom will always be the background music of my life. Amen.

---

[65] Jesus Saves - by Priscilla Owens (1829-1907)

September 13

CORNERSTONE

Behold I lay in Zion a chief cornerstone, elect, precious, and he who believes on Him will by no means be put to shame. Therefore, to you who believe, He is precious, but to those who are disobedient, the stone which the builders rejected has become the chief cornerstone, and a stone of stumbling and a rock of offense. 1 Peter 2:6-8

A cornerstone is so very important to a building. "Cornerstone" also means the "basic part of something," a foundation, the rock upon which the weight of the entire structure rests. As I consider this, it becomes clear why Jesus is called the Chief Cornerstone, because on Him and His work on the cross all the truth of our salvation rests.

Taking a look at our lives, it occurs to me that perhaps a good example might be that we all are given stones with which to build our lives. If we are wise we choose to make Jesus our cornerstone. If we reject Him, the Chief Cornerstone, we choose something else upon which to build...fame, money, power or success, for example.

Thus, lives become unsteady and unstable; and we stumble over the stones of love and truth lying rejected in our path. It is a choice each of us must make before we begin construction.

Heavenly Father, I realize I cannot make a wise choice in building my life without acknowledging the importance of the Chief Cornerstone upon which to build. I do not want to stumble, but instead to thrive on the hope of my salvation, which totally rests on Jesus. Amen.

September 14

SO MUCH RUBBLE

Then Judah said, "The strength of the laborers is failing, and there is so much rubbish that we are not able to build the wall."
Nehemiah. 4:10

Rubble...a tumbled-down wall, once the protection of a city, is now just a field of stones. Rebellion tore down the walls. Apathy crumbled the mortar, allowing the stones one by one, to fall unnoticed. The enemy sauntered in, unchecked.

Rubble now surrounds America; her God-given protection lies in heaps. The enemy has breached the wall and stands with defiant fist raised against the Most High.

"Let us rebuild!" voices cry out. Is there a chance for restoration? A leader stands tall calling workmen to the task, urging them on. Rubble and ruin can be recycled into building blocks. Old stones, once discarded, when placed by consecrated hands, create a solid foundation for the future.

There are steps that can be taken to rebuild, even if it seems there is too much rubble and the task appears impossible. First, erect a holy altar and on it burn the rubble of rebellion. Replace it with obedience. Secondly, take the waste of complaining; reclaim it by prayer. Permit God to redeem the ruin of hopelessness, and incorporate that into the wall. With these things in place, rubble is transformed and order is restored.

Father, You are the Master Architect. As I look around at the rubble I have allowed in my life, would you take the sacrifice I offer that I may find usefulness again? Rebuild the ruins that threaten to ruin me. Thank You. Amen.

September 15

THROUGH THE MOTIONS

I will praise you with all my heart; before the gods I will sing praises to You. Psalm 138:1

Is there life in my worship? Is there joy in my praise? Is my commitment hollow? Am I going through the motions?

Sometimes I feel like a cheerleader whose team is losing the game. I jump and wave my pom-poms but thoughts of winning are gone. I'm going through the motions. Yet I serve a *living* God! Rich abundance is promised and victory awaits; no matter that the contest at times seems hopeless.

I always wanted to be a cheerleader. But I was never thin enough, athletic enough, or popular enough to be voted in! I was loyal, however. Filled with team spirit, I ran for Pep Club President—and won! It wasn't quite the same, but I had a position and responsibility in that role. My little sister became the cheerleader—and the green-eyed monster took up residence in my heart.

Thinking back at those high school days, I can draw a parallel to my life today. I may never be the one out in front, waving the banner of God's love and redemption; but that doesn't mean that I don't have a position and responsibility to maintain my enthusiasm for the team I represent. I'm thinking how important it is that my joy and commitment stay strong and true, even if I'm only sitting in the stands waving and cheering.

God, help me see with new eyes your game plan that assures triumph in the final score. Put new springs in my feet, strength in my hands and purpose in my leaps...that I appropriate Your power and no longer just go through the motions. Amen.

September 16

BALANCE

Your ears shall hear a word behind you, saying, "This is the way, walk in it," whenever you turn to the right hand or whenever you turn to the left. Isaiah 30:21

Teetering down the sidewalk, my grandson bravely navigates his adventurous first trip on his two-wheeler... without training wheels!! Head bobbing from right to left, eyes scrunched tight in concentration he struggles, intent on keeping his balance.

I watch him and observe, also, his daddy running along beside, encouraging, instructing—ready to catch him should he tip too far to one side and lose that precarious balance. It brought a picture to my mind of my own struggles.

Riding the two-wheeler of my responsibilities and commitments, I am striving to find balance, careful not to lean too far in either direction. Too many duties, or too few? Too much relaxation or not enough?

I am learning a lesson today, as I watch this little child learn; discovering that balance is vital in keeping upright and moving ahead. But the most beautiful thing I see is my heavenly Father running along beside me, encouraging, instructing and sweetly waiting to catch me if I lean too far to either side. Speaking His word, the truth of His love and care for me, into my heart; He restores my balance.

Dear Father, I've used my training wheels long enough. I need only keep my eyes on You and listen for your voice to ride straight and true. Amen.

September 17

RECIPES

This Book of the Law shall not depart from your mouth, but you shall meditate in it day and night, that you may observe to do according to all that is written in it. Joshua 1:8

The other evening I was in the middle of cooking dinner, stirring a pot of lentils. The smells were delicious! Sausage, onions, spices, molasses and tomato sauce (among other things). Yum! This lentil dish is one that I have made dozens of times; it is one of our favorites, but I still had to go and drag out my old recipe collection to be sure I had it right. I'd forgotten all the specific spices.

I know I'm not alone in this but so often I wonder what direction God is leading. Where does He want me? What does He want me to be focusing upon? I ask it a lot! For answers I need to grab His recipe Book! A few years ago, at a Women's Retreat, the subject of our purpose in this life was discussed. It boiled down to this very simple "recipe", 1) to know God and 2) to make Him known.

God's "recipe" is well-stated by these two points. I must sharpen my listening skills and deliberately heed what I hear from Him and be faithful in the Word, getting to know Him. It follows that then I'll be ready to share Jesus when He presents the opportunity.

Heavenly Father thank You for the lesson learned today, the importance of following a recipe! It's as important for living as it is for cooking! May I learn to know You better through Your recipe – Your Word. It contains all the needful instructions, so nudge me always to check there first. Amen.

September 18

BEHIND THE FOOTLIGHTS

Trust in the LORD with all your heart; and lean not unto your own understanding; in all your ways acknowledge Him and he shall direct your paths. Proverbs 3:5-6

Looking back on my life I am chuckling as I remember acting in plays in my high school years. I did love being on stage! But I can't help contrasting that with my spiritual life. Trusting God's guidance, His direction, is rather like being an actor in a play. The script is written; God is Author, Producer and Director. I signed a contract at salvation, agreeing to follow the instructions of the director and producer. How disruptive and arrogant it would be for me to step to the front of the stage and say, "I think my part would be better if I…" How audacious!

But that's what I have insisted upon doing so many times. Instead of learning from Him I have kept trying to adapt the role to fit *myself*. So now I am waiting in the wings, ready for that first step onto the stage—again. I am determined to continue in the role God has designed for me—that of a disciple. And the curtain is about to rise anew on this very real performance in my life.

Father God, hearing Your voice in the scripture shows me I must become more familiar with the script, stay behind the footlights and follow You, my Director, more closely. It is on Your shoulders, after all, that the ultimate success of the production rests. Amen

September 19

DOORS

Ask, and it will be given to you; seek, and you will find; knock, and it will be opened to you. Matthew 7:7

Someone posted a little quote on Facebook. *"When life shuts a door, open it again. It's a door, that's how they work."* There's a measure of truth here. I tend to leave doors of unmet expectations closed, considering that opportunity as no longer available. I know I am too quickly discouraged, my faith in what I thought was my ministry tattered, because I haven't been "successful"—according to my definition anyway.

So often I feel like a failure. It's frightening sometimes to put myself out there for people to examine and choose whether or not to accept. I remember publishing my first book. My pastor asked me if I was ready to receive all the criticism that was bound to come. Oh. I hadn't considered what that might entail! I have always been leery of criticism. Anticipation faded and fear intruded. Was that door closed or should I move forward?

I was anxious, and no matter how I chided myself about trusting God, there was a knot of fear inside that I couldn't seem to untie. Though I felt guilty and wimpy, I had to find the willingness to lean on God's strength. Sometimes it takes courage to push through the doors we face, but God promises to be there on the other side.

Father, please grant me the courage to open the doors that I face with the grace only You can supply. What is waiting behind those doors is no surprise to You. May I always remember this lesson of learning to trust, until I truly learn it well. Amen.

September 20

THE SECRET PLACE

He who dwells in the secret place of the Most High shall abide under the shadow of the Almighty. I will say of the LORD, "He is my refuge and my fortress, my God, in Him I will trust." Psalm 91:1-2

Where is God's secret place? I yearn to go there to dwell, to rest beneath His wings. Only in that secret place will I find the certainty of His promise to keep me under His almighty shadow.

I search the pages of God's book and learn that Moses asked, like me, to discover Him in intimacy. God cleaved a rock, hid Moses there, and His glory passed close by.

My search leads to another Rock, this One cleft for *me*. Upon a cross, His breast torn, the heart of God is revealed. The secret place, a sheltering spot, is safe from the cares of the world; a place of peace and quiet and fulfilled longings. In Christ I find the secret place where I must dwell, and He in me under the shadow of the Almighty.

Father I hear the call of Your heart to mine, an invitation to rest, to abide, and find all that for which my heart longs. My gratitude knows no bounds to realize just what Jesus did to make the secret place available to me and to all who desire Your fullness. Thank you. Amen

September 21

MULTIPLICATION

A man's heart plans his way, but the LORD directs his steps.
Proverbs 16:9

One day not long ago, I had a big day planned, four events back-to-back; one beginning as the last one ended. I was a bit stressed about how it was all going to work out! Totally engrossed in working out how I was going to be wherever I was supposed to be at the right time, I was reading in my devotional. And it seemed I heard this word from God, *watch Me multiply your minutes,* further advising me how to trust Him for everything and to rest in Him (a subject close to my heart!)

So I told myself that I would do it all day—trust that He would do what He promised. And you know what? He did!! In every way He multiplied my minutes...the closest parking space; a server who brought my food first; a dentist who took me immediately...all kinds of things! And I was early for ALL my appointments!

The truth of Proverbs 16:9 is burning its way into my life. I know many of you have already learned this, and live your life in this way of trust. But I am still struggling to actually do what my mind—and God's Word—tell me is right. In contrast, I work and plan and put my confidence on what *I* can do, not what *God* can do. And so, if you are like me, I am here to say that God's way is best! He WILL work it out.

Dear God, would You teach us how You "multiply our minutes" when we trust in You and rest in Your care? Amen.

September 22

UNCERTAINTY

Our soul waits for the LORD; He is our help and our shield. For our heart shall rejoice in Him, because we have trusted in His holy name. Let Your mercy, O LORD, be upon us, just as we hope in You.
Psalm 33:20-22

Often I find the word "wait" coming to mind. I wait, and wonder the outcome of some issue I'm facing. Being quite sure of an outcome makes waiting bearable, don't you think? It's the uncertainty that wears on us. But, if we look at it correctly, it is uncertainty that should cause us to rest more heavily on God.

I hate to admit that I allow worry to paralyze me much too often. Worry is like sitting in a rocking chair—lots of movement but going nowhere! I have often placed quotes on my refrigerator like "Worry about tomorrow steals the joy from today."[66] God is sovereign and He has proved it to me many times, yet I still find myself stressing and obsessing over what I dread will happen or what I'm desperate to have happen.

Yet I'm learning. I hope you all are too, because it makes for a much easier life! You see, God loves us, and wants only our good But sometimes we struggle as we learn to experience God's love. We learn trust by relying on Him, but it takes time and experience for our souls to learn that trust. Thus, the waiting!

Heavenly Father, thank You for uncertainty—that we cannot see what is ahead. In that way we learn to be certain of You. The certainty of Your sovereignty chases worry away so that trust becomes our way of life. May we ever lean on the tenderness of Your heart toward us. Amen.

---

[66] Barbara Cameron (1949-)

September 23

DOUBT

Come unto Me, all you who labor and are heavy laden, and I will give you rest... Matthew 11:28

It is lonely to live in doubt. The intimacy with God, which had begun to feel familiar is fading as I turn my face from His with a gnawing suspicion that He is not sufficient for what I think I need.

Jesus cannot inhabit this place of doubt, so it is a dark and cold setting for my distrust—my sin. I don't like it here. I feel lost, fear-ridden, and, again, lonely. I've heard that He can handle my doubt, so why do I stay, trapped in misery?

His beckoning, light-filled presence awaits my repentance as He holds out His arms in welcoming grace. My steps are leaden, weighted with the pull of earthly desire. Yet I feel a stronger pull throbbing within the center of my soul. His voice calls, *Come unto Me all you who labor...* Such struggle, such labor—it should not be. Relief is offered.

Lifting my feet I head back toward the place where I left Him. One step of obedient trust and there He waits—my Father, my Friend! Warmth and light and tenderness shatter—as a laser beam— the loneliness of doubt.

Dear Father, You see all, You know all and You long for my trust.
Forgive me for pulling away; finding fake pleasure, for a while
in human endeavors. I long for your closeness.
Please keep calling. Amen.

September 24

THE TRUMPET SOUND

And the Lord spoke to Moses, saying: "Make two silver trumpets for yourself; you shall make them of hammered work; you shall use them for calling the congregation and for directing the movement of the camps."
Numbers 10:1-2

...in a moment, in the twinkling of an eye, at the last trumpet...
I Corinthians 15:52

I was reading the account in Numbers of instructions that God gave to Moses. Along with all the tabernacle plans, God throws in directions to make two silver trumpets.

There were many uses for these trumpets...I was amazed. Calling all the people to assemble—or simply the leaders to gather, sounding the signal to break camp—when and in what order to move out. And furthermore, when they needed to go to war, the trumpets were to sound the alarm calling forth God's help in rescuing them from their enemies.

Here's the highest and best use for these trumpets, in my opinion: They were to be blown in times of *gladness*! Gladness over their feasts, at the beginning of each month to rejoice over their offerings and remind the Lord God of His covenant.

Whose heart doesn't skip a beat at the sound of trumpets? *"Reveille"* is a call to assemble (or a call to wake up!) *"Taps"* is played, either peacefully at the end of a day or, mournfully at the end of a life. We hear military bands, marching bands and concert bands where the sound of trumpets is unmistakable.

God, I believe You have placed a longing for hearing the sound of trumpets within hearts. From thousands of years ago to the present day it evokes a response. Can it be that You want our ears to be attentive for the most glorious day in human history...the sounding of the last trumpet when Jesus comes to take us home? I want to be ready! Amen.

September 25

FALLOW GROUND

Sow for yourselves righteousness; reap in mercy; break up your fallow ground, for it is time to seek the LORD, till He comes and rains righteousness on you. Hosea 10:12

I was intrigued by the term "fallow ground" in this passage. Having been raised in a farming community, I would often see a field empty of crops. They told me it was lying fallow, but I didn't quite understand. Fallow ground is the tilling of land without sowing it for a season, that it might become more fruitful. Letting the soil rest. Often, however, when in this condition, it can become overgrown with thorns and weeds.

Thus the caretaker of the soil was careful to "break up" his fallow ground; i.e., to clear the field of weeds before sowing seed in it. In the spiritual realm, the prophet Hosea is saying to the children of Israel who are living in rebellion, "Break off your evil ways, repent of your sins, cease to do evil, and then the good seed of the word will have room to grow and bear fruit." As I consider my own life, I think my field has been empty for a while—unplowed, unplanted. It could be described as dormant, though I sense it is becoming fertile. I look forward to new growth.

Heavenly father, please plow my heart and plant your seed of righteousness. Let the crop be rich and abundant, with a harvest produced of cultivated patience. Upon reaping, may it show that seeds of faith and love can grow from earth that has lain fallow. Amen.

September 26

TROPHIES

Do you not know that those who run in a race all run, but one receives the prize? Run in such a way that you may obtain it... Now they do it to obtain a perishable crown, but we for an imperishable crown. I Corinthians 9:24, 25b

Pondering on this verse brings a long ago memory to mind. When our boys were young they were involved in Little League. One son was old enough to play; the other wanted to play but was only 5 years old. He was made a batboy for his friend's team. At the end of the season, our player received a "participation" trophy; while our *batboy* was given a big trophy engraved with his name. As you can imagine, this caused hard feelings between our boys!

How many times we work hard to receive a big trophy, wanting to win and have something to show for it! Then other people show up with accomplishments that make our effort seem small. I understand my son's hurt, because I have felt it in my own life. I want trophies to prove my worth, when all God really wants is to perfect the treasures with which He has blessed me. Instead of the envy that permeates my heart so often, because of someone else's perceived trophy, I must celebrate the work God wants to do through me, so at the last day I can lay an imperishable crown at His feet.

Oh, Heavenly Father, what a beautiful lesson! May I ever allow You to perfect the treasures You have already placed in me, learning to give You ALL the glory. Why would I ever desire to display a trophy? Help me! Amen.

September 27

PERCEPTION

You are my hiding place; You shall preserve me from trouble; You shall surround me with songs of deliverance. I will instruct you and teach you in the way you should go; I will guide you with My eye.
Psalm 32:7-8, 10

We used to live up in the hills outside of town. There were a lot of hills to navigate whenever we traveled anywhere. I remember very clearly, the day after an ice storm, that I found myself sliding toward the edge of the road where there was a deep drop off. I was terrified!

Strange how our perception alters in the presence of danger. What, in summer, is an unnoticed incline on the familiar road home becomes an insurmountable hill when coated with ice.

Panic heightens our awareness. I normally drove up and down that hill every day, without a thought of trouble. Yet as I slid sideways in my car, I saw it very differently: threatening and dangerous! Fortunately the car came to a stop as it hit the roadside gravel. It was so slippery I couldn't stand up when I got out of the car. I was so grateful when help arrived soon afterward.

Inching my way home later around a snow-packed curve, I was thinking of the need for my spirit to be aware of danger. God tells us He will guide us, surround us and deliver us. Life is full of pitfalls and we must learn to be watchful. The enemy lurks in the familiar and the routine. The complacency in which we tend to operate can turn life into a frightening slide if we are not attentive.

Heavenly Father, I must watch the road with Your eyes and grip the wheel of grace firmly so that You steer my course straight and true – and keep me out of the ditch! Amen.

September 28

MY MOUTH

I will bless the LORD at all times; His praise shall continually be in my mouth. Psalm 34:1

Out of the same mouth proceed blessing and cursing. My brethren, these things ought not to be so. James 3:10

Here we see the dichotomy of two distinct opposites spoken of in the same breath, so to speak. How can the same mouth blurt out a blessing, followed by a curse? But it happens so often, and it is a mystery. Every time I observe this duplicity in someone especially when it is me, I am challenged to be more careful of what comes from my mouth!

The prophet Jeremiah says that our words come straight from our hearts. I often, to my regret, allow an offensive word to slip out; mostly when I get hurt or angry. Before God got hold of my heart I always had a curse on the tip of my tongue, ready to be released. Now when I realize I have used a swear word, I immediately confess in prayer, asking forgiveness. I am quite sure the Holy Spirit is the one convicting me! It's a huge step toward my healing that I now claim forgiveness immediately. The cursing feels uncomfortable on my tongue and I am happy about that. I do not want to speak words that don't glorify God.

Dear Father, You always forgive me, clean up my tongue and set me straight once again. I want to keep the sense of Your presence within me, communing with my heart. My prayer is that I will pay heed to my every word. May I bless You and continually praise You never, ever dishonoring You with my mouth. Amen.

September 29

DETOURS

No temptation has overtaken you except such as is common to man, but God is faithful, who will not allow you to be tempted beyond what you are able, but with the temptation will also make the way of escape, that you may be able to bear it. 1 Corinthians 10:13

It is still summertime, and it seems there's a rush to get all the road repairs and construction completed in a short span of good weather. We all know what that means...we can be driving along and suddenly a bright orange sign pops up with an arrow and the dreaded word "DETOUR". And everything changes!'

As I look back on my own life's journey, I see detours that I didn't comprehend when I was younger. In so many instances when I was engaging in harmful behavior that could have absolutely ruined me, God would throw up a barrier to turn me from danger. Perhaps He would bring into my life a situation or a person to accomplish the turning aside; maybe even change my job or location. Oh, how I chafed under His discipline! Now, however, I am grateful for the detours.

Our life detours are not for punishment, although we often feel that way. They are to save us from getting stuck, from going where we would be in danger or to shape our character some other way. And the sweetness of this realization is that God always provides a way through or around that danger. I rest on the verse above, the perfect response to a detour.

Are you in the midst of an unwanted, painful, detour right now? Don't run from Him. There will be detours. Go obediently through them, but let your heart listen for His words of love and encouragement as you do.

Heavenly Father, teach me that often when I suffer, even if it breaks your heart to let it happen; in Your infinite love and wisdom You allow it because it is protection and care for me. Amen.

September 30

HARPS ON A WILLOW TREE

By the rivers of Babylon there we sat down, yes, we wept when we remembered Zion. We hung our harps upon the willows in the midst of it. For those who carried us away captive asked of us a song, and those who plundered us requested mirth, saying, "Sing us one of the songs of Zion!" Psalm 137:1-4

There is such a poignancy in these verses. The waters of Babylon's rivers, flooded by the tears of God's children, rolled endlessly on, unaware of the forlorn mourners on its banks. Joy had fled from the hearts of the captives; the victors' taunts rang in their ears. And, sadly, once-bright harps used for praises and song were abandoned and hung upon willow trees. *How could they sing the Lord's song in a strange land?*[67]

It seems to me that captivity still exists and we ask, "Can we sing as the waters of today's Babylon roll over us and carry our joy away? Or have the world's wicked ways captured our hearts, and engulfed the hope we once claimed?" The captors cry, "Let's hear you sing, show us your God." But with faces cast down, our lips fail to praise. Sad to say in our despair, with stiff, stubborn fingers, we've hung up our harps. Who will sing the Lord's song in our land if we don't?

Oh, God, as Your children may we pull down our harps from the weighted-down willow tree and cry out with thanksgiving and joy. Singing amidst the darkness of the turbulent night, help us pluck out a sweet melody. Amen.

---

[67] Psalm 137:4

October 1

UNDERBRUSH

And do not be conformed to this world, but be transformed by the renewing of your mind, that you may prove what is that good, and acceptable, and perfect, will of God. Romans 12:2

To console those who mourn in Zion, to give them beauty for ashes, the oil of joy for mourning, the garment of praise for the spirit of heaviness; that they may be called trees of righteousness, the planting of the LORD, that He may be glorified. Isaiah 61:3

Walking in autumn along the road I am gazing at the underbrush and, looking into my life, seeing a parallel somehow. A new layer of dead leaves covers budding growth, much as the stratum of disobedience I am struggling with today threatens to smother my faith, and the jungle of my tangled past strives to entwine my roots.

But then I look up. From tangled underbrush, twisted and dry, to trees standing tall against the sky, understanding that the leafy mulch and withered branches return to dust to be absorbed, nurturing the soil.

So it is within my soul. God says He will take away the former things if I will keep my eyes on Him, and from the snarl of sin and shame He'll straighten, nurture, rearrange, and raise me up to praise His name.

Holy Father, I beg You to transform me, renew my mind and use the mulch of my tangled past to nurture my life and make of me a tree of righteousness. Amen.

October 2

ON THE HEELS OF THE STORM

Restore us, O God of hosts; cause Your face to shine, and we shall be saved. Psalm 80:7

Snowbound—housebound—by the storm, I sit by the window contemplating the distortion it has created. Evergreens, shrubs and ferns are shrouded in white, their branches bowed low beneath the weight of the snow. All is silent, hushed under a canopy of gray-white sky.

Then through a gap in the frosty boughs a gleam of light appears and the sun breaks forth, transforming the overhead to blue. Experience tells me that soon the snow will melt from the sun's warmth and the laden branches will slowly lift as their burden vanishes; familiar shapes and colors will return.

Sometimes I am bent low beneath the burden left by a storm in my life; there is no color in the periphery of my vision. I need to remember that the Son of God longs to break forth in my heart. Experience tells me His presence will melt the cares and bring back sparkle and clarity. Then my arms will lift in praise.

Maybe I can only see a glimpse of Him through the shrouded trees of my pain, but it is enough; a harbinger of more to come.

Heavenly Father, I know sometimes that You allow storms into our lives; that gray sky distortion brings confusion and sadness. But Your promise is sure: You never leave us. So help us to watch for the light to break through. Amen.

October 3

GOD IN THE SHADOWS

And He said, "My presence shall go with you, and I will give you rest." Exodus 33:14

I have been reading and pondering the Book of Esther. I noticed that nowhere in the whole book is God's name mentioned. I think it is fascinating that a story such as this could be written without the name of the main character being mentioned! So I wonder...Does God disappear when His name is unspoken? Does His presence vanish when it is unacknowledged? NO! He is eternally sovereign, overarching all human history. God said to Moses, *"I AM WHO I AM".*[68]

Of all the names attributed to God in the Bible, "I AM" is one of the most intriguing. With this name, God declares His eternal, ever present existence; and reveals that He is always the same; has always existed and will always exist.

He has a **purpose**: to preserve His people. He has a **promise**: to redeem them and bring them home. He works by His **pattern:** conviction, mourning, repentance, redemption—a pattern repeated throughout Scripture. God is everywhere; perhaps in the shadows, yet in His sovereignty ever **present**; His **plan** is in place...working according to His purpose, His p**attern**, His **promise** to redeem His people.

I don't want Him only to be in the shadows of my life, but be *seen* through me. Whether or not I speak His name or acknowledge His presence He is there. He promised.

Heavenly Father, You are an amazing God! It is so important for us to comprehend the fact of Your presence, serving and redeeming Your people. Even unseen, un-named, perhaps unnoticed, You ARE. It's a promise we can cling to forever. Thank You. Amen.

---

[68] *Exodus 3:14*

October 4

MEMORIES

Do not remember the former things, nor consider the things of old. Behold, I will do a new thing, Now it shall spring forth; Shall you not know it? I will even make a road in the wilderness and rivers in the desert. Isaiah 43:19

Memories play a huge part in our lives! Good and bad, they are what make up our past, color our present day, and hopefully bring direction to our future. God dwells in the midst of all that makes up our memories.

I was nine years old when I lost my mother to polio. We were living in a tiny town in Wyoming, small enough that all the children in town played together. I have such wonderful memories of the things we did, the fun we had. It is amazing that as I think of that town what resonates is not the grief from losing Mother, but the happy memories; childhood adventures, running free. I believe it is God's mercy, covering the pain with joyful reminders in order that I can look into the loss with a heart that is healing because of the knowledge of His presence. He was there then. He is here, now.

Searching through my Bible, I found the above verse. Even though it says to forget the former things, I believe it means not to hang our hats there; we can't *forget*, our memories are part of us, but we can keep ourselves looking forward in hope of the new thing God promises. This passage jumped out at me today and couldn't be ignored!

Heavenly Father, I have been in a valley lately, but reading Your Word renews my spirit as I find that You are all about doing something new – in me! Please take my past – my memories – and breathe on them, forming a beautiful and useful stream in my desert. Thank You for memory; such a gift! Amen.

October 5

CONSIDERING JOY

Consider it pure joy, my brothers and sisters, whenever you face trials of many kinds; because you know the testing of your faith produces perseverance. Let perseverance finish its work so that you may be mature and complete, not lacking anything. James 1:2, 3 (NIV)

Looking unto Jesus…who for the joy set before Him, endured the cross…consider Him. Hebrews 12:2, 3

I'm staring heartache in the face…seeing a painful road ahead. And I'm certainly not eager to embrace it and call it joy. So it's with a bit of rebellion that I recall this passage of scripture. But as I look deeper into the words, God tells me why.

I am to walk through the trial, building a strengthening faith with each step. When this particular trial has passed, the joy that awaits, though it will be tinged with sorrow, will be a new knowledge of a faithful God. His sustaining presence along the road lifts me to a higher level of completeness in Himself.

It's difficult to quash the rebelliousness of my humanity; to open myself in anticipation when dread stalks each moment. But unless I do, I will never know the reality of faith-infused joy. Jesus walked a painful path, too, for the joy that was set before Him. So, considering Him…I'm ready for my path. I will consider it joy.

Heavenly Father. I am determined to seek Your joy. But we both know how quickly and easily that desire can dissipate. Please keep me focused on Jesus, my Savior. Amen.

October 6

YARDSTICK

...do not rejoice that the spirits submit to you, but rejoice that your names are written in heaven. Luke 10:20 (NIV)

Am I now trying to win the approval of human beings, or of God? Galatians 1:10a (NIV)

We so often get our priorities skewed! Jesus had commissioned 70 disciples to go out to share the gospel. They returned with joy and were so excited that "even the demons are subject to us in Your name."[69] Jesus cautions them, however, to be even more grateful that their own names were written in Heaven.

I lay in bed the other night and found myself ruminating, measuring the good deeds I had done, examining them against the yardstick of success that I tend to use to establish my worth. As night fell and my head rested on the softness of my pillow I contemplated the activity that defined my day and I wondered, "How did I do?"

I'm coming to realize I must use a different measuring tool. Should I not be asking my Maker..."Did I grow today? Did I draw nearer to You? Am I more like You?" Even though I know I cannot earn "Brownie points" with God, I still struggle with comparing my works to what I imagine His expectations to be.

Father, I think I should use a yardstick that measures distance rather than height; one that will show how near I am to You rather than how high the pile of good deeds. I must rest in Christ's completed work and simply enjoy fellowship with You, because as hard as I might strive there is no way to measure up by my works. I yield to You. Amen.

---

69 Luke 10:17

October 7

MERCIES

This I recall to my mind, therefore I have hope. Through the Lord's mercies we are not consumed, because His compassions fail not. They are new every morning; great is Your faithfulness. "The Lord is my portion,"' says my soul, "therefore I hope in Him."
Lamentations 3:23

I have been studying God's mercy, and lately I seem to see that word everywhere I look in the scripture. Mercy seems to run through the Bible like a silver cord. Last week, for no particular reason, I opened to the third chapter of Lamentations. Here is part of my journal entry for that day: "Mercies, compassions—plural! They are myriad; more and more noticeable the more I know Him. Every morning new ones." There are a couple of *therefores* here. When you see the word *therefore* go back and see what it's there for. Therein lies instruction!

It's so important, when in crisis, to call to mind past mercies. We are living *at* His mercy; *in* His mercy, *because* of His mercies that cover us—new every morning. It is *through* His mercies (the vehicle He uses) that we live—that we are not consumed. Think of how the flames of our desires and earthly failings would otherwise consume us. Think: bad decisions, the overt and covert rebellion and disobedience. Some of my negative behavior in the past (and today, too) would certainly have zapped me had it not been for His mercies; I am so aware of that!

I thank You, Heavenly Father. How I must have grieved You – and still do, often. I am so grateful for Your mercy; Your compassions. You have been, I recall with joy, merciful to me. May my soul always seek You. Amen.

October 8

HAND ON MY SHOULDER

And when I saw Him, I fell at His feet as dead. But He laid His right hand on me, saying to me, "Don't be afraid..." Rev. 1:17

There is an ocean of meaning in these few vital words that begin the book of Revelation. I wonder how I could have read this verse so many times, and missed the beauty of this truth.

What a sight to behold: Jesus, in all His transcendent beauty; His face shining like the sun! No wonder John fell on his face as though he were dead, overwhelmed with the vision to the point of unconsciousness. I stop for a moment to ponder, to consider if I have ever really *seen* Jesus in my mind's eye. I think not. I have skimmed over these words, taking for granted the power revealed here.

But then, gently, His hand reached out and He touched me! All that power and majesty swathed and channeled into the words that meet me in my need, "Be not afraid." I am chastened. I am challenged; I am changed by that tender voice, that nail-pierced hand on my shoulder.

So I ask myself...have I, living in abject fear, never really seen You, Jesus? Have I become so jaded in the efforts to run my life that I have ignored the splendor of Your majesty? Have I become so numbed by the noise of my frantic voice that I am insensitive to the sound of Yours?

Heavenly Father, You tell me that those who read these words, and hear them, are blessed. I realize I've been fearful all of my life, never allowing myself to hear the gentle voice of Jesus, and I cry my gratitude to Him, His hand on my shoulder, His voice in my ear, His promise to my heart is all I need. Amen.

October 9

MOONLIGHT GOLD

I will give you the treasures of darkness, and hidden riches of secret places, so that you may know that I the LORD, who call you by name am the God of Israel. Isaiah 45:3

Treasures of darkness. I don't see treasures very often when pain fills my days, and encompasses my nights, but God promises them to me. I have heard it said that it is possible to gather gold, where it may be had, by moonlight.

I guess it is true that gold is visible in the dimmest light if one but looks. Its brilliant nature doesn't need the sun to bring forth its gleam. Perhaps its beauty is more precious if it is glimpsed in the pale glow of moonlight than in the blaze of noonday sun.

And, so I think it is true that our faith, triumphing in the dark night of trial and suffering, shines with holy fire. A transcendent shimmer that could not be seen in the bright sunshine of seeming prosperity. So many gems and precious metals come from the deep parts of the earth. Treasures of darkness.

God, please make me shine for you with the gold you are mining by moonlight in my life. Amen.

October 10

THE REPENTANCE WAIT

Therefore the LORD will wait, that He may be gracious to you; and therefore He will be exalted, that He may have mercy on you. For the Lord is a God of justice; blessed are all those who wait for Him. And though the Lord gives you the bread of adversity and the water of affliction…your ears shall hear a word behind you saying, "this is the way, walk in it." Isaiah 30:18, 20

Recently I was involved in a personal incident that I am still attempting to resolve. I was challenged in a way that knocked me to my knees. As time moves on, I continue to seek comfort from God. He speaks gently to me through His Word. I read an old favorite of mine, *For thus says the Lord God, the Holy One of Israel… "In returning and rest you shall be saved; in quietness and confidence shall be your strength."*[70] As much as I treasure this verse, the passage doesn't end here. The last part of it reads, *But you would not.* God is speaking to stubborn, stiff-necked people, His children. Just like me.

Throughout experiencing the bread of adversity and the water of affliction there is a way to return, rest, repent and wait. In my crying out to Him He hears, and offers me the opportunity to repent and rest!

Waiting is a settled confidence, an awareness of His merciful guiding voice; a plan, if you will, for healing, acceptance and change. I can only truly wait within the blessing of repentance. How precious of Him to tenderly reach down and touch my wounded heart.

My dear Father, for Your justice and grace that surround me, I give You my willing, waiting heart in thanksgiving.
Work Your plan in me. Amen.

---

[70] Isaiah 30:15

October 11

BREATH OF LIFE

And the LORD God formed man from the dust of the ground and breathed into his nostrils the breath of life; and man became a living being. Genesis 2:7

Some time ago we were under a haze of smoky air here where I live as well as in most of our country. Forest fires, house fires, weather issues had us thinking about what exactly we are inhaling. Pondering about what we usually take for granted brings these thoughts on breathing to my mind.

A breath is taken without thinking. It began at my birth with a tender slap and continues until extinguished by the same Breath that made me a living soul. The ability to breathe empowers my physical body to flourish. How marvelous!

Are faith and trust as natural for me as inhaling and exhaling, the means by which I process elements from earth's atmosphere? The Source of my physical breath, the enabling Power for my soul to flourish, longs for my dependence upon Him. It doesn't take long when my breathing is compromised to become grateful for the normal ease of taking a deep breath and to feel strong compassion for those whose every breath is an effort.

Father, I am chagrined by the truth here. Incomplete trust and weak faith are like gasping for air, taking in merely enough to survive. And I wonder…am I inhaling the vital oxygen of Your presence? Processing it properly? Exhaling Your peace? Or am I simply gasping? It bears thinking about. Amen.

October 12

MOSAIC

Even to your old age, I am He, and even to gray hairs I will carry you! I have made and I will bear; even I will carry, and will deliver you. Isaiah 46:4

Glancing in the mirror the other day, I was not at all pleased at what I was viewing! It seemed that age has crept in swiftly and set its seal on my face. Wrinkles and spots have appeared overnight. Surely it wasn't this bad yesterday!

That was a bit of disappointment touching my morning. But it made me aware of how much importance I have attached to my appearance, figuring that it defined me somehow. Although I hate to admit it, unless I *looked* good, I considered myself NOT good. And so I began to ponder my life...looking into the mirror of God's Word.

My life seemed useless in my estimation, as it was all spent on pleasing myself. But those shards of shattered clay that I would have kicked aside have found usefulness in God's hand. He is creating an object of beauty from the broken pieces—a mosaic.

A mosaic cannot be made from wholeness, only from brokenness. The years of stumbling, running from God, selfishness and fear; though showing the jagged edges caused by rebellion, somehow form part of the pattern when placed into a mosaic by the loving hands of the Master Designer. He is able to take whatever I bring from wherever I've been, and use it for the mosaic He is creating with me.

Heavenly Father, forgive me for paying so much attention to how I look. As my aging becomes more and more visible, may the beauty of Jesus' polishing of my wrinkles with grace visibly shine through. Amen.

October 13

RUNNING WITH FOOTMEN

If you have run with the footmen and they have wearied you, then how can you contend with horses? And if in the land of peace, in which you trusted, they wearied you, then how will you do in the floodplain of the Jordan? Jeremiah 12:5.

Reading through Jeremiah the other day I was intrigued and challenged by this verse. What if, in the living of life, we can't keep up with footmen? I looked up "footmen" to help gain the meaning of this passage. As Jeremiah was complaining about his lot in life, God is reminding him through this comparison that it could get worse. There will always be hard things to endure. It's a given.

But God often allows these hard things into our lives to train us, to strengthen us and harden our resolve. Especially when we may be asked to run against "horses" someday. I realize it's an analogy, asking us to examine our efforts—whether or not we are doing our best. If challenged to run faster, could we? Would we? If we don't stand firm when things are easy, what will happen when things get tough, when persecution comes hurtling against us? Because it will.

God uses the strength we gain from running the race before us with determination and endurance to build up our confidence in His presence;, as we see Him sufficient for each battle. God's question to Jeremiah is so basic—an examination of thoughts and intents.

Heavenly Father, I am longing to run my race in a way that brings honor to You. May I take joy in where I am right now, even though I know there may be a harder race ahead. Thank you for the assurance of Your uplifting, encouraging presence. I lean into it. Amen.

October 14

SWEET FRAGRANCE

Now thanks be to God who always leads us in triumph in Christ, and through us diffuses the fragrance of His knowledge in every place. 2 Corinthians 2:14

Everybody loves a parade…but a triumphal procession is so much more. I remember a time when I was young and rode a home-town float in the 4th of July parade, wearing a black bathing suit and thinking I was hot stuff! The excitement and applause of the crowd was heady.

As I read this verse I thought of another procession, in which I now long to take part. This parade may only have the applause of One, but as I learn more and more of Him, that knowledge makes my heart glow.

You see, there is an eternal purpose in this parade. It is not simply to entertain, but to display and diffuse the fragrance of Jesus to the observing crowd. God is the drum major here, leading the community of His people in triumph as the band plays its rendition of *Hallelujah Chorus*. The onlookers become aware of a subtle sweet fragrance, the perfume of Christ's presence.

Father, as we march along behind You, our Leader, may we ever be conscious of the aroma we are spreading; trusting You to waft the peace of Your presence, letting you be known. Amen.

October 15

THE RIDE

Lord, my heart is not haughty, nor my eyes lofty. Neither do I concern myself with great matters, nor with things too profound for me. Surely I have calmed and quieted my soul, like a weaned child with his mother; like a weaned child is my soul within me.
Psalm 131:1, 2

I am sure that many of us have great memories of the county fairs and carnivals we enjoyed when we were younger. Perhaps many of you still do enjoy them. I remember my favorite, the Tilt-A-Whirl. Round and round, spinning rapidly. I never cared for rides that would turn me upside down, but loved getting dizzy—in a somewhat safe manner. My husband, though, tells me he got sick every time he climbed on! I loved the lights on the midway, the smell of cotton candy and the feeling of abandoning myself to a good time.

As age creeps up on me, I look back and view much of my life as if it were a carnival ride. The Tilt-A-Whirl, for example: faster and faster, the turning becoming more and more frantic. Oh, how I loved the spin, enjoyed the rushing, the demands and the thrill of importance.

But now it would seem, the ride is over. The spinning has lost its appeal. I have to acknowledge I am worn out. I can't keep up; I can't compete any more. I step out: dizzy, light-headed and reaching for support. God is waiting for me...to calm my spinning head, put my feet upon the ground and redirect my steps. At the same time however, I sense the flashing lights of the midway beckoning me still. I want to ride again...there is more to enjoy, more usefulness with which to serve You, but…

O, Lord, help me choose a slower ride this time. Amen.

October 16

OBSTRUCTION

Then the word of the LORD came to Jeremiah, saying, "Behold, I am the LORD, the God of all flesh. Is there anything too hard for Me?"
Jeremiah 32:26-27

Often on a trip we have parked beside a river. Maybe to have a picnic, or simply a rest on our journey. I remember one occasion in which I was sitting quietly, and I observed a log stuck there in the river…victim, perhaps, to a huge storm; laid flat with its roots to the sky, settled deeply into the bed of the stream. The river, undeterred, flowed on; its only concession to this obstruction was the pattern of ripples that resulted. So, as always when out in nature I ponder an application God may be showing me.

Yes, many times we find an obstruction in our lives that perhaps has us feeling stuck. But I see here that the river of God's love and grace flows steadily *around* all the obstacles that life's storms toss down in my path. Sometimes the obstruction is so large that it cannot be moved; sometimes I despair in my struggle to move past it.

But through the murmur of the water here on the riverbank, I hear God's whisper. He reminds me of His constancy, and I see anew the lovely lacy froth of bubbling ripples that is only made beautiful *because* of the obstruction.

Dear Father, I thank You for this beauty that only You can cause to happen. I'm remembering that You are able to create loveliness even from a situation that threatens to undo me, and trusting that You will keep the grace-filled river flowing around the obstructions that may come! Amen.

October 17

ROAD TRIP

You will show me the path of life; in Your presence is fullness of joy; at Your right hand are pleasures forevermore. Psalm 16:11

Both my husband and I enjoy road trips. He loves to drive, it relaxes him. And I, well, I love to lean on his alertness and abilities. THAT relaxes me!! We put music on and sing along with uplifting hymns and praise songs…as well as songs that bring back memories of our youth! I was thinking that driving with your best friend beside you, hearts in harmony, singing together and filled with expectation of what is ahead has to be among one of life's greatest pleasures. And I can't help but think there are many parallels corresponding to our spiritual journey. What do you think? Can you see them, too?

When I get ready for a trip, perhaps I am overly concerned with preparations and provisions. I seem to think it's up to me to have what we need at hand at all times. I wonder if I embark on my spiritual journey with the same mindset, thinking we ourselves are responsible in to provide for needs along the way, forgetting that God promises *His* provisioning, His protection and His preservation. Do I really have the faith to let go and hold only to His hand for all we will require? It bears considering. I understand that we have some responsibility to prepare, but perhaps it shouldn't be such an all-consuming effort as I've allowed it to become.

Heavenly Father, walking with You should be a joy-filled trust journey, free of concerns for the future. Teach me to let go in faith, and simply let You love me and lead me. Amen.

October 18

CRUMBS

I will be fully satisfied as with the richest of foods; with singing lips my mouth will praise you. Psalm 63:5 (NIV)

It seems to me we humans are very much ruled by our hungers. Cravings beg to be satisfied and we are not always careful where we seek satiation. Crumbs fall my way as I crouch beneath the world's table. Crumbs that tantalize, yet leave me begging for more—crumbs of approval, of material things or physical comfort. My mouth is accustomed to the flavors of the old life. They may taste good, but then they turn bitter, demanding more; always longing for more.

I need more to take away the dry acid taste of flavors that never satisfy, the leeks and garlic of the Egypt season in my life. It should be no surprise to me, but nonetheless I am often amazed at my emptiness after a banquet of crumbs.

Somewhere my ear picks up the call of the Lord of Hosts announcing a feast. Delectable, rich treats are offered, to be enjoyed by all who choose to attend. I'm invited, as is everyone. So why do I still sit here with hands extended toward the crumbs? As flavorful as they may be, there is no comparison between crumbling fragments and a full bite of satisfying richness.

Heavenly Father, I want to accept your invitation. I am really hungry, and long for the nourishment You can offer. Amen.

October 19

A-A – H-H!

Let your conduct be without covetousness; be content with such things as you have. For He Himself has said, "I will never leave you nor forsake you." Hebrews 13:5

I was wondering the other day if I have really let God say this to me? Would I behave differently if I allowed this powerful whisper to dominate my heart? *I will never leave you.* Perhaps I can liken it to coming home after a vacation, or other time away. The comfort of my home, my own bed and my own routine fills me with relief and contentment fills me.

I am learning the truth that God is at work in my life every moment. Every conversation, and every interruption is of Him. Though I may devise a plan for my day, I must be ready for Him to jump in with another. My tendency is to rush frantically about, trying to arrive at the place where I already am: in God's presence. I yearn for the deep rest that complete trust brings, to always feel the peaceful feeling of a first night back in my own bed. A-a – h-h!

It is true that one needs to get away sometimes in order to realize the blessings of home and to fully appreciate what we have. Each time I step inside our house after a long trip and inhale the familiar scent that is *us*, my heart lifts in praise. In the spiritual sense, as well, when I've been away from the familiar, not having my usual time with God, my longing to be alone with Him is palpable. I desire to reconnect with intimacy and breathe His pure air. In response I whisper, "A-a-h-h."

Heavenly Father, You show Yourself so faithful and patient with me. Accepting the truth of Your constant presence affords me the beautiful sense of A-a – h-h! May I rest contented in this way – always. Amen.

October 20

YOU WHO LABOR

Come to me, all you who labor and are heavy laden and I will give you rest. Take my yoke upon you and learn from Me, for I am gentle and lowly in heart and you will find rest for your souls.
Matthew 11:28-29

Exhausted, we took a week away at the beach. My body and spirit were in desperate need of rest. But what, exactly, is rest? That question followed me to the ocean's shore. The answer? We find rest when we give up control. When we stop working so hard to get things done and begin to trust completely in God's work in us and our lives. It takes time to stop and give up, in a sense, and let rest take over. God considers this quite important, as He tells us: *"Cease striving, and know that I am God."*[71]

I am learning that rest doesn't mean sitting immobile, doing nothing. Rest is walking along the beach, enjoying the power and majesty of Creation. Rest is finding unusual pieces of driftwood; cooking in a different kitchen; worshipping in a different church perhaps. Rest is a restoring of our mind, spending time in Scripture, finding the beauty of what <u>is</u>, and allowing that beauty to overtake the striving and rushing about that characterizes most of our struggling. It is taking the time to find a renewed joy in God, just for who He is. I spent a lot of time in the Scriptures, just reading and absorbing truth. What a luxury!

Yes, Father, I have found rest. Thank You for time with You, the Lover of my soul. May I never forget that Your promised rest awaits even in the midst of at-home busyness. Amen.

---

[71] Psalm 46:10

October 21

OVERSEER

For you were like sheep going astray, but have now returned to the Shepherd and Overseer of your souls. 1 Peter 2:25

What a fascinating concept, God as my overseer! Webster says an overseer is "a person who watches and directs the work of other people in order to be sure that a job is done correctly."

Somehow, the word Overseer has taken on a negative connotation...perhaps because of the tales of slaves being persecuted by them. In truth, however, it is a most blessed occupation, as we see when we tie this together with the truth of God's abiding presence within us. It brings a satisfying concept to light and consciousness. In order for God to be the Overseer, Bishop, Guard and Shepherd of our souls, it requires His constant consistent presence, and we can trust the One Who promises to oversee the whole of our lives.

We are like sheep going astray. I know I was, yet His presence never left me—never! He stayed until this precious little sheep came back to the fold where as my Shepherd He can—and will— fully perform the joyful job of watchfulness.

Oh Lord, You are my Shepherd! And as such You become the Overseer of my life. How very grateful I am to realize this, and begin a new awareness of the truth of Your loving watch care over me. Amen!

October 22

FLAMING SWORD

Then the LORD God said, "Behold, the man has become like one of Us, to know good and evil. And now, lest he put out his hand and take also of the tree of life, and eat, and live forever" – the LORD God sent him out of the garden of Eden to till the ground from which he was taken. So He drove out the man; and He placed cherubim at the east of the Garden of Eden, and a flaming sword which turned every way, to guard the way to the tree of life." Genesis 3:22-24

Banned from the Garden, Eden became only a memory for Adam and Eve, For us as well, the place where our hearts are at home is guarded by cherubim and a flaming sword; keeping us, as surely as it did Adam and Eve, away.

We call it punishment for our sinfulness, and feel a sense of sadness and loss. The truth, however, is that it is so much more than simply harsh discipline. It was—it is—an act of love by God, the beginning of the unfolding of His plan of salvation. Lest we partake of the tree of life and live forever in our miserable, human sinful, state; Jesus came, He died and rose!

So the cherubim guard the tree of life until we partake of its fruit in Heaven. And Jesus' blood now serves as the flaming sword, guarding us who trust in Him; knowing that one day we will be granted re-entry and live forever with Him in the brand new Eden.

Heavenly Father, we eagerly anticipate that day, our hearts thrilling with the truth that You are making all things new. And as part of that, You are making us new as well! Even on this imperfect earth, we dwell in joy! Amen.

October 23

PIECES

Do not be anxious about anything, but in every situation, by prayer and petition, with thanksgiving, present your requests to God. And the peace of God, which transcends all understanding, will guard your hearts and your minds in Christ Jesus. Philippians 4:6-7 (NIV)

Anxiousness slithers throughout my mind like a serpent, entwining itself in my thoughts. "What if's?" crowd into my prayers and peace seems far away. I look at my life right now and it appears to be like a new jigsaw puzzle just overturned onto the table, a pile of pieces.

There's a sort of method to putting together a puzzle, just as there is in our lives. God's recipe is clear in the above verse. Just as we begin putting a puzzle together by finding the corner pieces and then the border, so we begin in life by turning our anxiety into prayer. Next, petition accompanied by thanksgiving brings peace. The thanksgiving piece is really important, because by doing so we are yielding our control to God and acknowledging His sovereignty.

Using the puzzle analogy, we have then assembled the border. So life gets easier as piece by piece the whole picture begins to settle into place. Safely guarded by our faith in Jesus, we can move forward peacefully as a beautiful picture becomes visible.

Father, my petition is that You protect my heart. It feels as though it is shattered into pieces – my mind fragmented with anxious concerns. Guard it, please. Solve the puzzle by the peace beyond my understanding that is promised to me through Jesus's sacrifice. Anxiety ceases and I gratefully trust Your hands to put together all the pieces. Amen.

October 24

BROOMS

If we confess our sins, He is faithful and just to forgive us our sins and cleanse us from all unrighteousness. 1 John 1:9

I swept the floor clean of debris this morning. I did it yesterday morning and I will do it again tomorrow. It is autumn and wet outside; and somehow a constant stream of dirt tracks itself across my floor. I wonder why I am sweeping so vigorously when I know it will be clean for such a short time. Why do I do it over and over and over? It seems useless.

But I can hear God's voice nudging me and I remember how many times He has swept me clean, knowing that before much time has elapsed there will be dirt tracks across my heart and I will have to come running to Him and ask to be cleaned up again. How can He do it over and over and over? Does He ever consider it useless?

No. Because He promised to cleanse and forgive me when I confess my sins, as stated in the above verse. Perhaps the joy of a restored relationship sparkling like new brings satisfaction to Him, something like my momentarily clean floor brings me.

So, Father, with a new perspective I sweep and praise You, thanking you for Your broom of love that never rests, but ever waits to whisk the mud from the floor of my heart. Amen.

October 25

PARADOX

For you know the grace of our Lord Jesus Christ, that though He was rich, yet for your sakes He became poor, that you through His poverty might become rich.
2 Corinthians 8:9

...as sorrowful, yet always rejoicing; as poor, yet making many rich; as having nothing, and yet possessing all things.
2 Corinthians 6:10

A paradox is a statement or situation that may be true but seems impossible or difficult to understand because it contains two opposite facts or characteristics. Upon reading these passages I feel I can comment based on my own experience.

I am of the wealthy poor; my riches unseen by human eyes. I am surrounded by the poverty-stricken wealthy, proudly preening goods and success. They are empty-eyed and frantic, searching for one more dollar, one more accolade.

I was once as poor as they until I struck the gold of eternal wealth. I feel deeply the affluence of my soul; my heart abounds in the luxury of love that must be invested wisely. The penury of this world—its destitution—swathed in fragile veils of opulence needs desperately to mine the vein of gold that awaits at the foot of the cross. In so doing, people will exchange possessions for the possessing of treasure untold.

Heavenly Father, looking at the treasure You gave Your Son to provide for me makes my heart fill with gratitude and praise. Forgive my sometime search for worldly riches. I am satisfied with the wealth of Your merciful love. Amen.

October 26

POWER

He (Christ) is not weak in dealing with you, but is powerful among you. For to be sure, he was crucified in weakness yet he lives by God's power. Likewise we are weak in him, yet by God's power we will live with him to serve you. 2 Corinthians 13:3b, 4 (NIV)

As I sit contemplating the difficulty I'm having living a life of victory, I'm mesmerized by the tree outside my window in the midst of a windstorm. I have watched this tree grow larger, taller and fuller each Spring from its beginnings as a new young tree sapling. But today it is under attack by the wind. Gust after gust bends the trunk far to the right, yet during each pause in the onslaught it rights itself.

What keeps it rebounding to erectness?

It is the *life* in the tree; its deep roots vibrant, strong and healthy, powerful enough to bring the tree upright again. And I am coming to realize there is a power that I often fail to recognize—resurrection power—in me. And even though I might be bowed and bent by the tempting winds of comfort and old habits, this resurrection power rests in me to enable, strengthen and remind me that I am dead to sin. It can control me no more. That old life cannot break me nor throw me to the ground!

Heavenly Father, You have shown me that my soul is alive through Jesus' resurrection. He will stand me upright...with the power of His life in me. May I never be bent too low to respond to Your power. Amen.

October 27

NOT BY SIGHT

For we walk by faith and not by sight. 2 Corinthians 5:7

Do I need to have these above words emblazoned across each window, each mirror, in each direction I look? Indeed upon my forehead! Because I am anxious to know what awaits: I want to see ahead. Why, I wonder? Maybe it's so I can plan my day—my way.

My human nature pokes its nose into my thoughts and demands satisfaction, to know what to expect. I get frightened when I can't see the future. *Do not be afraid. Stand still and you will see the salvation of the LORD."*[72]

I'm discovering I trust the *illusion* that I am in control rather than the fact of God's sovereignty. The reality is that He rules, not I. Even though I have moments of faith; truly walking in faith must be a life-style, not merely occasional sprints. It is steadily plodding along the dusty road of life with a willing trustful obedience.

So maybe it *would* be a good idea to paste the words of this verse wherever I look, to remind myself that I cannot see. Indeed, faith means that I will not...but I must keep walking anyway. The only way I will be able to see is with eyes of faith, my spirit standing still before Him. In the words of yet another scripture, *Be still and know that I am God.*[73]

Heavenly Father, this brings me up short. To realize that I do not fully trust You but rather continue to be concerned with my own plans and how I can bring them to pass. Still my soul, and guide my steps. Amen.

---

[72] Exodus 14:13

[73] Psalm 46:10

October 28

KNEADING

For it is God who works in you both to will and to do for His good pleasure. Philippians 2:13

Sometimes I think that we neglect allowing God to "do His good pleasure." We somehow cling to the idea that we are in control. Reading this verse I am reminded of something I pondered after my mother-in-law had tried to teach me to make bread. Unfortunately, I never did master that skill! But I was amazed at the working of the dough beneath my hands—a first for me! Fascinated at the response of the dough: the more I push, the more it springs back. Mother says, "The more you knead, the better it likes it."

But as I read the verse again, I thought, "This is where I am right now—again—trying to understand my present situation. I feel a bit like a mound of dough on a floured board under God's hand. He is kneading me; and teaching me that just as kneading helps activate the yeast, thus making good bread, His working on me activates the Spirit life He's placed in me.

I know I am not alone in discovering this truth; and I am hoping that if you find yourself in a similar circumstance, when nothing seems to be going right, you may be reminded of how our heavenly Father's hands stay poised to work on us as we yield to His tender touch.

Father, help me to understand that to serve You well, I need to be kneaded. So, please knead me and form me into bread that will feed and nurture others. Thank You. Amen.

October 29

COMPARISON

And we all, who with unveiled faces contemplate the Lord's glory, are being transformed into his image with ever-increasing glory, which comes from the Lord, who is the Spirit. 2 Corinthians 3:18 (NIV)

For several years, my husband and I lived and worked on a small island as caretakers for a camp. I remember one day I was soaking up some sun, seated on a fallen log. With the beauty of nature surrounding me, I happened to glance up to see an eagle perched high in a tree. He was peering at me intently; at least so it seemed. While I marveled at the power and majesty of his existence, somehow I felt uncomfortable as the object of his scrutiny.

I never forgot that feeling. I thought of it later when I caught myself perched high in the tree of spiritual superiority, looking down upon another person; and I remembered the eagle. Stunned, I realized that looking down upon others is an uncomfortable perch when I look up into the face of the One to Whom I should be conforming.

Father, I have no doubt that You see this comparison. Help me remember always that I am called to see others through Your eyes. Forgive the pride that makes me ever feel superior to anyone. Amen.

October 30

CONFIDENCE

Now may the God of hope fill you with all joy and peace in believing, that you may abound in hope by the power of the Holy Spirit.
Romans 15:13

So many times I begin a year with plans and determination, only to watch days slip by without reaching any goals. I truly tried to be intentional, sticking to what I'd like to get done. Now as the year is winding down I realize that I haven't really appropriated this truth: *A man's heart plans his way, but the LORD directs his steps.*[74] So I must be open to interruptions in my plans, if God so directs! Yes, the year is winding down, but it isn't over yet, so there is still time to reach a goal or two!

I really do appreciate a couple of words I read the other day: "confidently anticipate," because they are balm to my soul, underscoring my intention to live in anticipation and wonder. Giving in to the discouragement the enemy throws at me is not a good idea! God promises if we will, hope will replace discouragement. Is discouragement nipping at your heels? Your hope sagging? Go to the Source of hope that you may anticipate with confidence!

Father, here I am coming to You, the true hope-Source. Let confident hope be what fills my heart, my mind, and my senses. May the hope that only You can bring overflow. Amen.

---

[74] Proverbs 16:9

October 31

AWAKENING

With my soul I have desired You in the night yes, by my spirit within me I will seek You early; for when Your judgments are in the earth, the inhabitants of the world will learn righteousness. Isaiah 26:9

I overslept this morning. God had awakened me, and I sensed Him asking me to spend some time with Him. The God of the universe, desired to talk with me! But I fluffed my pillow and turned over, mumbling "Later, God"; rebuffing Him. My dreams were twisted, troubling and unrestful and I later awakened, with no time to pray.

I'm sure I grieved Him this morning. Even while I accept the forgiveness He extends as I confess, I mourn the loss that is mine in indulging my selfish desire. The truth is, strength and energy, joy and purpose come from Him, not from another hour of sleep.

What treasure might I have discovered if I had only answered the soft ringing of the Heavenly alarm clock?

So many times, Father, I lie back down in the blankets, not content to get up and get going. And each time I do, I end up disappointed, rushing around empty. I so need to remember this when You invite me to spend time in Your Word, and carry my hopes and cares to You in prayer. Amen.

November 1

DREAM SPINNER

O LORD You have searched me and known me. You know my sitting down and my rising up; You understand my thought afar off. For You formed my inward parts; You covered me in my mother's womb. I will praise You for I am fearfully and wonderfully made; marvelous are Your works and that my soul knows very well.
Psalm 139:1-2, 13-14

Sharing the thoughts in this book is, for me, a long-held dream. I have often wondered, where do our dreams begin?

I believe they are spun by God, as His breath creates our souls. He places them in the depths of our spirits. Knitting us together, He forges the longings, desires, hope and imagination into the creative core that propels, moves, shapes, determines our path. He is aware of what His desires for us are, and so He shapes and forms us with the abilities that enable us to follow His leading on our path. I am aware that it is a fearful responsibility to heed and a wonderful reality to which we can cling.

That path was planned in the mind of God before we ever took a breath. In the place God knows so well...our very secret selves... yearnings are conceived. Though conscious thought seldom spends time there, we need to learn that allowing Him to be our God will grant those dreams He's spun within us and carry us to fulfillment on wings of His spirit.

Heavenly Father, yes, You have put dreams into my heart. May I follow Your leading and trust Your plan. And thank You for all the dreams You have already fulfilled. I praise You. Amen.

November 2

BOUNTY

Yet He had commanded the clouds above, and opened the doors of heaven, had rained down manna on them to eat…He sent them food to the full. He also rained meat on them like the dust, feathered fowl like the sand of the seas; so they ate and were well filled, for He gave them their own desire. Psalm 78:23-25, 27, 29

The similes the psalmist uses here ring true to life. Manna, the food of angels, rained down on them; but they were not satisfied.

Then He rained meat on them like dust. Imagine?!! No trips to the grocery store…it was just *there!* Plentiful, even when He was displeased with their disobedience and rebellion. He was not stingy with them. Neither is He with us.

I look around my home and begin to notice the bounty He has provided—the filled refrigerator, the cozy bed, the hot shower, and the delicious first sip of coffee. I am overwhelmed with His goodness; yet a feeling of dissatisfaction lingers. And thus, before the day is over I find myself wanting more even though I am full of what I truly need. The temptation to complain arises as discontent creeps in.

Not being thankful is disobedience, pure and simple. It is my rebelliousness that refuses to trust God. Does He withhold the manna from me because I am not grateful? No! He continues to rain down bountiful blessings. "Gratitude turns whatever we have into enough."[75]

Forgive me, Father, I am literally full from the blessings You rain down. May gratitude dispel the wanting, and may I be satisfied with Your bounty. Amen.

---

[75] P. Graham Dunn

November 3

QUILT OF PRAISE

I will praise you, LORD, among the nations; I will sing of you among the peoples. For great is your love, higher than the heavens; your faithfulness reaches to the skies. Psalm 108:3-4 (NIV)

I read these words of the Psalmist David, pulled from the rest of this lovely psalm, that express his courage to praise God even in the midst of dark and troubling times. I am reminded of what goes into the piecing together of a quilt. In this psalm David's thoughts create a quilt of praise, culled from experiences of God's faithfulness that enable him to declare his faith that God's love will continue to cover him and carry him.

I am not a quilter, but I can appreciate and admire the work that goes into making one. Our foremothers pieced together beautiful works of art from scraps filled with memories to warm them on their journeys. Perhaps these quilts were the only thing of beauty they had to brighten drab, hard surroundings. They recorded their joys and sorrows in the stitches; incorporating their memories, hopes, dreams and prayers that kept love alive.

Heavenly Father, what beauty can be made from scraps! What wholeness can be found from the fragments of our lives. My heart is filled with praise as I recall pieces of my life that, sewed together in my memory, create a quilt of praise which covers me with Your love. Amen.

November 4

GRACE AND GRATITUDE

For all things are for your sakes, that grace having spread through the many, may cause thanksgiving to abound to the glory of God.
2 Corinthians 4:15

Grace, spreading through many, causes thanksgiving to abound. A thought worth pondering. What causes gratitude, really? It's the realization of *grace,* I believe. True gratitude, that is—the kind that evokes worship deep in the heart of the believer.

So many times I think our expressions of gratitude are simply exhalations of relief, a hastily spoken "O, thank God!" There is a soul-deep gratitude attitude, however, that is expressed in a giant "Yes!" to God because the reality of His grace has permeated to our very core.

This is reflected in obedience, trust and worship. God appreciates our relief, of course—acknowledging and giving praise to Him for His display of protection or provision. But perhaps it is true, as well, that He waits for that surrendering sigh from our souls that acknowledges Him as our gracious all-in-all. Knowing that everything we have, temporal and eternal, is ours from His loving grace. When this recognition penetrates our hearts and spreads through us, thanksgiving will abound to His glory!

Father, I want to be more and more aware of the grace You shower upon me. Help me see it and respond with a surrender that delights You and fills my life with worship. Amen.

November 5

MIGHT AND MERCY

O give thanks to the LORD, for He is good! For His mercy endures forever. Psalm 136:1

In my Bible I have written "pulse" and "heartbeat" next to the verses in this psalm. It is a recitation of God's might and mercy, hand in hand; listing so many acts He performed to rescue Israel followed by the phrase *for His mercy endures forever.* How could I read this tribute and not find my spirit responding in praise?

And then, following all the accolades, comes verse 23. *Who remembered us in our lowly state, and rescued us from our enemies. Who gives food to all flesh. For His mercy endures forever.* He remembers us! There's no limit to His might! And yet, there's no end to His mercy!

I thank Him that He remembers me in my lowly state; that I can rely on His limitless might, and rest in His enduring mercy. It's the *pulse* that beats throughout scripture; it's the *heartbeat* of my faith.

This psalm is an exercise in gratitude. Often we take for granted God's incredible activity in the lives of His people! His goodness, His tenderness and His compassion are shown forth in the miracles listed here in Psalm 136. It behooves us to recall these miracles, especially when we are faced with what feels like an unsurmountable obstacle. He is the same today as then.

Heavenly Father, Your might and Your mercy have not diminished over the centuries. You are still able – still willing – to respond to our need. Oh, please help us to remember. Amen.

November 6

HIGH PRIEST

The High Priest will make atonement for the Most Holy Place because of the uncleanness and rebellion of the Israelites, whatever their sins have been. He is to do the same for the tent of meeting, which is among them in the midst of their uncleanness. Leviticus 16:16 (NIV)

There are many significant illustrations that God has provided for us in the Old Testament. The Tabernacle, His dwelling place on earth in that day, is one of them. Rules, law and ceremonies for sacrificing and cleansing were all duties of the High Priest as he ministered in the Tabernacle. As I read the repetitious precise directions from God I am impacted by the truth that the Tabernacle has significance for believers. It is a picture of who was to come—the fulfillment of the Law—our precious Savior, Jesus. Each of the High Priest's functions was fulfilled at the cross. Jesus is our High Priest. The Tabernacle is a picture of Him also.

So as I ponder the fact that the Tabernacle remained in their midst—the midst of their uncleanness—I am humbled to consider that Jesus remains in the heart of each believer, having cleansed and purified it by the sacrifice of Himself. Although God sees us as forgiven and clean, we still dwell in sinful bodies.

How difficult for holiness to dwell in the midst of uncleanness but amazingly, He does! He promised to remain in us,[76] because of His great love and the lengths to which He went to make us clean.

Heavenly Father, what a beautiful picture, a blessing inspiring my gratitude! I give You thanks for Jesus, my Savior, His sacrifice and the truth that by His Spirit, He <u>remains</u> in me. Amen.

---

[76] John 15:4

November 7

CORNUCOPIA

...the fruit of the Spirit is love, joy, peace, longsuffering, kindness, goodness, faithfulness, gentleness, self-control.
Galatians 5:22,23

"...be filled with the Spirit..." Ephesians 5:18

Filled with the Spirit! Filled completely to the brim with Him is what we are to be. "Filled" means there is no room for anything else.

It is Autumn, harvest time; that lush bountiful time of year when crops are gathered in and thanksgiving fills our hearts. Celebrating the season, we often decorate our homes with autumn-inspired objects. On my dining room table is a cornucopia with fruit and vegetables spilling out of it. This brought to mind the idea that of our lives should be filled with the Spirit.

I'd like for my life be like a cornucopia, a symbol of abundance and plenty. Not of material things, but rather the fruit of the Spirit, bubbling out of me. I want to brim over with love and joy and peace, kindness and gentleness to others and patience with self-control. Since fruit is a result of growth, so it is up to me to allow the necessary nourishment and tending to take place. My Holy Spirit Gardener stands ready and willing to provide these.

Father, fill me, flood me, with Your Holy Spirit, so there is no room for selfish goals that would grieve You. Let there be an overflow of fruit as I yield myself to You. Amen.

November 8

SEAWEED AND SAND

I acknowledged my sin to You, and my iniquity I have not hidden. I said, "I will confess my transgressions to the LORD," and You forgave the iniquity of my sin. Selah. Psalm 32:5

I am always amazed when I read of the magnitude of God's forgiveness, as well as the resulting grace and peace He provides. I recall a time when the natural world provided an illustration of this to me.

We were on vacation in Mexico and I was standing on a beautiful beach, focused on the sand, sea and sky. There was nothing on the horizon but waves breaking against the reef…the only sound the shrill cry of gulls and the quiet rustle of the surf on the sand.

Then…a low rumble interrupted my reverie. I watched man's effort to remove the piles of seaweed that each wave deposited on the shore. Seaweed makes the beach messy; so back and forth the machine labors, scraping with its blade, heaping up and dumping unwelcome slimy ocean growth out of sight. Then pristine sand can welcome vacationers.

But each wave hurls its new crop onto the tractor's fresh-cleaned path! I'm mesmerized, pausing ankle deep in the push and pull of the tide, and I think…it's sort of like forgiveness.

When I am confronted with my sin; I confess, my heart is scraped clean and the refuse carried away. But when a wave of unbelief and disobedience deposits another heap on my heart; how joyful to know that God hears my confession, forgives, and dumps my sin out of His sight.

Father, do I hear the approaching rumble of your merciful scraping blade? I'm ready to be cleaned up again. I confess, and accept the promise that You WILL forgive and cleanse. A pure white heart is mine. Thank You. Amen.

November 9

DESIRE

O LORD, we have waited for You, the desire of our soul is for Your name and for the remembrance of You. With my soul I have desired You in the night, yes, by my spirit I will seek You early, for when Your judgements are in the earth, the inhabitants of the world will learn righteousness. Isaiah 26:8-9

What caught my attention here was the mention of *desiring God*. I asked myself, "Is He the passion of my soul?" Thinking of the times I have fretted and wrestled with Him in the night reminds me that "I will seek you early" should be my rallying cry. As an inhabitant of this hurting, fallen world, I need to learn righteousness, or as I often think of it—"right-choice-ness!"

Our desires fuel our choices. Our choices determine our behavior. Our behavior determines our destiny. The beginning of an intimate journey must be desire. I need to check the devotion level in my soul. Is the desire tank full? And if not, why not? Even a seed of passion, if nurtured, can blossom into yearning that ignites the soul into action and results in a continuous flow of intimate connection with God through His word. And I realize that the only way that the seed of desire is present is through the touch of the Holy Spirit.

So God, in my supposed maturity I comprehend the difference between want and need, but the intense yearning for material things too often surpasses my yearning for You. Please take hold of my heart. May I gaze at You, hungering and thirsting for righteousness that will indeed fill my soul. Amen.

November 10

COVERING

Or suppose a woman who has ten silver coins and loses one. Doesn't she light a lamp, sweep the house, and search carefully until she finds it? And when she finds it, she calls her friends and neighbors together and says, "Rejoice with me! I found my lost coin!"
Luke 15:8-10 (NIV)

The reality in this verse was played out recently in my life! I've been noticing I'm doing a lot of silly, forgetful things, and it bothers me a lot.

I lost my checkbook…well, I didn't really lose it, I left it someplace. I started to write a check one morning, only to discover the checkbook was gone! As I frantically dug through and emptied my purse, checking all the desk areas; I had a terrifying flashback to the time I had my purse stolen and my identity compromised. So, trying to remain calm, I thought back over the previous days and remembered that the last time I had used it was at the grocery store. When I called the store, holding my breath; they told me they had it. Oh, did I rejoice! Just like the woman in the Bible. Isn't it incredibly wonderful—that feeling of fear replaced with relief and peace when we think what might have happened?

I have pondered how at-risk we truly can be due to carelessness. It staggers me to consider the sweet mercy of God, protecting us in our human weaknesses, even when we are most unaware.

Heavenly Father, I desire to become more and more conscious of Your overarching presence in everything I do. Teach me gratitude for the way You cover my carelessness with Your grace. I am humbled by the realization of that mercy. Amen.

November 11

SACRIFICE

Let this mind be in you which was also in Christ Jesus, who, being in the form of God, did not consider it robbery to be equal with God, but made Himself of no reputation, taking the form of a bondservant, and…humbled Himself and became obedient to the point of death, even the death of the cross. Philippians 2:5-7, 8

Veteran's Day. We will pay our respects and give our thanks to all who have served, and still serve, our country. But I wonder if we really grasp the deep meaning of sacrifice, even as we say the word.

Webster defines it. "Sacrifice: the act of giving up, destroying, permitting injury to, or forgoing something valued for the sake of something having a more pressing claim." We say it very lightly sometimes, I think, "Thank you for your sacrifice"; forgetting that the very act is a renouncing of something very precious for the greater good.

I can comprehend what a sacrifice means to someone in the military. As a Navy wife, every time I waved my husband off to sea, a sacrifice was being made. But ever so much more precious is Jesus' willingness to give up everything for something that had a more pressing claim…us. He proves His love for His broken world. A sacrifice can only be made if one is willing to give up something of value. He was. We must never say "Thank You" to Him lightly. May we always stop and think of the weight of importance the word "sacrifice" entails before it rolls glibly off our tongues.

Father, I am convicted and challenged as I read tribute after tribute to veterans; my heart also swells in gratitude to my Savior, who willingly gave the ultimate sacrifice for me. Amen.

November 12

MIRY CLAY

I waited patiently for the LORD; and He inclined to me, and heard my cry. He also brought me up out of a horrible pit, out of the miry clay; and set my feet upon a rock, and established my steps.
Psalm 40:1-2

Stuck in the mud! What an apt description of the way I was floundering for a foothold in the horrible pit of discouragement. I so identified with the Psalmist. But waiting patiently? Not really… more like a questioning whine, a wondering wail or a moaning cry.

I didn't have to stay there, though—mired in squishy unsteadiness. God leaned down to where I was, (that's what 'inclined' means) and heard my cry. Not only did He hear, but He grabbed hold…lifting me out of that pit and setting me on a rock where He could establish my steps and stabilize my walk.

You see, there is no way to gain stability in miry clay, like oozy mud, down in a pit. But on the Rock Christ Jesus, where God positions me, the foothold is sure.

From quicksand to a quickened life! From miry clay to the miracle of praise! Love lifted me!

Heavenly Father, it IS a miracle You have done, hearing my cries of pain and lifting my heart to praise You. How grateful I am to have firm footing again. Amen.

November 13

REDEMPTION'S SONG

Therefore, behold, I will allure her; will bring her into the wilderness and speak comfort to her. I will give her vineyards from there and the Valley of Achor as a door of hope. She shall sing there as in the days of her youth. Hosea 2:14, 15

The rebellious wife of Hosea, immersed in adultery, is a picture of the unrepentant child of God. It is a picture of me.

Once, a song of joy caressed her lips. A young bride, in love with her bridegroom, sang an anthem of innocence and thanksgiving that was replaced by a dirge of sadness and loss. I identify. I turned my back to Him, too; muffling my song.

But God doesn't leave her mournful; nor did He ever stop seeking *me*. How beautiful His words of promise: making her wilderness a door of hope, through which she can return, to sing once more her melody of delight.

His promise is to me as well. As He speaks tenderly to me in my wilderness I can walk through the open door of hope back to the shelter of His love. I will then sing redemption's song, the anthem of the forgiven; the loveliest of all music that bursts forth from the lips of a ransomed soul.

Dear God, Your song leaves my lips and my heart in gratitude. My song shouts the truth that You have redeemed me, saved my life and brought me back because of Your love. I cry Hallelujah! May I never forget, so that my song goes unheard. Amen.

November 14

PLACES

The lines have fallen to me in pleasant places; yes, I have a good inheritance. Psalm 16:6

As a navy wife it was necessary to relocate often. Usually every 3 years we would move to a new duty station: sometimes even less time elapsing between orders. It wasn't difficult for me because, as a child, we had moved almost that often!

I have such great memories of many places; and each one has its special space reflected in my mind. Strange how looking back and considering all these places—the locations of my rites of passage—I wonder if I could I have passed through them all and not left a part of me behind. Because each time I moved ahead, I gained a memory.

Houses, rooms, classrooms and sanctuaries contain, I know, pieces of my soul that are hidden there. In my mind I wander back, with thoughts enhanced by time. I smell the scents and hear the sounds. My fingers itch with the remembered touch of those I love.

And though it's true these special places have no intrinsic life, or character, on their own, I do not bid them farewell, but enfold them into my heart. For I know within their confines, I have achieved my place. My prayer is that the pieces of my heart left behind will bring honor to my Heavenly Father.

So, Lord, I must lift my hands in gratitude for all the places You have provided in my life; for the joys, sorrows, victories and disappointments that fill the memories and weave the precious fabric that now enfolds me. Thank You for all the pleasant places. Amen.

November 15

CHEERS!

What shall I render to the LORD for all His benefits toward me? I will take up the cup of salvation and call on the name of the LORD. I will pay my vows to him. Psalm 116:12-14.

In wondering just what the "cup of salvation" means, I discovered that it has the connotation of a toast, as when we lift a glass, so to speak, to honor someone. What a great way to honor the Lord, don't you think?

Digging a little bit deeper, I remembered the verse where Jesus says: *Father, if it is Your will, take this* ***cup*** *away from Me; nevertheless not My will but Yours be done.*[77] Jesus prayed and sweated that the "cup" be taken away, but it wasn't; and thus He died a horrific death. And *only* because He drank the cup of divine wrath on sin on our behalf can we lift up the "cup of salvation" to Him in worship. This, my friends, encapsulates worship: our worship is to be a celebration in action, fed by gratitude—lifting a toast to God and His Son in a very tangible sense.

I have never before connected the Jesus' cup of suffering with the "cup of salvation" in this Psalm 116. Talk about thanksgiving! If this were the only blessing we could think of each day, it would serve, wouldn't it?

Oh, Father, my heart is touched with truth once again. I want to honor Jesus and – not to sound irreverent – raise my cup, shouting "Cheers!" in the finest, most joyful, sense of the word! I give You praise and thanks. Amen.

---

[77] Luke 22:42

November 16

THANKSGIVING

Thanks be to God for His indescribable gift. 2 Corinthian 9:15

Come, let us sing for joy to the LORD; let us shout aloud to the Rock of our salvation. Let us come before him with thanksgiving and extol him with music and song. Psalm 95:1-2 (NIV)

Beside us to guide us, our God with us joining. Ordaining, maintaining His kingdom divine; so from the beginning the fight we were winning; Thou, Lord, were at our side, all glory be thine.[78]

I've sung these beautiful words almost every Thanksgiving of my life. Recently I was pondering them in light of the upcoming holiday and I found President Abraham Lincoln's Thanksgiving Proclamation in my files. I think it proper to share his wise words as my devotional as Thanksgiving Day nears.

"The year that is drawing toward its close has been filled with the blessing of fruitful fields and healthful skies. No human counsel hath devised nor has any mortal hand worked out these great things. They are the gracious gifts of the Most High God….It has seemed to me fit and proper that they should be solemnly, reverently, and gratefully acknowledged as with one heart and one voice by the whole American People. I do therefore invite my fellow citizens in every part of the United States…to set apart and observe the last Thursday of November next, as a day of Thanksgiving and Praise to our beneficent Father who dwelleth in the Heavens."

Dear Father, with hearts full of praise, we give You our thanks for the gracious gifts of fruitful fields. Amen.

---

[78] We Gather Together - Composer Unknown

November 17

SHIELDED

But let all those rejoice who put their trust in You; let them ever shout for joy, because You defend them; let those also who love Your name be joyful in You. For You, O LORD, will bless the righteous; with favor You will surround him as with a shield. Psalm 5:11-12

Surrounded. What a comforting thought! It penetrates my heart this morning, lifting my spirits in joy, just as the above verses instruct. What really sparks the rejoicing is what He promises to surround me with...favor.

Shielded with favor. Normally a shield is held in front to protect vital organs, but here I see that His favor surrounds me—covering, protecting and defending *all* of me. In the dictionary, favor means acceptance, approval. I'm becoming aware of my life-long plea for God's approval. I see now that He grants it, as shown here in His word, and gives me joy. Why the favor?

Because I am righteous, not for anything I have done; it is only through the sacrifice of my Savior, Jesus, and His righteousness bestowed on me. I trust in Him, I love His name; I hold tightly to the shield of His favor with rejoicing.

Dear Father, my Shield and Defender, my Joy-giver, how precious and cared-for I am feeling because of Your promises. I've so longed to be accepted. Why haven't I realized I already am? Covered and surrounded by Your approval...because of Jesus.
Oh, thank You! Amen.

November 18

FEEDING FRENZY

Trust in the LORD, and do good; dwell in the land; feed on His faithfulness, rest in the LORD, and wait patiently for Him...
Psalm 37:3, 7

This beautiful psalm addresses the subject of *waiting*. Many of us struggle with waiting. Over and over I've read this psalm, seeing the instructions not to fret, but instead to rest, to trust and to wait patiently. Reading it again this morning I realize that somehow I missed the phrase of advice to *feed on His faithfulness;* and I believe it's a key that key that unlocks successful waiting.

We feed to nourish ourselves...bread and meat for our physical bodies, and hopefully God's word for our spiritual provision. But I am wondering if we are struggling to trust and wait patiently, to rest, with undernourished souls?

I consider the feeding frenzy going on in my life... disappointment, discouragement and despair too often fill my daily plate. A sense of failure and unfilled desire crowds out the truly appetizing meal that could satisfy my longing.

To "feed on His faithfulness" I must nourish my heart and my soul with the truth of His promises—promises which I have known and experienced to be trustworthy.

Heavenly Father, I am waiting. I think. Patiently? Not so much. Waiting because there is nothing else to do, not because I'm sated from a banquet of Your faithfulness. I am really hungry. This feeding frenzy, this downward spiral of dining on defeat, must cease. It's time to come to the table where You spread out a feast, inviting me to fill my plate from the unending delicious supply of Your faithfulness. Amen.

November 19

COMFORT FOOD

Because Your love is better than life, my lips will glorify You. I will praise You as long as I live, and in Your name I will lift up my hands. I will be fully satisfied as with the richest of foods; with singing lips my mouth will praise You. Psalm 63:3-5 (NIV)

My soul shall be satisfied—not simply with the richest of foods, but AS with it. The way that rich foods (comfort foods) satisfy the deep longing of my body, my soul can be satiated only by praising my Father.

Who has not pushed away from the table after a meal of, say, fried chicken or meat loaf, mashed potatoes and gravy; with ice cream for dessert—comfort food—without a deep sigh of satisfaction? Possibly tinged with guilt for having eaten too much?

There is such significance to me in these few beautiful verses from Psalm 63. His love IS better than life. So do I really believe and accept that? Or do I rush to the comfort food offered by the world? True satisfaction must come to my soul by way of praise, surrender and joy. Thus, sated with the sweet truth of His life-changing love, of which I can never eat too much, I will pour forth His praise with joyful lips!

Heavenly Father, You are only too aware of my appetite for comfort foods versus my longing for true comfort from Your table. So I ask for Your grace to point me to You, the Source of all comfort, that my soul can truly pour out praise to You. Amen.

November 20

CONTRASTS

For God so loved the world that He gave His only Son that whoever believes in Him shall not perish, but have everlasting life. John 3:16

Last year we suffered through a heat wave—temperature in the triple digits. In the normally temperate Northwest, it was a rare phenomenon; we simply are unused to heat like that. Someone in my hearing remarked, "If we get through this heat, when it hits the 80's we will probably freeze to death!" A rather humorous exaggeration, but it brings to my mind the subject of contrasts.

Do we ever really consider just how many contrasts make up our daily lives? Darkness/Light. Cold/Hot. Smooth/Rough. Sunshine/Rainfall—to name a few. If these contrasts did not exist, would we lose an appreciation for the way God put the universe together? If every day were calm and peaceful, with no ups and downs, we would likely not feel our need for God. We must have the struggles, the troubles, so that when life smooths out we can celebrate the peacefulness.

God allows night to be modified by starlight or moonlight, as well as by the approach of dawn. His marvelous distinction and purpose have made the contrasts of night and day, summer and winter, storms and tranquility. How wonderful it is that He has provided a way for us to transition from the pain and struggle of a life without Him to a life of peace in His presence. We would not know one without the other.

Heavenly Father, thank You for the reality that permeates life, of which we are often unaware. As I consider the contrast between eternal life and eternal death, I praise Your name for eternal salvation given to me, through faith in Your Son, Jesus. Amen.

November 21

FAITHFUL

Now may the God of peace Himself sanctify you completely; and may your whole spirit, soul, and body be preserved blameless at the coming of our Lord Jesus Christ. He who calls you is faithful who also will do it. 1 Thessalonians 5:23-24

A relationship is made up of interactions. We tend to take for granted so many attributes of God. I believe one of His most amazing characteristics is His *faithfulness*. Let's take a deeper look at how we, as believers, depend on that faithfulness to us—our spirit, soul and body…

- Without His faithfulness there would be no basis for my faith.
- Without His steadfastness there would be no firm ground where I can stand.
- Without His fidelity there would be no anchor for my allegiance.
- Without His unchanging nature there would be no cause for my devotion. Without the security of His love there would be no shelter where I could rest.

Oh, yes, He calls us to *come* to Him, *lean* on Him and *rest* in Him. And He is faithful! He will make it happen—He will sanctify us and preserve us blameless. Hallelujah!

Heavenly Father, my God of peace, I yield myself, all of who I am, to You. Please do Your work in me. Amen.

November 22

EXPECTATION

The LORD upholds all who fall, and raises up all who are bowed down. The eyes of all look expectantly to You, and You give them their food in due season. You open Your hand and satisfy the desire of every living thing. Psalm 145:14-16

The turkey is moist and full of flavor, cranberries sweet and tart, potatoes smooth and the stuffing well-seasoned, a favorite meal to savor. Wrapped in joyful memories, it is more than a dinner; it is living…an experience. Thanksgiving!

Everything tastes the same as it should. I can close my eyes and, once again, be at my huge round table with loved ones gathered near, relishing the closeness of family…though that's not the case this year. Our gathering is small and the absences of loved ones are deeply felt.

There's a scattering taking place even as the Holidays approach. Our children are forming new families and shaping their own traditions. While I know it must be so, I can't deny a still small space where sadness takes control. The expectation I can hardly admit I have has not been met, and my dining room is somehow empty though loaded with God's bounty.

So I invite my Lord Jesus to my Thanksgiving table. May I welcome Him with joy and gratefulness for the delicious dinner spread out before me, the sound of memories pouring through my heart and the hope of new things to celebrate.

Jesus, please fill the empty places as only You are able. And may I, through this holy season, release expectation…so giving freedom to my loved ones. Then I can receive gratefully from Your hand – unexpected blessing! Amen.

November 23

HAVEN

He calms the storm, so that its waves are still. Then they are glad because they are quiet; so He guides them to their desired haven. Oh, that men would give thanks to the LORD for His goodness, and for His wonderful works to the children of men. Psalm 107:29-31.

As you know by now, I am a Navy wife and as such have waved my husband off to sea many times. This psalm ministered to me as I released the man I love to do his sworn duty to protect our country. Yes, I was proud of him and respected him for the sacrifices he made. I, too have sacrificed, enduring many lonely nights, solving problems and caring for our children.

So, when I read these words about *those who go down to the sea in ships,*[79] I can identify! And I was cheered by the promise of a desired haven to which God guides the ships and the men. Additionally, I myself found peace and stillness amidst the storm of loneliness and concern by being guided into my own haven—a haven of peace and comfort from my God who holds everything together. He helped hold me together in order that our home was a haven as well, where my sailor was grateful to return.

The lessons we learned throughout those years of separation and reunions have stood us in good stead over and over, and conditioned us to a trust in God's direction that has never been shaken.

Oh my dear Heavenly Father, I, like the psalmist, give You thanks for Your goodness to us, Your wonderful works. We have rested, and will rest, in the haven of Your care. Amen.

---

[79] Psalm 107:23

November 24

KEPT

For I know whom I have believed and am persuaded that He is able to keep what I have committed unto Him until that Day.
2 Timothy 1:12

For as long as I can remember, I have been terrified of being rejected, given away. The fear comes from an incident in my childhood. After our mother died we were threatened, if we didn't behave, with being sent to an orphanage. It never actually happened, but that threat of rejection has crippled me for so many years; caused pain and dashed hope to the ground.

Thus, I trembled as I read of God's covenant with His people, offering His protection and preservation – simply because of His love and care for us, whom He has created. He made a promise thousands of years ago, and since He is a Covenant-keeping God, that promise holds true for me! Why?

Because I have entered into a covenant with Him, choosing to trust Christ as my Savior, thereby becoming His child, His Beloved. Do I trust that promise? Yes, increasingly, the more as I look into His Word, learning His ways and learning to know *Him*. I find comfort here in its pages, especially in the following verses:

Now to Him who is able to keep you from falling, and to present you faultless before the presence of His glory with exceeding joy, to the only wise God our Savior, be glory and majesty, dominion and power, both now and forever. Amen.[80]

Heavenly Father, what have I committed to You? Simply put, my all. Praise to You, I am kept – never rejected, never abandoned. Amen.

---

[80] Jude 24-25

November 25

CASTING

Cast your burden upon the Lord and he shall sustain you.
Psalm 55:22

…casting all your care upon Him, for He cares for you. 1 Peter 5:7

For so long I have had a misconception: I thought "casting upon" meant "throwing it at," thus relieving myself from carrying it. I'd consider casting my burden on God, yet somehow that never seemed to rid me of it. I have reconsidered my idea of casting.

I'm discovering that God allows burdens and wants *us* to carry them sometimes—but He wants us to ask and depend on His help in doing so. Matthew 11:28 tells us He desires us to yoke up with Him and use His shoulder to share the load; whether it is of Him for my growth and strengthening or from a misplaced sense of guilt or responsibility.

I grew up in an area where fly fishing was a way of life. As I consider the word "casting" I can't help but think of a fisherman, fly-casting. He expertly tosses his hook across the water…not throwing it to rid himself of it, but to catch something…a fish! He still holds the pole, still is part of the process, but casts his line in hope to receive. Never does he cast without hope.

When I "cast" my burden on God, may it be with a sense of hope…for His strength to help bear it. I think we are not to be *care free*, nor *careless*. Rather, we are to let ourselves be cared *for*.

Heavenly Father, when cares come, please help me remember that You long for me to lean on You. Your love supports me no matter how heavy the burden may seem when I try to go it alone. Thank You for the promise of a burden shared. Amen.

November 26

PACKAGING

But the LORD said to Samuel, "Do not look at his appearance or at his physical stature, because I have refused him. For the LORD does not see as man sees; for man looks at the outward appearance, but the LORD looks at the heart." 1 Samuel 16:7

What an incredible, personal God we serve! I often have opportunities to mail out copies of my books and I remember a couple of incidents that have shown me this truth! My sister ordered several copies, so I boxed them up, taped heavily and fortified with extra cardboard! Unfortunately the mailman had stuffed the box into her mailbox, pushing and twisting the carton to fit. The box was mangled and torn, but when she fearfully opened it, the books were in perfect condition!

Later, I opened an email from another friend: "received your book yesterday, it looked like it had been run over by a semi, was torn and dirty, sad on the outside. But the book was in perfect condition*!!*" This wonder was highlighted by her last comment: "I couldn't help but think about us, sin makes what others see and hear from us not so pretty, but God sees the inside as beautiful because we've been washed in the blood".

We assume from looking at torn, dirty packaging that whatever is inside is ruined. If we look at ourselves with earthly eyes, that is all we might see, but God is more concerned with the *inside*, and will go to great lengths to protect and preserve it. Hallelujah!

Father, I praise You for Your power and Your love; for taking my messed-up life, however torn and dirty, and cleaning me up so that You can get the glory. Because You truly see into my heart. I thank You. Amen.

November 27

IMAGES

A man shall be as a hiding place from the wind, and a cover from the tempest; as rivers of water in a dry place, as the shadow of a great rock in a weary land. Isaiah 32:2

Isaiah speaks prophetically of Jesus, God in the flesh. Let's examine all the descriptions of Jesus mentioned here in this verse. First, a *hiding place* from the wind. Is it not true that our lives often feel buffeted by a strong wind? That we are tossed around in what feels like a violent tempest of pain, loss or confusion?

Isaiah also says that Jesus is as *rivers of water* in a dry place. Maybe we're not in a storm, but instead feel dry and empty. Here is Jesus to meet that need—not with merely a trickle, but with rivers of water. Water that satisfies completely.

And that's not all! Every one of us can identify with the need for rest—the *shadow* of a great rock in a weary land. Weariness attacks us; discouragement and disappointment may wear us down. But we can take heart. There is rest awaiting. It is Jesus, His outstretched arms to welcome the weary soul.

All these images of safety, refreshment and rest describe Jesus, but I find I often fail to notice Who You truly are. My head recognizes You in these pictures, but my heart fails to avail itself of Your marvelous wonder.

Heavenly Father, Your reminders are sweet indeed! These images of Jesus You describe are life-giving and I hereby ask You to keep pouring the truth of Your provisioning into my heart. They bring Your strength. Amen.

November 28

NIGHT LIGHT

Those who are wise shall shine like the brightness of the firmament. And those who turn many to righteousness like the stars forever and ever. Daniel 12:3

We were vacationing in Cancun, Mexico. One evening after dinner we strolled back to our lodging at the resort. The full moon was a pale golden disk sliding through a veil of fog as sheer as mist, playing tag with umber clouds; its reflection on the water a path of subdued light. It was strikingly lovely.

The moon is merely a reflector, having no ability to give light on its own. Its fullness is visible only when it is in perfect alignment with the sun.

Remembering this, I am contemplating my own life. Since I am to reflect God's glory—to appear as a light in this dark world (2 Peter 1:19)—it is so vital that I stay in alignment with Him! Because when I move away and attempt to shine on my own, the reflection of His glory that I cast on the water is dimmed.

The fog-shrouded moon, however, encourages me. It is still beautiful, still visible. And in me as well, even through the veil of my humanness, the reflection of God's glory can still be seen. May it always appear as a light in the dark night around me.

Heavenly Father, Your creation has so much to teach me. I long to be a bright reflection of You, so I ask You to keep my heart in alignment with the Son, the One who gave His life for me. Amen.

November 29

POVERTY

Blessed are the poor in spirit... Matthew 5:3

There are different kinds of poverty. There is the kind we generally associate with the word: not having sufficient income. There is, however, a spiritual poverty, one that indicates a person's need for God; being at the end of one's own resources.

My own poverty—have I ever been truly aware of it? I consistently feel an urge to do something in my own strength and abilities to make myself more worthy. Often I say, "I can't do it. I need to rely on Jesus," but I say it with a sense of discouraged failure. That makes it all about me.

What I need to say is, "I can't do it. However, I don't have to. God will." This expresses my spiritual poverty, a realization of my need.

The words are much the same; the difference is huge because it indicates the condition of my heart. Instead of a joyful abandon to obedience does God hear only my complaint? "Oh dear, I messed up. I guess I can't do it without Your spirit. Oh, well, You're going to have to intervene and haul me out of trouble. Again."

When I look deep inside, I discern that the whining voice expresses how I truly feel, no matter how noble-sounding my words.

Father, forgive me. I so need You. Without You I am definitely destitute. Admitting my poverty of spirit will bring the blessing of Your Spirit's filling. With that I am rich. Amen.

November 30

SKILL

Rejoice in the LORD, O you righteous! For praise from the upright is beautiful. Praise the LORD with the harp; make melody to Him with an instrument of ten strings. Sing to him a new song; play skillfully with a shout of joy. Psalm 33:1-3

These verses tell us that our praise is beautiful; it is fitting that we who love God express our praise to Him. Further, it says that He inhabits our praise. And I think that's what makes it beautiful: His presence, in all its beauty, fills us as we praise.

But I noticed something else while pondering this psalm. It says, *Play skillfully;*, and it occurs to me that skill takes *practice*! Unless one is a complete prodigy, he doesn't approach an instrument and begin to play skillfully. God is instructing us to gain skill so that praise is much more than simply an off-key cacophony.

So I think there is a lesson here. Praise requires practice; an intentional, conscious effort to learn, to press down worry and fear and lift up a heart and voice of worship. Skill doesn't come without some sour notes played on occasion; our motives may not always be pure.

But how important to persist in practicing so that the notes and melodies become pure and beautiful and the shouts of joy tuneful and triumphant. Thus , praise will become our habit.

Father, I must practice praise! Let it fill me, moment by moment, with the new song You're writing in my heart. Amen.

December 1

OKAY!

Behold the maidservant of the Lord! Let it be to me according to Your word. Luke 1:38

My friend was describing the children's Christmas program at her church. The "angel" was placed on a chair to raise her above Mary and Joseph; and from that perch, she gravely announced to Mary, "You're going to have a baby." To which Mary replied, "Okay." Then the angel turned to Joseph, "And you're going to be the baby's daddy," and Joseph answered, "Okay." We stood there and chuckled, visualizing the scene, but at the same time, comprehending the simplicity and beauty of their childlike responses.

Pondering that little story on Christmas morning, I turned in my Bible to Luke 1, and read again the story of Gabriel's announcement to Mary of her imminent pregnancy. Her response awakened a song of joy in my own heart! In essence, she was saying, "Okay." I read on. "*My soul magnifies the Lord, and my spirit has rejoiced in God my Savior. For He has regarded the lowly state of His maidservant; for behold, henceforth all generations will call me blessed. For He who is mighty has done great things for me, and holy is His name.*"[81]

I want Mary's song to be my song as well. She had the ultimate blessing to carry God's Son to His birth, which is why we call her blessed. We, too are blessed to have so many opportunities to carry His word, His hope, His joy and peace wherever we go; to whomever we meet.

You, Heavenly Father, my mighty God, have done great things for me and gratefully I praise You. Holy is Your name. I will trust You. Amen.

---

[81] Luke 1:46-49.

December 2

CHRISTMAS MORNING

The Light shines in the darkness... John 1:5

One of the lovely things about our Christmas celebrations is the use of lights. We decorate with lights, hanging them on Christmas trees; we light candles, big and small, to cast a sweet glow. It is easy to see, as dawn breaks on Christmas morning, why our hearts might turn to the birth of Jesus, and contemplate the sparkling beauty of the Light of the World, Jesus. The Light, first dispelling the murky dimness of a stable, brings into the world the dawn of our deliverance, the end of our darkness.

That morning of hope enables the beginning of our salvation, the end of mourning in our hearts; changing the darkness there to brightness, and despair to rejoicing. The Light of the World once wrapped in swaddling clothes, this Child of Bethlehem, now shines with mercy, forgiveness and everlasting love.

Shepherds basked in the glow of angelic praise, lost in the wonder of experiencing Heaven's rejoicing. Moving quickly to Bethlehem they found a dark stable glowing with the newborn Light of the World. May the windows of our own hearts reflect the beams of Jesus's beauty and shimmer with the Light from heaven brought down to earth—God with us, Emmanuel.

Heavenly Father, how lovely You are! You sent the Light of the World into our world, and now ask us to reflect it to those around us. Amen

December 3

A MANGER AND A CROSS

But when the fullness of time had come, God sent forth His Son, born of a woman, born under the law, to redeem those who were under the law, that we might receive the adoption as sons. Galatians 4:4

I often think of Mary, the mother of Jesus, during these days leading to Christmas. God's perfect timing revealed a newborn babe lying in a manger, shrouded in swaddling clothes that protected Him from the roughness of His bed. The soft security of His mother's arms cuddled Him sweetly as she gratefully offered Him sustenance. She was so aware of the miracle of this birth, and her mother heart beat with the joy of its fulfillment. Her only regret at that moment must be having had only a crude manger, an animal feeding-trough, in which to lay Him.

We know in hindsight that the future held for this mother a mixture of all-surpassing joy and all-encompassing heartache, as the shadow of a cross waited behind the manger, dimly shrouded in time.

Unaware of the whole plan, she held her Savior, rocked him, fed him, loved him, and at that moment did not know that someday she would lay him in a hollowed tomb, swaddled once more, this time in burial clothes.

Dear God, we celebrate the baby in a manger, singing "Glory to God." We gather beneath the cross, weeping at the price He paid. We lift our hands in praise at the empty tomb, understanding with grateful hearts that, for us, there would not be such joy at the manger without the promise of the shadowed cross. We bow in gratitude. Amen.

December 4

CHRISTMAS DREAMS

Then Joseph her husband, being a just man, and not wanting to make her a public example, was minded to put her away secretly. But while he thought about these things, behold, an angel of the Lord appeared to him in a dream... Matthew 1:19-20

What are your dreams for Christmas? Desires, hopes and anticipation always fill us at this season. Perhaps it is a longed-for gift, a hoped-for reconciliation, or simply a wistful yearning for what used to be. We often do not recognize these yearnings as coming from God's heart of love, but these dreams are part of His plan for us.

The telling of the first Christmas story holds accounts of dreams, too. Joseph was thinking of his beautiful Mary threatened by scandal; yet as he slept, an angel appeared in a dream, and told him what to do. His obedience brought them, as husband and wife, to Bethlehem for the birth of Jesus; as prophets had foretold.

The Magi were warned in a dream not to go home through Jerusalem because the wicked king planned to take the life of the Child Jesus. Because danger threatened that Child, in a dream Joseph was warned to take his family to Egypt until the danger passed. Once more, the angel appeared in a dream to direct them home again.

Christmas dreams: supernatural means that God used to protect and advance His plan for the ages. And today we ask, "Does God still send dreams?" Yes! But He also brings the fulfillment of our deep unspoken yearnings.

Heavenly Father, help us to see that what we dream for at Christmas has already been fulfilled. The longings for what we hope are met in Your Son...Jesus. He satisfies. Amen.

December 5

ANGEL VOICES

Bless the LORD, you His angels, who excel in strength, who do His word, heeding the voice of His word. Psalm 103:20

Filled with joy and anticipation, at Christmas, we sing familiar carols; the melodies inviting us to remember. Carols tell the beautiful story of the first Christmas: a miraculous birth, shepherds…and angels! The angels are the *voice* of Christmas. They are God's messengers, speaking His word; announcing His plan…to Mary, to Joseph in a dream and to humble shepherds on the night of Jesus' birth.

What did the angel voices say? "Do not fear, there is news of great joy!" Their words evoking a response of praise: "Glory to God in the highest!" That message of the angels invites us and we fall on our knees and listen.

What do the angel voices say to us? The very same…all the glory must go to God. Let us hear again the angel voices; and heed their message, shifting our attention and our focus, to God. Our hearts respond to the wonder of the miracle announced long ago by angels— its echo heard down through the years—with a whispered "Thank You" and a shouted *Glory to God in the highest!*[82]

Father, faced with the truth of this story my heart can do no more than cry out in praise along with the angels, the shepherds, Mary and Joseph, and all of Christendom: "Glory to God in the highest!" *Amen.*

---

[82] Luke 2:14

December 6

THE MAGI MIRACLES

Now after Jesus was born in Bethlehem of Judea in the days of Herod the king, behold, wise men from the east came to Jerusalem, saying, "Where is he that is born King of the Jews? For we have seen his star in the east, and have come to worship him." Matthew 2:1-2

Encountering isolated oases and dirty villages, camped night upon night on chilly highlands; enduring dark skies and swirling dust in endless deserts; threatened by insects, hardships, thieves and terrors. These men whom the scripture calls wise traveled on. Impelled by the lure of a star glimpsed in the eastern sky and driven by a desire to sacrifice everything to worship the King, they embarked on a fearsome journey, following the supernatural. For God's sovereignty had placed a kernel of understanding in the hearts of these distant ones that someday He would send a king and a star would light the way.

Grimy, gritty and saddle-sore, the Magi determinedly descend upon Jerusalem. No glittering robes and jeweled crowns here; just anxious, sweat-stained and weary travelers. Their questions ignite a frenzy; even as scribes and priests search the scriptures and direct the seekers to Bethlehem.

Miracles, threaded through the needle of God's plan, weave the story across the tapestry of time; gathering His chosen ones to Bethlehem to celebrate the birth of His Son. The hope of redemption embodied in a star that compelled wise men from afar to come. In Bethlehem, gifts are opened in worship and hearts receive Him. Thus takes place this greatest of miracles.

Father God, thank you for this example of faith and worship. May we follow these intrepid travelers to seek Your Son now as we celebrate His birth as well as every day that follows. We realize that wise men still seek Him. Amen.

December 7

THE VOICE OF GOD

God, who at various times and in various ways spoke in time past to the fathers by the prophets, has in these last days spoken to us in His Son... Hebrews 1:1,2

As we enter into this blessed season of expectancy, I wonder if we are straining to hear God's voice. We have to understand that He has been speaking throughout history, and perhaps we should look at some ways God allows His voice to be heard.

The voice of God, revealed in His Son—the voice which thundered over the formless void and brought forth all life—spoke again: the Word transformed into a tiny scrap of flesh, the fulfillment of prophetic message. The voice of God, heard in a baby's cry. A blessed miracle.

The voice of God is revealed in His Son, no longer a babe, echoing incredible words from a cruel cross. Words which reverberate throughout history: *It is finished.*[83] Our redemption is paid.

The voice of God truly rings...now in the Christmas season, through the carols we sing and the scriptures that speak; telling the oft-repeated story of a Child in a manger. And I wonder, through all the festivity, can we hear the voice of God whispering in invitation..."What about my Son? What will you do with Him?"

Oh Heavenly Father, we pray that our ears not be shut against Your voice. It pleads with us, reminding us over and over that we need to be in communion with You. To hear and respond. And we pray that You continue wooing us. Amen.

---

[83] John 19:30

December 8

O LITTLE TOWN OF BETHLEHEM

But you, Bethlehem Ephrathah, though you are little among the thousands of Judah, yet out of you shall come forth to Me the One to be Ruler in Israel, Whose goings forth are from of old, from everlasting. Micah 5:2

O little town of Bethlehem, so small and insignificant among the cities, virtually unnoticed, you waited in obscurity. Eyes, once fastened on you in hope, turn away in disappointment as history passed you by. You were to be the place from which Messiah would come, but bondage and darkness seem to have extinguished your light.

You are not insignificant in God's plan however, and tonight, amid the hustle and bustle of a tribute-paying crowd, an event of cosmic proportions is rousing you from oblivion. Your light, nearly forgotten, reflects from a star floating above a shadowy stable. A commotion occurs, shepherds arrive, animals are disturbed and voices are raised.

Ancient prophecy is fulfilled in the birth of a Baby and, little town of Bethlehem, you have achieved your destiny. Your dark streets are illumined by the Light of the World.

Heavenly Father, though we may feel small and insignificant, we find hope in the promise that You fulfilled that long-ago night. You brought Your love to earth in a tiny baby, born in an obscure stable in a town that had almost forgotten how to anticipate. May we reach out to receive the Gift born that night. Our waiting is over. O Come to us, abide with us, our Lord Emmanuel. Amen.

December 9

HOLDING THE PROMISE

The people who walked in darkness have seen a great light;
those who dwelt in the land of the shadow of death,
upon them a light has shined. Isaiah 9:2

Lord, now You are letting Your servant depart in peace, according to Your word; for my eyes have seen Your salvation which You have prepared before the face of all peoples, a light to bring revelation to the Gentiles, and the glory of your people Israel! Luke 2:29-32

From ages past, through the darkness of human night, the promise of a Light sustained hope in the hearts of men. Prophets foretold this Light, but time passed and gloom obscured the promise. Centuries later, when hope seemed nearly extinguished, Simeon, a man righteous and devout, held on to the promise that in *his* lifetime the promised Hope would be revealed. He would see the Messiah!

And one day in the temple, into aged Simeon's arms the child Jesus was placed. With light exploding in his heart from on high, he knew. He knew for a certainty he was holding the promise.

Do we realize that we, too, can hold the promise? The Light of the World is our Savior. Our darkness is dispelled and our hope renewed by the fact that Jesus, the Messiah, is born to us. His hands extended in mercy, He awaits. To what are we holding?

The promised Light has come.

My dear Heavenly Father, when I consider the way You move to keep Your promises I am filled with awe. And to read about a faithful man who trusted You for all the years of his life, it gives me confidence to continue holding onto the promises I have in Jesus; and my awe turns to praise. Amen.

December 10

O CHRISTMAS TREE

I will plant in the wilderness the cedar and the acacia tree; the myrtle and the oil tree; I will set in the desert the cypress tree and the pine and the box tree together, that they may see and know, and consider and understand together, that the hand of the LORD has done this, and the Holy One of Israel has created it. Isaiah 41:19-20

Christmas is all about the birth of Jesus, the Gift of God, given for our redemption. The book of Isaiah speaks much in prophetic form of this miraculous birth, the coming of the Messiah. As I am thinking about Christmas and decorating, it intrigued me to read the above passage with God's promise to plant the beautiful trees of the forest to bring beauty to the barren desert.

We have a custom of bringing trees of the forest into our homes at Christmas to make them beautiful in celebration of the birth of the One called Emmanuel, God with us. As we string twinkling lights of hope on our Christmas trees and hang ornaments filled with precious memories; we must not forget there was another tree of the forest fashioned into a rough cross, where the One who was born to die gave His life for all who would believe in Him.

O Heavenly Father, may you always remind us of the hope and joy that we can experience in relationship with You, the One Who created the trees of the forest. You dwell with Your people, adorning our lives with Your glorious beauty. Amen.

December 11

HOPE

Therefore my heart is glad, and my glory rejoices; my flesh also will rest in hope. Psalm 16:9

There is hope in music; music that rings in the heart of all who believe. Especially at this time of year, we hear in the chill of December the warmth of chiming bells or a Christmas carillon. Anticipation enhances our senses and we embrace the sound of bells ringing from street corner to church steeple.

Hope comes alive in the eyes of a child filled with expectant desire. And hearts of the downtrodden longing for transformation find solace in the possibility of something new. This is hope, and the harmony of its tune enables the taking of another step when all seems dark.

A hurting world hungering for peace listens for the strains of angel song, singing the promise of a Savior. This song peals for all.

The eyes of our Heavenly Father look down in love. The heart of a Savior beats with longing. The Prince of Peace says, "Come."

And hope rings the bells!

Dear Father, You are the Composer of hope's refrain. May our ears be ever alert for the intricate melody of Heaven as it fills our souls with expectancy. Amen.

December 12

A CHRISTMAS HEART

Unto us a Child is born, unto us a Son is given... Isaiah 9:6

We are nearing the end of a quickly-passing year. The "holidays" are just around the corner, and it would be wise of us to take time to pause to make our hearts ready. Because Christmas should really be all about *hearts*, right?

So how do we keep Christmas alive all year? We need to foster and develop a Christmas heart. What would that look like?

First of all, it would be a heart filled with **anticipation...** anticipation akin to that of Mary and Joseph, celebrating the truth of this tiny phenomenon...anticipation that will not dwindle amid the grooves of everyday routine.

Secondly, we will need a heart filled with **excitemen**t... excitement like that of the shepherds, their eyes burning from the glory-heat of fiery angels...excitement that will not dim in simply being satisfied with the Gift. We might wonder just what the difference is between anticipation and excitement...well, I think anticipation is for what God is *going* to do, and excitement is for something He has *done*!

Also necessary is a heart filled with **amazement**... amazement for the miracle of humanity and deity combined in one small baby; amazement that will not diminish as a new year enters and Christmas passes by.

Lastly, a heart filled with **wonder**...the wonder of our own gaze upon this child, our Redeemer... wonder that will not decline into complacency.

Dear Father, as we approach the manger this Christmas season, may we not leave the manger until anticipation, excitement, amazement and wonder throb within us and begin to flow out as streams of compassion from Your Christmas heart. Amen.

December 13

VACANCY

And she brought forth her firstborn Son, and wrapped Him in swaddling cloths, and laid Him in a manger, because there was no room for them in the inn. Luke 2:7

Some time ago we were gifted with an anniversary getaway at a lovely resort on the ocean. While there I was remembering once more the story of Jesus' birth in a stable. In contrast to Him we had a room at the inn. Our windows were open to the sea breeze; the fireplace flickered with cheer. Every human comfort was accessible to us. We rested there, abandoned to pleasure. And it was sweet.

But I thought how, long ago, two special travelers sought a room at an inn. Carrying burgeoning new life, weary and worn. No space available there—no clean sheets or towels to swaddle a babe, no cooling breath of air; just a food trough filled with hay. And, dependent on man's care there Baby Jesus lay.

My senses soaked up those pleasant surroundings: sounds, smells and scenes so luxurious. I stopped to wonder, amid all the ease: is my "Vacancy" sign aglow? Have I made room in my heart for the life Jesus brings, or am I trying to fill it up with comfort and material things?

Heavenly Father, I don't want my Savior to wander outside my inn. Instead I want to welcome and give Him His rightful place; the "Vacancy" sign extinguished, with no room for anything but Him. Amen.

December 14

THE FULLNESS OF TIME

But in the fullness of time, God sent His Son, born of a virgin…
Galatians 4:4

"Fullness of Time" also means an "appointed time." God, who exists beyond time and space, employs time in our human sphere to bring about His plan. Omniscient, all-knowing, He was aware of the precise moment to send Jesus and, nine months before His birth, Gabriel was sent to Mary with his incredible announcement. It was not on a whim, nor a last-minute choice, but a time appointed from eternity. I do love to ponder how God moves in the events of history!

Into the dark sealed womb of a virgin entered the seed of the living God, empowered by His Spirit to grow into a fully human baby. We ask how. We don't know. But we do know nothing is impossible with God. And Mary, wrapped in God's glory, embraced the miracle in faith.

And in a similar way, there is an appointed time for each of us when, into the dark pocket of our need, the light of Christ approaches for entrance.

Father, may we face the fullness of our own time to embrace the Word of Life for which our hearts hunger. You have promised to come and meet us in the darkness of our situation, whatever it may be; and will spread the light of Your glory there. Amen.

December 15

GRATITUDE

"And she will bring forth a Son, and you shall call His name Jesus, for He will save His people from their sins." *Matthew 1:21*

I found this lovely description of Christmas! I'm not sure who wrote it, but it certainly tells us why our gratitude on this holy day is so important. Ponder these words for just a moment, as the clocks ticks forward to the celebration:

"His future coming was proclaimed by all the prophets. The virgin mother bore him in her womb with love beyond all telling. John the Baptist was his herald and made him known when at last he came. In his love Christ has filled us with joy as we prepare to celebrate his birth, so that when he comes he may find us watching in prayer, our hearts filled with wonder and praise."

And we pray:

Father, all-powerful and ever-living God, we do well always and everywhere to give you thanks through Jesus Christ our Lord. Through Him we are saved from our sins. Amen.

December 16

TIDINGS!

How beautiful upon the mountains are the feet of him who brings good news, who proclaims peace, Who brings glad tidings of good things, Who proclaims salvation, Who says to Zion, "Your God reigns!" Isaiah 52:7

I've always loved this imagery…the poetry of beautiful, loving, obedient feet. Normally feet are not considered "beautiful"—more like useful. But they are so very important, and God describes those feet who carry His message to be lovely in their usefulness. Here in these verses the prophet is speaking of the time God will redeem Jerusalem; but to me it also speaks of all those who carry the message of His Son's coming to redeem us. And so, the image works at Christmastime.

On the holy night of His birth the mountains ring with Heavenly music; Hallelujahs fill the valleys. Good News! Beauty spreads, like the break of dawn, shedding light upon the dark and weary world. Angels radiate God's glory; pounding shepherds' feet hasten to Bethlehem in breathless wonder! How beautiful are those feet, the very first to carry precious tidings. Glad tidings of great joy!

Promised peace: the Prince of Peace, slumbers against his mother's breast, biding time until the day His beautiful feet will carry Him, the Truth, to Calvary's mountain to shout salvation's tidings, Our God Reigns!

Dear Father! What a day that will be! But in the days before Your plan reaches its finale, may I be one whose feet are beautiful in the bringing of Your Good News to all those I meet. Amen.

December 17

OVERSHADOWED

He who dwells in the secret place of the Most High shall abide under the shadow of the Almighty. Psalm 91:1

And the angel answered and said to her; "The Holy Spirit will come upon you, and the power of the Highest will overshadow you; therefore, also, that Holy One who is to be born will be called the Son of God." Luke 1:35

We are told in Scripture that nothing shall be impossible with God. Yet this angelic announcement rings with seeming impossibility, even while Mary bows in surrender. I wonder if she had any idea how it would be accomplished. What faith! This boggles my mind even as I acknowledge it to be true.

There is a word here that brings a soothing warmth to my wondering: "overshadow". I love visualizing abiding under God's shadow, as the psalmist describes. To accomplish His purpose, God the Father—the Most High—commissioned the Holy Spirit to overshadow the body of a tender young girl abiding under His shadow. He filled her womb with the seed of the child Who is the *Son* of God. Holy! Holy! Holy! Blessed Trinity!

As Christmas approaches, with awe-filled eyes I'm rejoicing, realizing how God in three persons was actively involved in this "impossible" miracle. And Mary consented; experiencing the truth of God's sheltering shadow.

Oh, dear Father, may we all abide there: overshadowed by the Almighty, because of the birth and sacrifice of Jesus. Amen.

December 18

CERTAINTY

So it was, that while they were there, the days were completed for her to be delivered. And she brought forth her firstborn Son, and wrapped Him in swaddling cloths, and laid Him in a manger, because there was no room for them in the inn. Luke 2:6-7

The Christmas story, as we read it, has a lot of unknowns! We have to use our imaginations on occasion, to read between the lines. Imagine Mary and Joseph, even though accepting the assignment from God, surely they were wondering. Especially considering the fact of Mary's amazing conception!

Remember when we were expecting our children—those of us who are blessed to be mothers, how anxious we were to see their faces? And prospective fathers—is it not difficult to wait and make sure that your child is perfect? How could it have been any other way in Bethlehem?

Mary, privileged by God's touch, heavy with child—and apprehension—surely finds a stable, dark and musty, to be a crude confinement in which to endure the pangs of birth. She was so anxious to see the outcome of the miracle—her son. And Joseph, drenched with weariness and fear, rushes to find a lamp with which to examine the newly-born Wonder. Counting fingers and toes, waiting for tiny eyes to open and lips to elicit a human cry...he holds Mary tenderly and whispers, "He's real." What a moment it must have been! We don't need imagination perhaps; but we do need eyes of faith.

Dear Heavenly Father, may we be anxious to see Him as we celebrate His birth; to peer into His face, view His humanity and acknowledge His deity. Let us examine Him in all His wonder, hear His whisper in our hearts and shout with joy, "He's real!" Amen

December 19

THE KNOWING

So all this was done that it might be fulfilled which was spoken by the Lord through the prophet, saying: "Behold the virgin shall be with child and bear a Son and they shall call His name Immanuel, which is translated, 'God with us." Matthew 1:22

Several different characters populate the story surrounding Christ's birth. I would like to talk about two of them, because they each dealt uniquely with an angel visitation, One of those is Zacharias. Absolutely incredulous upon hearing from the angel that his aging wife, Elizabeth, would bear him a son, he mocked the words in unbelief. God then struck him dumb and he would be unable to speak until his son was born! But oh, think of the spoken song of glad praise that ultimately burst from lips silent for so long! His arms were now filled with a sweet burden, a gift from the Holy One. Months of silent pondering God's ways gave way to a knowledge of the holy reaffirmed in his newborn son!

And consider Mary! Her song was sung freely, a song of joy in God her Savior. Her humility was ennobled, as she embraced the unimagined. Completely compliant with God's plan for her life, her heart was at rest in a knowledge of the holy from the Spirit's joining; sensing a moment no one else could ever know. And as time passed, her body filled with the blessed Gift.

It makes me wonder about my song...do I sing from a knowledge of the holy? Intimacy with Himself, in a sacred love exchange, is the very gift He brings. Hope and joy resound in my heart's song, because when my heart knows the Giver, it is in the knowing I can receive.

My dear Father, I am humbled by the realization that I, too, have received the Gift, and intimacy with the Giver carries it straight to my heart. I sing with gratitude and praise. Amen.

December 20

WHOM SHALL WE TELL?

Now when they had seen Him, they made widely known the saying which was told them concerning this Child. And all those who heard it marveled at those things which were told them by the shepherds.
Luke 2:17-18

Consider the angels' perception of the Incarnation: An expectant hush fills Heaven, God's plan is about to unfold. We marvel, not understanding. The Son is leaving? In wonder we gaze as He sheds His cloak of glory and slips into the tender skin and mortal flesh of a baby. Suddenly we are ordered to announce this birth. "Whom should we tell?" God points, and a dozing group of humble shepherds awakes to see us! Yes, actually see us, praising God, glorifying Him and shouting His plan.

An expectant hush fills a stable. Crowding in upon each other, these same shepherds jostle for a look. They gaze in wonder at this Messiah-child, Do they sense His holiness? Hearts answering the call of God, rising on trembling legs, they back away in awe. "Whom should we tell?"

Joy beaming from faces that have seen a miracle, they announce the news to all they meet. Were any of the shepherds standing around the cross when He gave His life for them? I wonder. Angels were silent then.

Now as we look back; we too see an infant; and knowing the end of the story...how this Babe became a man, died and rose again... an expectant hush fills our hearts and we rise from our knees in awed wonder. "Whom should *we* tell?" Everyone!

Heavenly Father, I see the answer clearly! May I ever carry the good news to everyone, everywhere! Amen.

December 21

THE SEED

For as the rain comes down, and the snow from Heaven, and do not return there, but water the earth, and make it bring forth and bud, that it may give seed to the sower and bread to the eater, so shall My word be that goes forth from My mouth,; it shall not return to Me void, but it shall accomplish what I please and it shall prosper in the thing for which I sent it. Isaiah 55:10-11

I was walking along a wooded trail, my thoughts kicking sideways the way my feet were pushing branches from the path. But suddenly I bent in wonder to see….nestled amid evergreen boughs a pinecone rested. Newly fallen to earth, bearing within it a seed that is capable of growing into a majestic tree.

It looked so small and insignificant as it lay there, drops of sap adhering it to its new bed. I would have crushed it beneath my foot had God not caused me to pause and ponder.

Nestled in a manger, newly come from Heaven, a Child rested, swaddled in unfamiliar flesh; yet bearing within all the power needed for mankind's redemption. Perhaps the lowliness of His birth made all the more amazing His majesty as He rose in splendor from the grave. Seeming insignificance—grown to radiant glory!

What of the seeds of grace planted within me—placed by God's fingers into the soil of my life? Insignificant? No! Nestled within me His power becomes boundless potential.

Oh, my Father, I must take care not to crush the seed. Help me, guide me, show me the seed; make me aware of its presence, and the responsibility I carry to let You nurture it to fruition. Amen.

December 22

EMMANUEL

And a virgin will be with child and will give birth to a Son, and his name will be called Emmanuel, which is translated, "God with us." Matthew 1:23

Pondering the way we use our senses to experience the beauty of Christmas, I have been thinking of just what Emmanuel means.... God with us. And questions take shape.

Do we *look* for Him? Blithely we sing, "Joy to the World, The Lord is come." He is here...can we see Him? Are our eyes, bright with expectancy, only capable of seeing shiny tinsel and twinkling lights. Do we reflect the gaiety of the Season, but reject the Joy of the Season?

Emmanuel. God with us. Do we *listen* for Him? Reverently we sing "Silent Night, Holy Night..." He is here...do you hear Him? Are our ears, alert for new sounds, only met with hollow laughter or empty cheer? Do we echo the songs of the Season, yet remain deaf to the gentle voice of the Son of the Season?

Emmanuel. God with us. Do we *reach* for Him? Happily we sing, "O, Come Let Us Adore Him." He is here...do we want to touch Him? Are our hands, busy with preparations, only filled with packages to wrap, tasks to be done and tying the bows of the season, yet empty without the Gift of the Season?

May we pause, cease our labor for a moment and lower the volume of the external sounds. Let our eyes open with understanding and our hearts become aware that He has come. His hands reach out and He sweetly speaks, "I am here." Do we truly realize He is both Gift and Giver?

Emmanuel, You are God with us. Please help us to comprehend the true meaning of that name – to watch for You, listen for You and reach out in Your name. To know the joy of Your presence WITH us. Amen.

December 23

HOME FOR CHRISTMAS

Whom have I in heaven but You? And there is none upon earth that I desire besides You. My flesh and my heart fail; but God is the strength of my heart and my portion forever.
Psalm 73:25-26

We sing and hear sentimental songs, and memories stir us with yearning. We want to be home, to be cherished and accepted, where burdens are lifted. Wrapped in love and caring, with our longings met; we can rest. Or, so we hope, anyway. Home. It has such a strong appeal. But where is home, truly?

Do we not all experience an essential longing inside to be home for Christmas? God reminds us through the psalmist in the passage above that He is our home, the place of our strength, our portion—all we need, all we should desire. He bids us to come to Him and has built within us the desire to rest in Him.

I believe we sing "*O Come, O Come, Emmanuel*"[84] because it brings hope. For centuries people of God had waited for this promised coming. But actually, Emmanuel now sings to our hearts. God is with us; the miracle has occurred. The Word has been spoken: *Come unto Me*. God has displayed His heart by sending His Son. He longs for us to come home to Him so that our yearnings are satisfied in Himself, our Creator. He is the One who truly cherishes and accepts us. Lifts our burdens and gives us rest. Home.

Dearest Father, as we celebrate the birth of the Prince of Peace Who directs our hearts to You, we find true rest during the waiting, the expectation of His second coming. We come to You, acknowledging that when we know You, our hearts are home at Christmas, at rest forever. Amen.

---

[84] Orig. Latin text translated by John Mason Neale (1818-1866)

December 24

This hymn, written long ago, expresses so much of what Christmas means to me. I trust all who read it will rejoice in its truth.

COMMUNION HYMN FOR CHRISTMAS

Gathered round Your table on this holy eve,
viewing Bethlehem's stable we rejoice and grieve
Joy to see You lying in Your manger bed,
Weep to see You dying in our sinful stead.

Prince of Glory, gracing Heav'n ere time began,
Now for us embracing death as Son of Man
By Your birth so lowly, by Your love so true,
By Your cross most holy, Lord we worship You.

With profoundest wonder we Your body take—
laid in manger yonder, broken for our sake;
hushed in adoration we approach the cup
Bethlehem's pure oblation freely offered up.

Christmas Babe so tender, Lamb who bore our blame,
How shall sinners render praises due Your name?
Do Your own good pleasure in the lives we bring;
In Your ransomed treasure reign forever King!
—Margaret Clarkson

Dear Father, I can only echo "Amen."

December 25

LIGHT OF THE MORNING

"The Light shines in the darkness..." John 1:5

I remember one particular Christmas in which we didn't do any of the usual Christmas things. No decorations, no tree, no presents, no baking, no candy! It wasn't planned to be that way; it simply happened. Time ran out. We were empty nesters by then, so there was no pressure to perform the normal family routines.

Although we had no idea of what we would do when we got out of bed on that Christmas morning, as dawn broke we put on some Christmas music and let our hearts turn to the birth of Jesus, contemplating the loveliness of the story that often is taken for granted amid the activities in which we have involved ourselves. Without any distractions, we experienced the Light of the World.

Reminded by the candles we had lit earlier, we allowed the music to fill our hearts, celebrating the joy of our togetherness and the fact of our redemption. Redemption that was made possible by the future sacrifice of the Babe we were now honoring. It was a time of pure worship and thanksgiving. Never before, and never since have we had a Christmas morning like this; but we will never forget.

Precious Father, the true meaning of Christmas brings a brilliant glow to our hearts when we contemplate Your gift of Your Son. He is the Light of the Morning, our Savior and we bless His name today. Amen.

December 26

O COME, O COME EMMANUEL

Therefore the LORD Himself will give you a sign: Behold the virgin shall conceive and bear a Son, and shall call His name Immanuel.
Isaiah 7:14

O come, O come, Emmanuel, and ransom captive Israel that mourns in lonely exile here until the Son of God appear...[85]

There's a kind of longing in the words of that song, isn't there? They are words that could come right out of the depths of your heart when you feel captive by doubt or despair. Maybe you feel your own life could be sung in a minor key just now... saddened by a recent loss in the family or a trial that only piles your problems higher and higher, pressing your spirit down further and further.

The text of that carol reflects such a mood. But there is more to that song! The words go on to include a triumphant chorus which echoes, *"Rejoice, rejoice, Emmanuel shall come to thee, O Israel."*

That's the hope that Christmas gives. Even though we may feel shrouded by gloomy clouds of night, we have reason to rejoice. Yes, even in the middle of Christmas glitter and tinsel, our hearts may be in pain for one reason or another. That's a bitter feeling, but also a sweet one. It's sweet because we have the promise that Emmanuel—*"God with us"*—shall come to us and abide with us.

God, will You meet us where we are during these sometimes dark winter days? We know Christ has come for our redemption, and we have every reason to break forth with the resounding words, "Rejoice! Rejoice!" May we do so with Your help and strength. Amen.

---

[85] Orig. Latin text translated by John Mason Neale (1818-1866)

December 27

JESUS!

And His name shall be called Wonderful, Counselor, Mighty God, Everlasting Father, Prince of Peace. Isaiah 9:6

With joy and thanksgiving we celebrate His birth. In His name, the Name above all names, we find our all in all. It's fascinating to consider the names of Jesus, and in looking at them I find it amazing that so many of them contrast with one another. Let's look at them for a moment.

A Savior dying on a cross – a Redeemer rising from a tomb.
A gentle Shepherd – a warrior King.
The Mighty God – the Everlasting Father.
Light of the World – the Word made flesh.
Prince of Peace — the King of Kings.
The Lion of Judah – The Lamb of God.
The power of the Lion sheathed in the meekness of the Lamb.
The suffering servant – one day to reign over all.
A Baby in a manger Emmanuel – God with us.

The most glorious truth of these names is that they portray Jesus as He is, encapsulating the promises of God. He is Himself God! And I can't help but ask...Isn't He wonderful?

Oh, yes, Heavenly Father, He is wonderful and we are filled with praise as we consider Him and look upon His beautiful face with thanksgiving. Help us to see Him as He is. Amen.

December 28

I AM GABRIEL

"Zacharias, I am Gabriel, who stands in the presence of God, and was sent to speak to you and bring you these glad tidings.'" Luke 1:13, 19

"... the angel Gabriel was sent by God to a city named Nazareth, to a virgin whose name was Mary. Then the angel said to her, 'Do not be afraid, Mary, for you have found favor with God..."
Luke 1:26, 30-31.

So many times in Scripture God tells us not to fear. We find fear is rampant in our country; yes, even in the whole world. It is disturbing, and represents a turning away from God and His gifts.

But we have this intriguing story, a familiar one; of the angel sent by God to bring good tidings and to banish fear. To Zacharias the priest, announcing the birth of John the Baptist. And thence to the virgin Mary to prepare her for the birth of Jesus.

Gabriel came straight from the presence of God, which brings authenticity to his words. God was ready to move, and He sent His angel to draw those He had prepared into His plan. God is still moving today. Can we hear Him whisper, "*Do Not Fear*?" Or are we so buffeted by anxiety and dread that we stoop in misery and doubt? Oh, this Christmas, may we let faith whisper into our hearts, "Be not afraid." Might it be possible, if we listen closely, we may hear the voice of an angel?

Oh, Father, let not my ears be closed to the story brought by Gabriel, and may I ever hear his words and not let fear take hold of my heart. I trust in Your truth. Amen.

December 29

THE WATCHERS

Blessed are those servants whom the master, when he comes, will find watching. Luke 12:37

I read the following quote by John Henry Newman, a 19th Century theologian. In it he describes those who truly wait for Christ's coming. I am reminded that for centuries the people of God watched for their Messiah. But their waiting had grown a bit stale by the time of the first Christmas. But notice just what real waiting and watching entail:

"They watch for Christ who are sensitive, eager, apprehensive in mind; who are awake, alive, quick-sighted, zealous in honoring Him. Those who look for Him in all that happens, and who would not be surprised, over-agitated or overwhelmed if they found that He was coming at once. This then is to watch: To be detached from what is present, live in what is unseen. To live in the thought of Christ as He came once and as He will come again. To desire His second coming, from our affectionate and grateful remembrance of His first."[86]

I wonder. What about us? Do we who look back, as Newman writes, from an affectionate and grateful remembrance of His first coming to His promised coming? In the euphoria of celebrating His birth, let us not stifle the zeal of anticipation that should fill our hearts with longing for His return.

Heavenly Father, may we be awake, alert and watchful, because we believe Jesus is coming soon. We want to be ready, to live in the thought of His coming. Help us, please. Amen.

---

[86] John Henry Newman (1801-1890)

December 30

THE GIFT

Every good gift and every perfect gift is from above, and comes down from the Father of lights with whom is no variation or shadow of turning. Of His own will He brought us forth by the word of truth, that we might be a kind of first fruits of His creatures. James 1:17-18

Whenever Christmas rolls around, the subject of gifts arises and pervades the atmosphere. It's astounding to behold the lengths to which advertisers go to sell their wares, to foster a desire for an object—something we didn't know we needed. Thinking of the gifts God gives in endless measure, I wonder if there are gifts given to us that we never bother to unwrap. Perhaps the wrappings do not appeal and we leave a gift on the shelf, not intrigued enough to open it and discover what surprise might await us. Or maybe we don't realize that we have a need!

Long ago a tiny Baby lay in a manger, blanketed by straw and swaddling clothes. So unattractive perhaps, this humble birth; that many did not bother to find the treasure brought to earth, wrapped in human flesh. He was God Himself, born to be our Savior. A gift we had no idea we wanted.

So I ask—have you unwrapped the Gift God sent? We all need it; indeed we have no hope without it. May we not leave it unopened on the shelf.

Heavenly Father, You have generously provided the Christmas Gift of Your Son. May we see with opened eyes our need of Him, unwrap and accept the Gift. Then we, with joyful heart, can worship Him, Jesus Christ, our Lord. Amen.

December 31

RETROSPECTION

Through the LORD's mercies we are not consumed, because His compassions fail not, they are new every morning, great is Your faithfulness. Lamentations 3:22-23

This familiar verse brings great comfort to me. Especially now at this time of retrospection as one year ends and a new year begins. We look backward and forward at the same time. When anticipation rolls in, regret over the undone can fade in light of hope.

I am a lover of words and the power they can wield. I also collect words—quotes, thoughts and poetry, keeping them in a huge file.

Feeling a bit nostalgic, I have been looking through that folder; and I found the following prayer. I didn't write it, but there must have been a reason that I kept it for all these years. So now I find it speaks my heart for the coming year; and I hope it speaks to you, and bolsters your faith and trust in our wonderful merciful God. I am praying these words with a heart full of hope.

Lord, may the days ahead lead straight to You. May Your hand be in mine through all coming trials and victories. May Your words ring true from my mouth and may my walk stay on Your path each passing day. Amen.

About the Author

Lois Williams has published four volumes of her reflective meditations, *Psalms From the Pathway, "Heart Chords, Pages, and Signposts.* One of God's able communicators, she is a poet, a speaker and an enthusiastic advocate of keeping a spiritual journal, using this method of writing thoughts based on scripture to grow in intimacy with God.

Many have come to appreciate the gift that she has been given and her courage to express her thoughts and feelings before her readers. Sometimes they are like a reassuring hug, sometimes a bandage on a wounded heart. At other times they are strength for the day and sometimes they bring conviction, but the most important thing is that they lead back to the Lord through the scripture that she uses.

Lois currently resides in Lacey, Washington with her husband Fred. You may contact Lois at any of the places below. She would love to hear from you.

Email:
fredlowill@msn.com
Her website:
www.LoveLettersFromLois.com
or visit her Facebook page

Lois Williams, Author-Speaker